TEACHING FINANCIAL CRISES

COUNCIL FOR
**Economic
Education**

Teaching Opportunity®

AUTHORS

Brett Burkey
Economics Teacher
Social Studies Department Chair
Spanish River High School
Boca Raton, FL

Rick Fenner
Associate Professor of Economics
Director, Mohawk Valley Center for Economic Education
Utica College
Utica, NY

Cheryl H. Morrow
AP Macroeconomics, Economics, AP Government and Politics Teacher
Spain Park High School
Hoover, AL

M. Scott Niederjohn
Charlotte and Walter Kohler Associate Professor of Economics
Director, Center for Economic Education
Lakeland College
Sheboygan, WI

This publication was made possible by the generous support of the NYSE Euronext Foundation

ISBN: 978-1-56183-742-7

5 4 3 2 1

CONTENTS

Authors ii

Acknowledgments iv

Foreword v

Downloading Visuals, Activities, and Related Materials vii

Introduction viii

Lesson 1:   A Comparison of the Panic of 1907 to the Crisis that Began in 2007 1

Lesson 2:   How Economic Performance from 2007-2009 Compares to Other Periods in
U.S. History 43

Lesson 3:   Manias, Bubbles, and Panics in World History 57

Lesson 4:   The Japan Comparison 79

Lesson 5:   Monetary Policy in the Recent Financial Crisis 107

Lesson 6:   The Role of Housing in the Financial Crisis of 2007-2009 137

Lesson 7:   The Instruments and Institutions of Modern Financial Markets 169

Lesson 8:   Understanding Financial Markets, 2007-2009 185

ACKNOWLEDGMENTS

PROJECT DIRECTOR:

Stephen Buckles
Department of Economics
Vanderbilt University

PROJECT COORDINATOR:

Christopher Caltabiano
Vice President for Program Administration
Council for Economic Education

EDITORS:

Suzanne Becker
Dian Coleman

FIELD TEST TEACHERS:

Cindy Fitzhum
Princeton High School
Princeton, MN

Garrick Grace
Foley High School
Foley, MN

James Redelsheimer
Robbinsdale Armstrong High School
Plymouth, MN

Ann Scharfenberg
New Richmond High School
New Richmond, WI

Howard Thomas
Manning High School
Manning, SC

FOREWORD

The Council for Economic Education's *Teaching Financial Crises* comes at an opportune moment for teachers of economics and personal finance. The financial markets have dominated the headlines in recent years and likely will continue to do so for some time. Teachers are confronting a teachable moment they have never before encountered: they now have students who want to know more about topics such as hedge funds, credit default swaps, deposit insurance, market volatility, and expanding tools of monetary policy. They have students who need clarity as well as context — that is to say, they need to be taught how the recent financial crisis is similar, and how it is dissimilar, to financial crises in the past. Students will also need to know how the recent financial crisis and any yet to come will help shape their personal and professional lives in the future.

Unfortunately, teachers have no organizing framework for putting into context the media attention that has been paid to the financial crisis. All they have is a set of current events articles, opinion pieces, and other popular media pieces unconnected to educational objectives, historical analysis, and economic processes and concepts that are used in the high school classroom.

Teaching Financial Crises is an attempt to fill this void with lessons that bring current issues and economic thought into economics, government, social studies, business and history classrooms. The volume makes a challenging series of events accessible to teachers and students by exploring the causes of and potential solutions to financial crises with creative, tested classroom activities.

There is a lot we know and there is much we still do not know about the recent financial crisis. A financial crisis reminds us that many economic events do not have simple, obvious causes or solutions. As teachers, we should not fall into the trap of suggesting that the causes and consequences of the crisis of 2007–2009 were as simple as some would have us think. The list of possible causes is as long and deep as the presumed solutions that have been advanced by countless commentators. Was it low interest rate targets maintained by the Federal Reserve in the first half of the 2000s? Was it the glut of worldwide savings that found its way into U.S. financial markets? Was it a lack of financial education on the part of borrowers in the mortgage market? Was it financial service providers offering complex financial instruments about which few people understood the exposure to risk? Was it that government either regulated too little or too much? Or was it simply about greed? Students must be taught that the potential causes of and solutions to the crisis are numerous, complex and interconnected. They must understand that both the causes and solutions require careful thought and discussion. And that is what we hope that this publication will encourage.

This resource is unique in that it is not applicable simply to recent events. It also takes a look at previous financial crises, which allows for exploration of both similarities and differences among these defining events. The first four lessons discuss common elements of financial crises in different time periods and different parts of the world. Lesson 1 compares the 2007-2009 crisis with a similar event in 1907. Among other things, this lesson uses compare-and-contrast analysis and asks students to solve a mystery that helps them see the very different outcomes that resulted from the two crises. Lesson 2 compares the recession that officially began in December 2007 with five earlier contractions, including the Great Depression. Students are asked to do independent research and engage in small-group discussions. Lesson 3 takes a historical look at five bubbles and panics that occurred at different times and places. Using a group activity, students discover that the same basic structure exists in each bubble. They will be struck by how difficult it seems to be to identify a financial bubble in the making. In Lesson 4, students participate as members of the President's Council of Economic Advisors to make comparisons to the Lost Decade in Japan—a serious long-term crisis that began in 1991 and continues to this day.

The final four lessons focus specifically on the crisis of recent years. Lesson 5 explores monetary policy during the crisis. Students serve as Federal Reserve Board governors to explore several monetary policy tools used by the Fed to promote economic and financial stability. Lesson 6 examines the housing bubble that occurred in the first several years of the 2000s. Students interpret data, review basic supply-and-demand models, and simulate a securitization process to see the effects of increasing leverage. A quiz bowl game in Lesson 7 helps students learn the concepts necessary for thinking and talking intelligently about modern financial markets. *Teaching Financial Crises* ends with Lesson 8, an exploration of the interaction between modern financial markets and monetary and fiscal policies. Students take part in a mock trial and work in small groups in an attempt to order events that occur in a logical sequence.

Benjamin M. Friedman's introductory essay on the crisis discusses what we, as teachers of economics and related subjects, can learn from the recent crisis. This informative and highly engaging essay is a good starting point for the study of financial crises.

Many people are responsible for bringing this publication to completion, starting with Richard MacDonald, Senior Adviser for Program Development at the CEE, whose idea it was in the first place. Stephen Buckles, Senior Lecturer in Economics at Vanderbilt University, deserves the highest praise for his role directing this project, drawing the best out of the authors and coordinating closely with CEE every step of the way. Lesson authors Brett Burkey, Rick Fenner, Cheryl H. Morrow, and M. Scott Niederjohn contributed first-rate classroom lessons and then reviewed other authors' lessons. Classroom teachers then tested the lessons and gave us their thoughtful comments and made creative suggestions that helped shape the publication.

As noted above, Benjamin M. Friedman, the William Joseph Maier Professor of Political Economy at Harvard University and a CEE board member, wrote a thoughtful introduction that anyone thinking about teaching the economics of the crisis of 2007–2009 will find to be truly helpful. The project could not have been completed without the careful and creative work of Suzanne Becker who edited the volume, making it much better than the rest of us had any right to expect.

Finally, CEE gratefully acknowledges the NYSE Euronext Foundation, whose generous support made this publication possible.

Council for Economic Education

DOWNLOADING VISUALS, ACTIVITIES, AND RELATED MATERIALS

On the Web

To download the visuals and activities for each lesson, find online lessons to extend the student activities, and find related materials to each lesson, visit:

www.councilforeconed.org/financialcrises

INTRODUCTION

Benjamin M. Friedman
William Joseph Maier Professor of Political Economy, Harvard University
Director, Council for Economic Education

Large-scale and unusual events often present occasions for learning, especially when they bring unwanted consequences. Even if no one is at fault for causing some event in the first place (an earthquake, for example), it is only natural to ask what might be done differently to mitigate the consequences should a similar catastrophe recur. When what went wrong was itself the result of human action, the question at issue is not merely containment but prevention.

What can we learn from the 2007-2009 financial crisis? What can policymakers, bankers, and others in positions of responsibility do to render this kind of disruption less likely to recur? If another such crisis does happen, what steps should policymakers take to contain its extent within the financial system, and to limit its contractionary impact on nonfinancial economic activity? Can what policymakers and bankers and other lenders did or did not do during the crisis shed light on how they should conduct monetary and fiscal policy, or regulate banks and other financial institutions, or run the affairs of the private institutions that they manage, in more normal times?

The 2007-2009 Crisis

The 2007-2009 crisis and downturn constituted one of the most significant economic events since World War II. In many countries the real economic costs — costs in terms of reduced production, lost jobs, shrunken investment, and foregone incomes and profits — exceeded that of any prior post-war decline. In the United States the peak-to-trough decline in real output was 3.8 percent, slightly greater than the previous post-war record, set in 1957-1958. Unemployment among the American labor force did not reach the level that followed the 1981-1982 recession, but (as of the time of writing) it seems likely to remain abnormally high for much longer than it did then. To an even greater extent than is usual, the decline also affected countries in all parts of the world — though, of course, some more so than others. The overall volume of world trade declined by 12 percent in 2009 alone.

It is in the financial sector, however, that this latest episode primarily stands out. The collapse of major financial firms, the decline in asset values and consequent destruction of citizens' wealth, the interruption of credit flows, the loss of confidence both in firms and in credit market instruments, the fear of default by individuals and institutions, and above all the intervention by central banks and other governmental institutions — both in scale and in form — were extraordinary. Whether this latest episode constituted the worst real economic downturn since World War II was, for many countries (the U.S. included), a close call. But there is no question that for the world's financial system what happened was the greatest crisis since the 1930s.

By now there are few people who do not acknowledge that major American financial institutions and the markets they dominate turn out to have served the country badly. The surface evidence of this failure is the enormous losses (more than $4 trillion on the latest estimate from the International Monetary Fund) that banks and other lenders suffered on their mortgage-related investments, together with the consequent need for American taxpayers to put up still larger sums in direct subsidies and guarantees to keep these firms from failing. But the financial failure also imposed real economic costs. Unemployment reached nearly 10 percent of the labor force, industrial production declined by 15 percent, business investment in new factories and machinery shrank by 21 percent, and what had been robust profits at most companies turned into significant losses.

How Government Responds

The U.S. Government moved aggressively, and on several fronts, to stanch the immediate damage. The Federal Reserve System not only eased monetary policy to the point of near-zero short-term interest rates but created a profusion of new facilities to extend credit to banks as well as other lenders. Congress enacted nearly $800 billion of new spending and tax cuts aimed at stimulating business and consumer spending. First the Bush administration and then the Obama administration experimented with one new program after another to rescue lenders and reliquify collapsed credit markets.

But despite the universal agreement that no one wants any more such failures once this one has fully passed, there has been a troubling lack of attention to reforms that might prevent this from happening. By now everyone acknowledges the excessive risk-taking, poor evaluation of the worth of both houses and financial assets and, often, plain reckless behavior (not to mention some instances of criminality, although to date surprisingly few of these have come to light) that caused the financial mess. But everyone recognizes too the dynamic character of many parts of the American economy, and most people sense that the financial markets have played a major role in allowing that to happen as well. And, so the argument goes, what is the alternative? Substantive government interference with financial markets would amount in the end to centrally planned allocation of an economy's investment process, delivering only technological stagnation and wasted resources. Softer attempts at regulation either prove ineffective — the private sector can afford better lawyers than the government can — or at best merely lead financial institutions to relocate to more lightly regulated jurisdictions.

Lessons to be Learned

As in past financial declines, what has been mostly missing in this discussion is attention to what function an economy's financial system is supposed to perform and how well it is doing that. Attention has mostly focused on investors' losses from buying mortgage-backed assets at inflated prices, not on the consequence that if the bond prices were too high then mortgage interest rates were too low and so the economy built, and Americans bought, too many houses. In just the same way, when the 1990s stock market boom crashed what everyone talked about was investors' losses on their telecom stocks, not the fact that if the stocks' prices were too high the cost of capital to the firms that issued them was too low, and so the industry laid millions of miles of fiber-optic cable that nobody ended up using.

In both instances, the cost was not just financial losses but wasted real resources. True, over longer periods of time the American financial system has seemed pretty good about allocating resources rather than wasting them. The economy's long-term pace of technological advance and growth in production suggests that American banks, and the U.S. stock and bond markets, steer investment capital reasonably effectively to firms that will use them productively, often including start-ups trying out a wholly new idea (think Microsoft, or Google, or, earlier on, Apple). But the issue ought to be an empirical one, subject to serious investigation, not a matter of faith.

Moreover, framing the question in terms of just how efficient a financial system is in allocating capital provides a natural point of entry for also asking at what price that efficiency comes. In recent years the financial industry has accounted for an unusually large share of all profits earned in the U.S. economy. The finance sector's share of all corporate profits rose from 10 percent, on average from the 1950s through the 1980s, to 22 percent in the 1990s, and an astonishing 34 percent during 2001-2005. In a fundamental sense, those profits accruing to the financial sector are part of what the economy pays for the mechanism that allocates its investment capital (and also provides other services, like checking accounts and savings deposits). But even a bare-bones notion of the cost of running the financial system includes not just the profits financial firms earn but also the salaries, the office rents, the travel budgets, the advertising fees, and all of the other expenses they pay. The finance industry's share of U.S. wages and salaries has likewise been rising, from 3 percent in the early 1950s to 7 percent more recently. The relevant question is what portion of the economy's total returns to productively invested capital is absorbed by this all-in cost of allocating it?

How, then, should the 2007-2009 financial crisis change what economists think about the world that we are trying to understand? And how should the financial crisis change what, and how, we teach students who are interested in gaining an understanding as well?

A Monetary Economy

The first lesson from the crisis is to recognize, much more explicitly than we often do, that we live in a monetary economy and it matters. At one level everyone knows this; but sometimes it seems as if economics education is aimed at persuading ordinary people that the monetary and financial aspects of our economy do not much matter: that aggregate supply depends only on technology and factors of production; that aggregate supply is in turn what determines output and employment; and that while aggregate demand depends on monetary and financial influences, it only matters in so far as it plays a role in determining prices.

The fact is that we buy goods and services not in exchange for one another, but for either government-issued pieces of paper ("currency") or for claims for those government-issued pieces of paper. As a result, the aggregate demand for those goods and services matters for the determination of output and employment, and monetary and financial influences in turn matter as well because they affect aggregate demand. Today most economists realize that the story under which aggregate supply depends only on preferences, endowments, and technologies, and this is what determines output and employment, and there is consequently no role for aggregate demand (and in turn monetary or financial factors) to affect anything except prices and inflation, is a fiction. But especially for teaching purposes, we often treat it as a useful fiction — a benchmark, or base case, from which to begin our analysis. Unfortunately, it turns out that moving past that base case is conceptually difficult. As a result, students often come away thinking that the base case, from which we were supposed to proceed, bears some relationship to the world in which we live. It does not.

The Importance of Credit

A second lesson is that while we live in a monetary economy, or at least what we call a monetary economy, what actually matters for the purposes that we are describing is not money, but credit: that is, what households and firms borrow, not the deposits that they hold. Indeed, with the benefit of hindsight the economics profession's half-century-long fixation with money — how to measure it, how to control it, why people hold it, and the like — stands as a tragic distraction. Think, for example, about some of the statements, all staples of the familiar monetary analysis of economic downturns, that we did not hear during this downturn:

"The money stock is falling."

"The Federal Reserve is allowing the monetary base to contract."

"Households and firms are not spending because their holdings of real money balances are too small."

"The Federal Reserve is being too restrictive in supplying reserves to the banking system, and so interest rates are too high."

No one heard any of these statements, or many more like them, because they were demonstrably false. Instead, we saw a dramatic demonstration that aggregate demand depends on the volume, the availability, and the price of credit, as well as on changes in the prices of non-money assets. It is the amount and ease of borrowing that matters for these purposes, not deposit-holding. In teaching our students what aspects of the economy make the difference between expansion and recession, we should aim their attention at what, and how, and at what price, people and firms borrow.

In some simple representations of the economy, of course, money and credit are the same thing, or at least they co-vary identically. Picture, for example, the simple textbook model of a banking system in which bank assets consist of loans and reserves, the liability side of each bank's balance sheet consists of deposits and the bank's capital, and, in the aggregate, reserves and capital are both fixed (the former by the central bank, and the latter by accumulated past profits and losses). In those circumstances, money and credit co-vary identically. But in the world in which we live, depository institutions have many ways of funding loans other than issuing money; their capital is not fixed (just ask your favorite banker what happened to the capital of his or her institution in the crisis, once it started booking losses); banks' ability to lend depends not only on their holding of reserves but also on their capital, and often the constraint that is binding is the one on capital; and lots of lending is done by institutions that are not traditional banks accepting deposits and that do not hold reserves at the central bank at all. (This also includes lending in which a close relationship between the borrowing firm and the lending officers who are intimately knowledgeable about its affairs plays a central role — which, according to the textbooks, is the special province of banks. General Electric Credit, for example, does just as much "relationship lending" as any bank.)

Without doubt, modeling all this is both difficult and complex. Economists would surely like to find a model that is simple, elegant, and right. But that is no reason to continue to equip our students with only the usual money-centered models — which are simple, elegant and wrong. The United States is now engaged in what will be a historic test of something as basic as whether even very large-scale changes in the quantity of central bank liabilities matter at all for prices and inflation. The question in brief is: Are we about to have a massive inflation? No one really knows the answer yet. But given the huge magnitude of the changes in the U.S. monetary base in the last two years, the current episode is almost certain to dominate the findings of empirical research in this field for at least the next generation. Students who are equipped with only the usual money-oriented models will simply not understand how to interpret what the data show about monetary policy and its economic effects.

The Role of Financial Institutions

A third lesson is that most credit (to recall, what households and firms borrow) comes from lending institutions, rather than from individuals doing the lending. What determines an institution's willingness or ability to lend? Like an individual, a financial institution exhibits profit motives, risk preferences, diversification objectives and balance sheet constraints. Unlike individuals, however, institutions face capital requirements, and therefore are subject to the influence of accounting rules. In the years leading up to the 2007-2009 crisis, many financial institutions took on unusually large "leverage" — the ratio of the value of their total investments held to the underlying capital they had to support it. That act rendered those institutions highly vulnerable when they began to incur losses. Many effectively took on even more leverage than their official accounts showed by assuming responsibility for assets that they were able, under the prevailing accounting rules, to keep off their balance sheets, and therefore against which they held no capital whatever.

Financial institutions, again unlike individuals, also face a wide variety of other regulatory constraints, some of which expand their capabilities instead of limiting them (the most obvious example is deposit insurance and other forms of government guarantees of their liabilities). Further, financial institutions mostly operate subject to limited liability (they are corporations), and they need to raise their own capital in competitive securities markets. What ends up being at risk when financial institutions lend is what Louis Brandeis, in the title of his 1914 book, famously referred to as "Other People's Money." For all of these reasons, financial institutions face different incentives, compared to what would motivate individual lenders, and so it is hardly surprising that their behavior as lenders is different too.

In addition, most of these institutions, at least when scaled by their volume of lending, are large and complex and professionally managed. The resulting conflict of interest between principals (a firm's owners) and their agents (the hired managers) adds to the problem created by limited liability for the firm's losses. The incentives that motivate the actual decision makers at these lending institutions are not the same as the incentives that would govern decisions by the firms' owners — the shareowners — were they to run the firm themselves. This difference in incentives between managers and shareowners compounds the difference in incentives between shareowners and debt holders. As the 2007-2009 crisis showed, in one financial institution after another, the managers who made the decisions were able to do well for themselves even while the firm's shareowners lost much of their investment and, in a few cases (except for government intervention there would have been far more) the debt holders lost as well.

Rationality in Markets

A fourth lesson, as the economist, Hyman Minsky emphasized years ago, is that our markets — and especially our financial markets — are not characterized by the level of rationality to which we all aspire. The Minsky hypothesis, to recall, is that the form of rationality that he labeled "euphoria" increases with the length of time that has elapsed since the last crisis. In the wake of the 2007-2009 financial crisis, this phenomenon is all too familiar.

What we usually do not mention, however, is how fundamentally subversive this lack of rationality is for even our most basic notions of how our economy works. At the macroeconomic level, the prices that are set in speculative financial markets determine the aggregate share of our national product that we devote to fixed investment of all kinds. At the microeconomic level, the prices determined in speculative financial markets steer the composition of that investment: hence too many houses built in the last expansion, and too many miles of fiber-optic cable in the previous one. To take another example, now looking into the future: is the appropriate price of oil $150 per barrel, as it was several years ago; or $30 a barrel, as it was more recently; or $70 a barrel, as it is today? The difference matters enormously for the amount we will invest in oil exploration, in refineries and other processing installations, and in alternative sources of energy. What about the boom in Las Vegas casino construction that the high prices of gaming industry stocks spurred in recent years to a level greater than the entire gross private domestic investment of many of the world's countries? In each of these cases, the central economic process involved is the determination of the allocation of investment by prices that are not necessarily themselves the result of rational behavior.

Economic Frictions

A final lesson of the crisis is that frictions — difficulties of shifting from one set of arrangements to another, whether those arrangements be personal, institutional, or governmental — are much more important than we normally let on in either our teaching or our research. Consider, for example, the most recent decline in the U.S. gross domestic product. From the peak in the fourth quarter of 2007 to the trough in the second quarter of 2009, U.S. GDP fell by 4.1 percent. Why was it such a tragedy, one might ask, that the nation went back to the GDP it had had in early 2006? Was our standard of living so horribly depressed then? Were Americans mostly poverty-stricken before the downturn that the financial crisis triggered? Of course not.

There are two reasons why this 4 percent downturn in our nation's total economic output was so troubling. First, we make arrangements in our daily lives — where we live, what car we drive, where we send our children to school, and the like — in ways that turn out to be very difficult for most people to alter once we have them in place. Second, the impact of economic fluctuations on individuals is usually highly uneven, on both the way up and the way down; and arranging for the winners to compensate the losers is just as difficult in the macroeconomic context as it is in the standard free-trade example. (Ask why free trade is so controversial, despite the well-known result that it makes the nation better off in the aggregate. The reason is that the winners from free trade are many and widely diffused through the population: everyone who gets to buy cheaper goods made abroad. The losers are fewer but easy to identify and far more sharply affected: workers in the auto industry, for example, or textile mills, or shoe factories. In principle the rest of us could compensate the auto and textile and shoe workers, and still be better off. But we somehow cannot, or at least do not, do that.)

In 1772, in the midst of the worst Scottish banking crisis in two generations, the philosopher and economist David Hume wrote to his closest friend, Adam Smith. After recounting the bank failures, the spreading unemployment, and even the doubt cast on the soundness of Britain's central bank, Hume asked Smith: "Do these Events any-wise affect your Theory?" As is evident from a reading of Smith's great book, The Wealth of Nations, published just four years later, they certainly did. Today's economists and teachers of economics should likewise learn from what happened in the financial crisis of 2007-2009. We should change how we think, and how we teach, accordingly.

A Comparison of the Panic of 1907 to the Crisis that Began in 2007

Lesson 1
A Comparison of the Panic of 1907 to the Crisis that Began in 2007

LESSON DESCRIPTION

This lesson provides an overview of the similarities and differences between the Panic of 1907 and the financial crisis that began in 2007. Students will assess the financial systems, economic events, and government responses in both periods. They will organize their analysis through a compare-and-contrast organizer.

Students will read a summary of events surrounding the San Francisco earthquake of 1906 and Hurricane Katrina in 2005 and resolve a mystery surrounding their impact on the nation's financial system. The students will participate in an oral reading illustrating the abandonment of traditional lending policies in the expansion of credit to 21st century borrowers.

INTRODUCTION

The Panic of 1907. Seldom is there a single, clearly identifiable cause of significant economic growth periods or economic collapses. The Panic of 1907 was created by a number of events, some related and others completely independent of one another.

The U.S. economy had no central bank to supply reserves or to act as a lender of last resort. The nation's money supply depended upon the amount of gold owned by banks and the federal government. As a result, if demand for money increased in one part of the country, **interest rates** would increase, money would flow to that part of the country, and money availability in other parts of the country would decrease.

Economic growth had dramatically increased the demand for loans and many institutions nationwide took on more **risk** than was prudent. The San Francisco Earthquake of 1906 was a disaster of historic proportions, and much of the world's money and gold was sent to cover claims and begin repairs. This made credit difficult to attain in New York and London. Banks lost reserves and had to reduce lending.

The excess of the Gilded Age spawned the Progressive movement at the turn of the century. Industrialization had created a great wealth disparity in the nation and attracted millions of immigrants to the country, exacerbating income differences in the crowded urban centers. The titans of business and the financial community fell under increased scrutiny by average citizens and their politicians. Reflections of the mood were manifested in 1907 by speeches given by President Teddy Roosevelt that raised the level of hostility. In one he called Standard Oil's John D. Rockefeller a "predatory man of wealth."

Increased government regulation of railroads and antitrust suits aimed at the burgeoning oil industry caused stock prices to fall. These actions and the critical public attitudes increased the level of uncertainty surrounding financial markets.

Leading financial investors attempted to buy much of the stock of a major copper company, to force others to pay high prices. The scheme failed and caused significant losses to several well-known investors. That, in turn, caused several banks to fail. Runs on other banks became serious as no central bank existed to help with panics.

In the absence of a strong federal regulatory structure or significant safety nets, the response to this crisis was delivered by a private citizen. J.P. Morgan, the world's most powerful banker, used all of his influence to convince fellow titans of industry to pool their resources and salvage the nation's financial institutions and the economy. The crisis led to the creation of the Federal Reserve System in 1913.

The Crisis of 2007-2009. A massive worldwide investment in the U.S. housing market led to the most calamitous financial crisis since the Great Depression. The irrational faith in the buoyancy of prices of housing and a changed and less regulated means to finance housing created a formula for unprecedented disaster.

Coming out of a mild recession in 2001, interest rates were lowered and credit flowed. Home ownership became a priority of the nation and lending agencies were encouraged to provide mortgages. A rapidly growing world was flush with cash and investors were looking for opportunities. Financial firms obliged by creating complicated packages of mortgages that were sold as securities promising higher rates of return and less risk to investors.

Lending standards eased, new forms of insurance for the packages of mortgages were created, risk-rating agencies gave solid reviews to the packages of mortgages; as a result, funds flowed to mortgages, and housing prices soared. Expectations of even higher prices by housing buyers and securities investors created an ever-growing demand for housing.

Increases in housing supply eventually caught up with the rising demand. Interest rates began to increase due to concerns about economy-wide inflation. The increase in supply and interest rates slowed the growth in housing prices. With changed expectations and more houses on the market, prices began to fall. With the fall in housing prices, many owners and speculators could no longer refinance their housing loans and the value of the packages of mortgages fell. Many financial institutions could not attract funds to purchase the securities holding the mortgages. As investors attempted to sell with very few buyers at current prices, financial institutions struggled to attract investors and deposits. Investors in financial institutions withdrew their funds and those institutions were forced to sell their securities at whatever prices they could get.

The full array of federal resources was brought to bear as the government tried to mitigate the crisis. Aggressive fiscal policy and federal government purchases of loans and stocks of affected financial firms, combined with extremely stimulative monetary policy efforts, were undertaken in efforts to slow the panic and make the financial system function smoothly. Central banks around the globe coordinated their efforts in response.

CONCEPTS

- The causes and effects of the Panic of 1907
- The causes and effects of the Crisis of 2007-2009
- Gold standard
- Risk
- Interest rates
- Mortgage-backed securities

OBJECTIVES

Students will:

1. Understand the causes and effects of the Panic of 1907 and the Crisis of 2007-2009.

2. Identify the similarities and differences between the two events.

3. Explain the benefits of an economic role for government in a market economy.

4. Understand the costs of a market economy with no central bank.

CONTENT STANDARDS

- Effective decision making requires comparing the additional costs of alternatives with the additional benefits. Many choices involve doing a little more or a little less of something: few choices are "all or nothing" decisions.

- Prices send signals and provide incentives to buyers and sellers. When supply or demand changes, market prices adjust, affecting incentives.

- Costs of government policies sometimes exceed benefits. This may occur because of incentives facing voters, government officials, and government employees, because of actions by special interest groups that can impose costs on the general public, or because social goals other than economic efficiency are being pursued.

- Federal government budgetary policy and the Federal Reserve System's monetary policy influence the overall levels of employment, output, and prices.

TIME REQUIRED

Three class periods

MATERIALS

- Activity 1: Comparing Crises (one copy per student)

- Activity 2: Catalysts for Economic Decline (one copy per student)

- Activity 3: Characters in the Financial Crisis (one copy per student)

- Visual 1: Pandemonium in the Markets (a PowerPoint or slide presentation)

PROCEDURE

1. The core of information for this lesson will be delivered with the help of a presentation using Visual 1: Pandemonium in the Market. This thorough visual aid begins with events at the center of the Panic of 1907 and finishes with a comparison of that panic with the financial crisis that began in 2007. Distribute a copy of Activity 1: Comparing Crises to each student. Have them list similarities and differences of the two financial struggles as you progress through the presentation. Slides 27 and 28 are a review of the similarities and differences between the two events which will serve as a confirmation of students' work in Activity 1.

2. Summary of the slides:

Slides 2 to 4 introduce students to the devastation of the San Francisco earthquake of 1906. The event is widely cited as a catalyst for the Panic of 1907 because of the massive drain on the world's stores of gold, required to pay the insurance claims and rebuild the city.

Slide 5 defines the **gold standard** and the parameters it sets on the supply of money. There were runs on banks in 1907, and there was no lender of last resort. In 2007, the Federal Reserve had the ability to prevent bank runs, but not runs on other financial investment firms.

Slide 6 illustrates the consequences of those limits on the world's ability to respond to the circumstances in San Francisco and the weakened state of the U.S. economy.

Slide 7 conveys the optimism at the beginning of the 1900s and the healthy business climate that led to the founding of some of America's greatest companies.

Slide 8 describes one of the sparks that ignited the compromised economy in late 1907. The failed attempt to corner the copper market was only the beginning.

Slide 9 implies that perceived market manipulation by many of the nation's prominent financiers was what really troubled investors and depositors.

Slides 10 to 12 demonstrate the role that the new financial institution, called a trust company, played in the crisis. This is one of the important similarities between the economies of 1907 and today in that a new and underregulated entity (similar to today's hedge funds) had accumulated a great deal of business in a short period of time. The search for greater return left many investors exposed when the tide turned and led to attempts to withdraw funds from trust companies and banks alike.

Slides 13 and 14 bring to light the impact on the economy from the 1907 Panic which has similarities to the scope of damage of the 2007-2009 crisis.

Slide 15 points out one of the real differences between the two crises. With the creation of the Federal Reserve still six years away, a private citizen brought the economy back from the edge. J.P. Morgan wielded unprecedented influence in bailing the economy out. This is a good time to note that this was not the first time Morgan came to the rescue of the U.S. economy. In 1895, with the country in the depths of a two-year-old panic, the federal treasury was nearly out of gold. President Grover Cleveland arranged for Morgan to create a private syndicate on Wall Street to supply the U.S. Treasury with $65 million in gold.

Slide 16 demonstrates an additional element of the Panic of 1907 that manifests in a similar form currently. Bucket shops were an early century phenomenon that allowed people to bet on the fate of a security without actually owning it. There was so much concern over them that they were banned by states beginning in 1909.

Slides 17 to 19 introduce students to the causes of the crisis of 2007-2009. The unusually long period of low interest rates and the concerted effort to promote home ownership to all levels of society set the stage.

Slides 20 and 21 reference complex innovations developed to securitize home mortgages for investor consumption. This is an important similarity to 1907 conditions: both periods originated sophisticated financial devices that exponentially increased profits for some but were not widely understood. Companies that provide ratings on investments failed to indicate the risks involved with the **mortgage-backed securities**.

Slide 22 describes the cataclysm that occurred when the government and investors began to come to their senses. The Federal Reserve, concerned primarily about rapidly expanding spending and the potential of increased inflation, raised interest rates squelching the demand for houses and new loans and increasing the payments on many existing loans. The demand for homes decreased and home prices began to tumble. Borrowers began to default and lenders went out of business. Mortgage-backed securities, so widely subscribed to around the world, became worth significantly less.

Slide 23 makes another connection with the Panic of 1907. Similar to the bucket shops 100 years before, credit default swaps enabled buyers and sellers to speculate on the health of the housing industry, and further encouraged speculation.

Slides 24 and 25 reflect the impact of the crisis of 2007-2009 on the world economy. As of this writing, the effects of the recent crisis are still unfolding. The Panic of 1907 lasted for about six weeks; the crisis of 2007-2009 has lasted much longer. However, both shocks to the respective economies have much in common.

Slide 26 illustrates a significant difference between the two events. From the fall of 2008 onward, the federal government spared little expense in an attempt to corral the problem. In 1907, government intervention in economic matters was not the rule.

Slides 27 and 28 summarize the differences and similarities between the two crises and are probably best shown after the next step.

3. Repeat that the purpose of this lesson is to compare and contrast two events in history to better understand economic crises and of the role of the government in the U.S. economic system. At this point, students can be asked to present their results from Activity 1.

   a. Some of the common characteristics your students will find for the two events are:

   Highly complex and linked financial systems existed in both crises.

   Strong economic growth leading up to the events generated a great demand for capital.

   Many people and institutions were highly leveraged and lenders were willing to take more risk.

   Innovative and largely unregulated forms of finance had been created: trust companies, hedge funds and mortgage-backed securities.

   Stock markets were setting all-time highs and companies were reporting record earnings.

   There were somewhat limited roles for government and the absence of relevant safety buffers.

Markets swung from great optimism to great pessimism quickly.

In both crises, the panics resulted in reduced production and rapidly increasing unemployment.

Corrective responses resulted in both crises, albeit from different sources.

b. Some of the possible differences your students will mention are:

In 1907, there was no Federal Reserve, J.P. Morgan became the de facto central banker, drawing together mostly private funds to resolve the crisis.

The Panic of 1907 lasted six weeks while the effects of the 2007-2009 crisis have continued for more than three years.

The 1907 crisis was felt at the commercial bank level in the absence of any kind of bank deposit insurance. The 2007-2009 crisis has focused on investment and financial companies; individual bank depositors have not lost their deposits. However, many individuals lost their houses.

In 1907, the nation was on the gold standard and the supply of money was fixed to the quantity of gold. In 2007, the Federal Reserve could expand the money supply in response to financial and economic pressures.

The Panic of 1907 was precipitated by a cataclysmic natural disaster in San Francisco. The events associated with Hurricane Katrina in 2005 were generally benign as catalysts for the 2007-2009 financial crisis.

In 1907, the government was sending numerous signals of its displeasure in the growing capacity of big business. In 2007, the administration was friendly to and supportive of big business.

In 1907, big business came to the rescue of the country and J.P. Morgan was hailed as a hero. In 2007, big business

and financial firms were heavily criticized and blamed by many.

4. Distribute a copy of Activity 2: Catalysts for Economic Decline to each student. It describes the details of the San Francisco earthquake and Hurricane Katrina. It poses a mystery for your students to solve as to why one event had such a large effect on an economy and one did not. Have students read the details and the data silently. Allow them several minutes to absorb the information and write down a possible solution to the mystery at the bottom of the page.

The most significant economic difference between the two events was the nature of the monetary systems. In 1907, the amount of money depended upon the gold supply and in fact gold flowed to San Francisco away from the rest of the country. In 2005, the supply of money was not fixed to the amount of gold and could be expanded by the Federal Reserve in response to financial pressures.

Once this is completed, divide the class into groups of three and designate each student as "A," "B,"or "C." Have all "A" and "B" students pair up and read their ideas. Integrate elements from each into one statement. Then, invite the "C" students to read their statement and integrate it with "A" and "B" development. This should all be accomplished within the groups of three. Have a spokesperson read the integrated statements aloud for class discussion.

5. Distribute a copy of Activity 3: Characters in the Financial Crisis to each student. Have students take turns reading the characters' lines aloud, starting, for instance, with Seat 1 Row 1 and moving around the room. Indicate to them that the characters and circumstances are based on actual people and events whose lives have played out during the financial crisis. The scenarios were created from interviews with local mortgage lenders and reports that aired on *60 Minutes* and

CNBC during the 2007-2009 crisis. When students have finished the recitation, have them answer the following questions:

a. Based on the surprised response of the announcer in frame three, speculate on the types of documentation requirements borrowers might have been subject to in more regulated times.

   Tax returns, W-2 forms, bank statements, credit reports, wage statements and payroll check stubs.

b. What financial innovation, popularized over the last 10 years, might have allowed lenders to accept a greater amount of risk?

   Mortgage-backed securities. This meant that the original lender would not suffer if a borrower could not make the mortgage payments. Even if one or two mortgages failed, it would be only a small loss to the buyers of the securities.

c. In retrospect, former Fed chair Alan Greenspan has admitted that keeping interest rates low for so long was not a sound policy for housing markets. What was the effect on housing markets? What might have been the motivation to keep interest rates so low?

   Low interest rates mean that more people could afford to buy larger, more expensive houses. Interest rates were kept low by the Federal Reserve in an effort to stimulate the economy following the 2001 economic recession.

d. Why were investors as far away as Narvik, Norway, willing to invest in U.S. mortgage-backed securities?

   There was the general belief that U.S. housing prices would continue to increase, the risk was spread across many mortgages, and the mortgage-backed securities came highly recommended from risk-rating agencies.

e. What financial move by the Federal Reserve had a dramatic impact on borrowers holding adjustable rate mortgages?

   The Federal Reserve moved interest rates upward as the economy recovered and the possibility of increased inflationary pressure became a concern. The rates on the mortgages increased rapidly.

CLOSURE

Review the fundamental points of this lesson. Two similar panics occurred for different reasons and under different conditions. Both had serious effects beyond those individuals directly involved in financial markets. Employment, production, and incomes all declined.

Help students understand that while the details of the two events might have been quite different, they are both rooted in similar systemic problems. The great desire to feed on optimism can lead to reckless decisions in the pursuit of profit. Innovative financial advancements can be introduced faster than people can fully comprehend. Runs on financial institutions (commercial banks in 1907 and investment banks in 2007-2009) caused failures and contributed to the panics.

The faith in market solutions and presumed safety nets can lead to inefficient decisions. Without a reasonable respect for risk, uninformed choices may accelerate. Prices can rise at a rapid pace until the profit taking begins to occur. The optimism that fuels the markets quickly turns to pessimism. Prices fall precipitously and investors wake up to the reality of overwhelming leverage and disenchantment with financial markets. This cycle has occurred repeatedly throughout history.

As predictable as each episode is, the only reasonable hope for a reduction in the costs of these types of events is for regulatory reform that creates some degree of containment and solution. The creation of the Federal Reserve was an example in 1913 and the current crisis may spawn another example, yet to be seen.

ASSESSMENT

Constructed-response questions

1. Although both financial crises affected the banking systems of their respective eras, one spread rapidly through commercial banks causing significant losses to individual depositors and one did not. What was the critical difference that contained the current crisis at the banks, protected individual depositors and allowed for an orderly contraction of the banking system where banks did have problems?

No central banking authority existed in 1907. Central banks can function as lenders of last resort to add liquidity to strapped banks. The effect is to reduce bank runs and panics. The Federal Deposit Insurance Corporation (FDIC) was founded much later (in 1933) and further reduced the likelihood of bank runs.

Without a lender of last resort or insurance, the mere scent of trouble would result in instantaneous queues outside of banks. The Federal Reserve and the FDIC in 2007 were able to prevent bank runs and support banks that failed until suitable buyers were found.

2. How can mortgage-backed securities seem to be so safe and yet at the same time apparently increase risk significantly?

One mortgage failure will severely damage the owner of that single mortgage. But one failure out of 100 mortgages means only a 1% loss if all the mortgages are owned as a package. Thus, mortgage-backed securities appear to be safer.

However, banks and mortgage brokers sold the mortgages they made to someone else. This meant that they could afford to be less concerned with the safety of any single mortgage and may have tended to make more risky mortgages.

3. What were the roles of changing interest rates in the housing crisis of 2007?

Falling interest rates several years prior to the crisis of 2007 led to falling costs of mortgages and rising demand for housing. That contributed to an increase in housing prices. Rising interest rates just prior to the crisis of 2007 meant that the purchase of houses had become more expensive and thus the demand for housing fell, placing downward pressures on housing prices.

Activity 1
Comparing Crises

Directions: Use this compare and contrast organizer to explore similarities and differences between the Panic of 1907 and the crisis of 2007-2009.

THE PANIC OF 1907   **THE CRISIS OF 2007-2009**

How are they alike?

_____
_____
_____
_____
_____
_____

How are they different?

_____   _____
_____   _____
_____   ⟷   _____
_____   _____
_____   _____

ACTIVITY 2

CATALYSTS FOR ECONOMIC DECLINE

The San Francisco Earthquake of 1906 and the toll exacted on New Orleans of Hurricane Katrina in 2005 are both American disasters of unprecedented proportions. The events were similar in the scope of damage. But they also are linked because the initial natural disasters were exacerbated by physical failures that caused even more losses. The earthquake caused numerous natural-gas lines to rupture, resulting in massive fires fed by the vast amounts of wood-frame construction common in that day.

Hurricane Katrina was a Category 3 storm when it made landfall on the outskirts of New Orleans. Though the winds were powerful, it was the storm surge that breached the man-made levees and engulfed the low-lying city in as much as 20 feet of flood water that wrought great suffering.

Both events are also connected because they occurred in advance of destructive economic crises that gripped the nation and much of the world. The earthquake in San Francisco is credited with being the external shock that weakened the economy so greatly that it became vulnerable to events leading to the Panic of 1907. Hurricane Katrina, although in proximity to the credit crisis that began in 2007, is not considered as a catalyst for economic decline. Why did the San Francisco earthquake play such a large role in prompting financial crisis while Hurricane Katrina was largely benign?

SAN FRANCISCO

- 7.8-magnitude earthquake

- Over 80 percent of the city destroyed

- Over 3,000 deaths (an estimated 500 shot as suspected looters)

- 250,000 left homeless

- 25,000 buildings destroyed on 490 city blocks

- 90 percent of the destruction resulted from subsequent fires

- Many buildings destroyed by firefighters using dynamite to create fire breaks

- Water main breaks depleted the means to fight the fires

- Overall cost of the property damage was about $10 billion in 2009 dollars, an amount equivalent to 1.50 percent of the nation's GDP in 1906

NEW ORLEANS

- The third-most-intense U.S. land-falling hurricane on record, Category 3 with 125 mph winds

- Levee breaches and overtopping resulted in floodwaters of 15 to 20 feet covering about 80 percent of the city

- An estimated 1,353 direct fatalities and 275,000 homes damaged or destroyed

- An estimated total of $81.2 billion in damage, slightly more than 0.5 percent of GDP in 2006

- Tens of thousands of jobs were lost due to severely damaged or destroyed businesses and supporting infrastructure

- Major highways in and around New Orleans were damaged or destroyed, disrupting commerce

- Katrina also affected the oil and gas industry by damaging platforms and shutting down refineries and interrupting operations at two major U.S. ports in Louisiana

ACTIVITY 3
CHARACTERS IN THE FINANCIAL CRISIS

"I need money for my kid's college tuition now, in 2006," said Joe. "The problem is that I don't have steady employment, I don't really have any money in the bank, and I already have a mortgage on my house with a big monthly payment. Is there any hope for me?"

"No problem!" said Bruce, the mortgage broker, "I don't need you to verify employment, and you can simply tell me how much you earn. I won't be checking whether you have money in the bank. I'll get you your money from the equity in your house."

Our announcer asks, "How can that be? Doesn't Joe need to prove he's a worthy borrower? Doesn't Bruce want to know what kind of risk he's taking by making this loan? How does he know that Joe will repay, and how does he know that the value of Joe's house will always be there?" He pauses and then asks, "What happened to the rules of banking?"

Mortimer, the old-time banker says, "Since World War II, the U.S. housing market has continued to go up, bankers made safe loans to thoroughly vetted borrowers and then serviced the loans until they were paid off. Many people stayed in those homes for decades, and less than 1 percent of borrowers defaulted."

Uncle Sam said in 2001, "Nothing is safer than the American housing market and nothing is more important than making sure every American is a homeowner. We're going to lower interest rates and keep them low so that home ownership becomes an affordable dream. We want to see the ownership rate rise. How can they lose? Prices never go down!"

ACTIVITY 3, CONTINUED
CHARACTERS IN THE FINANCIAL CRISIS

(Announcer) "Meanwhile, the rest of the world was getting a lot wealthier. The global pool of cash had doubled to a whopping $70 trillion between 2000 and 2006. Formerly poor countries like China, Brazil and India were now making things the world wanted to buy. Add that to the dollars from oil-producing nations and the world needed new places to invest. What would keep this money safe and generate a nice return?"

"Why, mortgages of course!" said a Wall Street banker. "We'll buy mortgages from the loan originators, bundle them in large quantities so that we mix in the very few bad ones with all of those good ones and sell shares in these investments to people around the world. There's a constant stream of income because what we see is that prices always go up and homeowners always pay. We'll call them mortgage-backed securities or MBS."

By 2003, Bruce (the mortgage broker) said, "We're running out of people interested in mortgages. Rates have been low for so long and everyone who qualifies under our guidelines has gotten a loan. There are a lot of people who have asked but they seem too risky for mortgage financing."

Uncle Sam says, "We really want people to own homes and we want to continue to stimulate the economy. We're going to keep interest rates low."

"Gosh" said the Wall Street banker, "we're getting gloriously wealthy from the fees generated by mortgage-backed securities and I would hate to see the gravy train end. Hmm, let me look at those statistics again. As I thought, we can loosen our guidelines for mortgage qualification. The way these mortgages are bundled, when we mix the risky ones with the sound ones, even if 10 percent of the borrowers default, the investor will still make a tidy profit.....I think?"

ACTIVITY 3, CONTINUED
CHARACTERS IN THE FINANCIAL CRISIS

"Wow, what a lovely village you have here in Narvik, Norway, and so close to the Arctic Circle," said the investment salesman in the Armani suit. "Yes, these investments are absolutely safe…look, they come with an 'AAA' rating from Wall Street rating companies. What more do I have to tell you? Look at these statistics, housing prices always go up and borrowers always pay."

The village treasurer responded, "Alright, it looks good. The people of my village trust me to make our nest egg grow so that we can have more school buses, care for our elderly population, and provide more services. I'm not really sure what an MBS is, but the American borrowers always pay and Wall Street says that it's a 'AAA' investment, the safest in the world. Where do I sign?"

"This doesn't seem right, I don't have to ask for tax returns or pay stubs?" asked Bruce. "I don't need to access bank records or look at existing debt? I can accept a borrower with a 500 to 600 credit score? I thought we liked to see at least 700? I don't feel comfortable selling these mortgages; if they don't pay, won't I get in trouble? What do you think, boss?"

"Don't worry Bruce, we're going to sell these things to Wall Street, we'll pass the risk on to them," said Bruce's boss. "Our hands are clean and you will make a nice income. The more you sell the more you will earn. Besides, if we don't sell them, somebody else will. The financial customers are clamoring for them."

(Announcer) "So, lenders kept lowering the guidelines for mortgages. First it was state your income, then no income but state your assets, then it was no income, no assets, then something called a "NINJA" loan…no income, no job or assets. Most of these were adjustable rate or deferred interest deals where the interest rate was low in the first months of the mortgage but then increased dramatically to a much higher rate."

"Uhh, I can't make my mortgage payment anymore," said Joe. "The rate jumped and the value of my house is plummeting because builders built more houses and everyone with an adjustable mortgage is trying to sell at the same time. Now I can't refinance my home. The last I read, a huge number of borrowers were delinquent on their mortgages and many of those were entering or close to foreclosure."

AARRRGHHH!!!!!

ACTIVITY 3, CONTINUED
CHARACTERS IN THE FINANCIAL CRISIS

QUESTIONS FOR DISCUSSION

A. Based on the surprised response of the announcer in frame three, speculate on the types of documentation requirements borrowers might have been subject to in more regulated times.

B. What financial innovation, popularized over the last 10 years, might have allowed lenders to accept a greater amount of risk?

C. In retrospect, former Fed chair Alan Greenspan has admitted that keeping interest rates low for so long was not a sound policy for housing markets. What was the effect on housing markets? What might have been the motivation to keep interest rates so low?

D. Why were investors as far away as Narvik, Norway, willing to invest in U.S. mortgage-backed securities?

E. What financial move by the Federal Reserve had a dramatic impact on borrowers holding adjustable rate mortgages?

VISUAL 1
PANDEMONIUM IN THE MARKETS

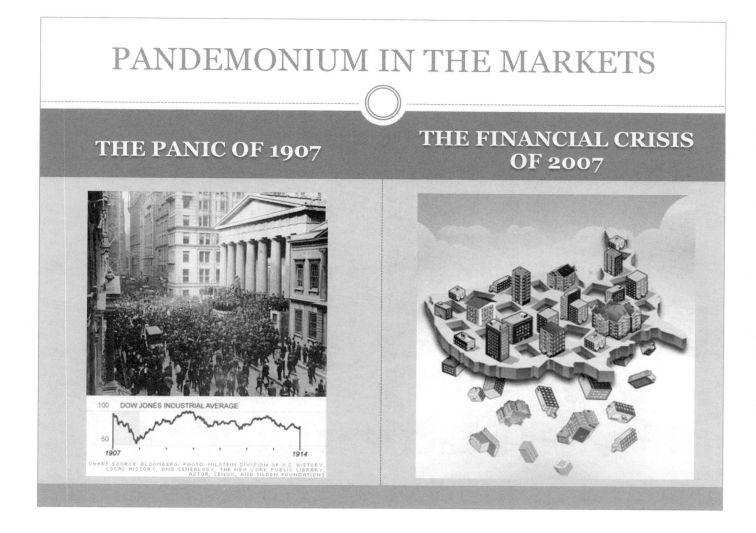

VISUAL 1, CONTINUED
PANDEMONIUM IN THE MARKETS

EVENTS IN 1906

DEVASTATION

SAN FRANCISCO EARTHQUAKE

- Shortly after 5 a.m. on April 18, a 7.8-magnitude quake, unleashed offshore, shook the city for just less than a minute.

Visual 1, Continued
Pandemonium in the Markets

SAN FRANCISCO EARTHQUAKE 1906

UNCONTROLLABLE BLAZE

80 PERCENT OF THE CITY DESTROYED

- Though the damage from the quake was severe, the subsequent fires from broken gas lines caused the vast majority of the destruction.

VISUAL 1, CONTINUED
PANDEMONIUM IN THE MARKETS

REMEMBERING THE SAN FRANCISCO EARTHQUAKE OF 1906

3,000 PEOPLE DIED

THE FIRES RAGED FOR FOUR DAYS

VISUAL 1, CONTINUED

PANDEMONIUM IN THE MARKETS

THE GOLD STANDARD

TOUGH BALANCING ACT

INFLEXIBLE CURRENCY

- Between 1870 and 1914, many countries adhered to a gold standard.

- This strictly tied national money supplies to gold stocks.

- Currency was redeemed for gold at a fixed exchange rate.

VISUAL 1, CONTINUED
PANDEMONIUM IN THE MARKETS

THE WORLD'S FINANCIAL SYSTEM HAD BECOME COMPLEX & INTERRELATED

- At the end of 1905, nearly 50 percent of the fire insurance in San Francisco was underwritten by British firms. The earthquake gave rise to a massive outflow of funds—of gold—from London.

- The magnitude of the resulting capital outflows in late summer and early autumn 1906 forced the Bank of England to undertake defensive measures to maintain its desired level of reserves. The central bank responded by raising its discount rate 2.5 percent 1906.

- Actions by the Bank of England attracted gold imports and sharply reduced the flow of gold to the United States. Interest rates rose and by May 1907, the United States had fallen into one of the shortest, but most severe, recessions in American history.

VISUAL 1, CONTINUED
PANDEMONIUM IN THE MARKETS

GREAT ECONOMIC PROMISE

At the beginning of the century, the nation was brimming with a great amount of optimism.

Here is a list of familiar companies founded between 1900 and 1905.

- Eastman Kodak
- Firestone Tire
- Ford Motors
- Harley-Davidson
- Hershey
- U.S. Steel
- J.C. Penney
- Pepsi-Cola
- Texaco
- Sylvania Electric

VISUAL 1, CONTINUED

PANDEMONIUM IN THE MARKETS

EVENTS IN 1907

- In October 1907 two brothers, Otto and F. Augustus Heinze, teamed up with a Wall Street banker in an attempt to manipulate the stock of a copper company.

- They planned to corner the market in the copper company's shares by buying aggressively in hopes they could later force short sellers to buy them at high prices.

- The plan did not have sufficient backing and failed.

Visual 1, Continued
Pandemonium in the Markets

PANIC IN THE STREETS

- News that a number of prominent New York bankers were involved in the failed scheme began a crisis of confidence among depositors.

- As additional institutions were implicated, queues formed outside numerous banks as people desperately sought their savings.

VISUAL 1, CONTINUED
PANDEMONIUM IN THE MARKETS

FURTHER COMPLICATING MATTERS

Trust companies were a financial innovation of the 1890s. They had many functions similar to state and national banks but were much less regulated.

KNICKERBOCKER TRUST COMPANY

VISUAL 1, CONTINUED
PANDEMONIUM IN THE MARKETS

GREATER RISKS WERE TAKEN

Illustration from Harper's Weekly December 20, 1913 by Walter J. Enright

- They were able to hold a wide array of assets and were not required to hold reserves against deposits.

- They earned a higher rate of return on investments and paid out higher rates, but, to do this, they had to be highly leveraged.

- They took more risks than traditional banks.

VISUAL 1, CONTINUED
PANDEMONIUM IN THE MARKETS

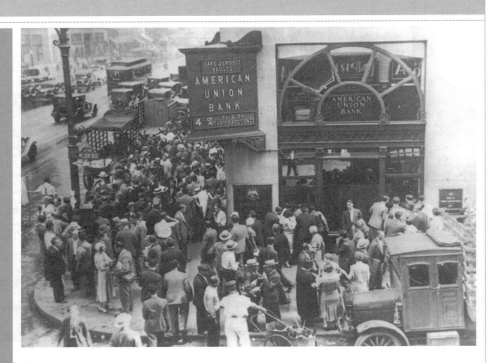

The runs on deposits that sparked the Panic of 1907 were at two of the largest New York City trust companies: Knickerbocker Trust and Trust Company of America.

A NEW YORK CITY BANK RUN IN NOVEMBER 1907

VISUAL 1, CONTINUED
PANDEMONIUM IN THE MARKETS

THE IMPACT

The crash and panic of 1907 had a dramatic effect on the health of the American and worldwide economies. In the United States:

- Commodity prices fell 21 percent.
- Industrial production fell more than in any other crisis in American history to that point.
- The dollar volume of bankruptcies declared in November was up 47 percent from the previous year.
- The value of all listed stocks in the U.S. fell 37 percent.
- In October and November 1907, 25 banks and 17 trust companies failed. Thousands of depositors lost their life savings.
- Gross earnings by railroads fell by 6 percent in December and production fell 11 percent.
- Wholesale prices fell 5 percent.
- Imports shrank 26 percent.
- In a few short months, unemployment rose from 2.8 percent to 8 percent.
- Immigration reached a peak of 1.2 million in 1907 but fell to around 750,000 by 1909.

VISUAL 1, CONTINUED
PANDEMONIUM IN THE MARKETS

WHAT WAS DONE?

J.P. MORGAN

NEITHER ELECTED NOR APPOINTED, HE FELT IT WAS HIS TIME TO ACT

- In the absence of a strong federal regulatory structure or any safety nets, the response to this crisis had to be delivered by a private citizen, J.P. Morgan the world's most powerful banker.

- He used all of his influence to convince fellow titans of industry to pool their resources and salvage the nation.

- The Panic subsided after six weeks.

VISUAL 1, CONTINUED
PANDEMONIUM IN THE MARKETS

LESSONS FROM THE PANIC OF 1907

SPECULATION IN OFF-STREET MARKETS

A BUCKET SHOP IN 1907

Bucket shops were blamed for fueling the speculation in 1907. They enabled people to speculate on the value of a stock without having to purchase the stock itself. The actual order to purchase went in the "bucket." Beginning in 1909, New York banned bucket shops and other states followed.

CUSTOMERS GENERAL OFFICE, HAIGHT & FREESE, N. Y.

VISUAL 1, CONTINUED

PANDEMONIUM IN THE MARKETS

THE FINANCIAL CRISIS OF 2007

THE WORLD MADE HUGE INVESTMENTS IN THE U.S. HOUSING MARKET...

...AND LOST!!

- By ignoring risk, remaining irrationally optimistic, and forgoing transparency through an array of fantastically complicated investment vehicles, the world's financial markets were extremely dependent on housing prices.

- The underlying assumptions were that housing prices never fall and homeowners almost always pay their mortgages.

VISUAL 1, CONTINUED
PANDEMONIUM IN THE MARKETS

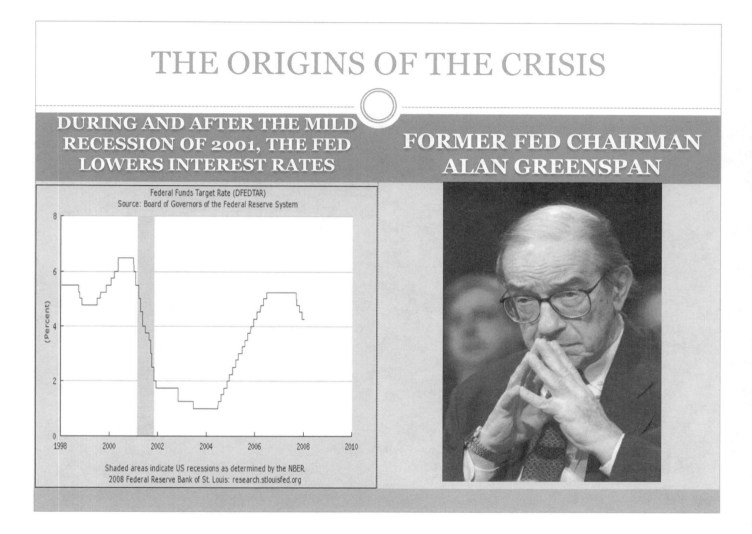

VISUAL 1, CONTINUED
PANDEMONIUM IN THE MARKETS

THE ORIGINS OF THE CRISIS

FORMER PRESIDENT GEORGE BUSH

STRONGLY PROMOTED HOMEOWNERSHIP

- "We can put light where there's darkness, and hope where there's despondency in this country. And part of it is working together as a nation to encourage folks to own their own home" –President Bush, October 15, 2002.

VISUAL 1, CONTINUED

PANDEMONIUM IN THE MARKETS

CAUSES OF THE CRISIS

HIGHLY COMPLEX FORMS OF FINANCING

- The momentum behind the expansion of homeownership led the government to reduce regulations and capital requirements for making loans.

- This led to a dizzying number of innovative ways to get less-qualified borrowers a mortgage and seemed to reduce risk for the lender.

- Mortgages could be bundled and sold around the world as securities.

THIS WAS TOO TEMPTING FOR THE FINANCIAL INSTUTIONS

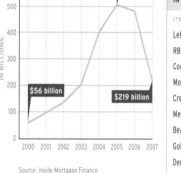

Total Financing of Mortgage-Backed Securities (2000-2007)

Banks and other investors poured more than $2 trillion into the mortgage-backed securities market between 2000 and 2007.

$508 billion

$56 billion

$219 billion

IN BILLIONS

Source: Inside Mortgage Finance

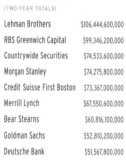

TOP UNDERWRITERS IN PEAK YEARS: 2005-2006 (TWO-YEAR TOTALS)	
Lehman Brothers	$106,444,600,000
RBS Greenwich Capital	$99,346,200,000
Countrywide Securities	$74,533,600,000
Morgan Stanley	$74,275,800,000
Credit Suisse First Boston	$73,367,000,000
Merrill Lynch	$67,550,600,000
Bear Stearns	$60,816,100,000
Goldman Sachs	$52,810,200,000
Deutsche Bank	$51,567,800,000

VISUAL 1, CONTINUED
PANDEMONIUM IN THE MARKETS

CAUSES OF THE CRISIS

TRUSTED AGENCIES FAILED TO WARN INVESTORS

RISK-RATING AGENCIES

- Mortgage-backed securities were constructed of mortgages of differing quality levels.
- The obligations of solid and sub-prime borrowers were mixed in a manner that made it very difficult for experts to calculate risk.
- The assumption that U.S. housing prices would continue to rise and incentives to provide good ratings led agencies to rate these securities as AAA, lowering investors' concerns.

VISUAL 1, CONTINUED

PANDEMONIUM IN THE MARKETS

EFFECTS OF THE CRISIS

WHAT WERE WE THINKING?

THE PERFECT STORM

- Homeownership peaks in early 2005 at 70 percent of households.
- The Fed raises interest rates.
- Home prices fall.
- Higher adjustable interest rates increase payments for borrowers.
- Borrowers default in waves.
- Dozens of subprime lenders file for bankruptcy.
- Mortgage-backed securities lose value as investors question their contents.
- Financial institutions struggle to find buyers.

VISUAL 1, CONTINUED
PANDEMONIUM IN THE MARKETS

"FINANCIAL WEAPONS OF MASS DESTRUCTION"

Financial institutions could purchase credit default swaps. A CDS is a private insurance contract that paid off if the investment failed. One did not actually have to own the investment to collect on the insurance. These promises were unregulated, and the sellers did not have to set aside money to pay for losses.

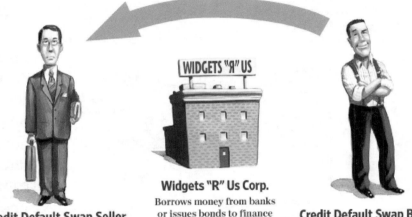

What is a Credit Default Swap?

A credit default swap is an agreement between two parties that works like a side bet on a football game. Swap sellers promise swap buyers a big payment if a company's bonds or loans default. In return for the promise they get quarterly payments. Neither needs to hold the underlying debt when entering into a swap.

WIDGETS "Я" US

Widgets "Я" Us Corp.
Borrows money from banks or issues bonds to finance operations.

Credit Default Swap Seller
Promises to pay swap buyer a set amount if Widgets "Я" Us defaults, often $10 million

■ Receives annual payments from swap buyer in return for "insurance"

■ Can include banks, insurance companies, hedge funds or others

Credit Default Swap Buyer
Promises quarterly payments to swap seller

■ Receives promise of large payout if bond defaults

■ Can include banks, insurance companies, hedge funds or others

■ If Widget's financial fortunes turn sour, the swap becomes more valuable. A swap holder can resell it and get high payments in return

Visual 1, Continued

Pandemonium in the Markets

THE FINANCIAL CRISIS OF 2007-2009

- Bank failures: 183 (2%) 12/07-2/10 (No deposits lost)
- Unemployment rate: 10.1% (10/09)
- Economic decline: -4.1% (4Q 2007-2Q 2009)
- Biggest drop in DJIA: -53.8% (12/07-3/09)
- Change in prices: +1.5% (12/07–6/09)
- Emergency spending and tax reduction programs: 2.5% of GDP in 2008 and in 2009
- Aggressive increase in monetary stimulus by the Fed

VISUAL 1, CONTINUED
PANDEMONIUM IN THE MARKETS

6.7 million jobs lost in 2008 and 2009

Capital investment levels lowest in 50 years

Domestic demand declines 11 consecutive quarters

Industrial production down worldwide: Japan 31 percent, South Korea 26 percent, Russia 16 percent, Brazil 15 percent, Italy 14 percent, Germany 12 percent

THE FINANCIAL CRISIS OF 2007-2009

VISUAL 1, CONTINUED
PANDEMONIUM IN THE MARKETS

The federal government unleashed a series of remedies in an attempt to limit the contagion.

Massive sums of bank reserves were created to ease fears.

In the process, the taxpayers took over or funded several familiar financial and nonfinancial companies.

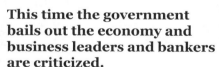

This time the government bails out the economy and business leaders and bankers are criticized.

VISUAL 1, CONTINUED
PANDEMONIUM IN THE MARKETS

SIMILARITIES

1907	2007
• Highly complex and linked financial system	• Global interdependent financial system
• Strong growth in the economy starting in 1900	• Vibrant economic recovery after recession in 2001
• Many people and institutions highly leveraged	• Lenders willing to take more risk in making loans
• Innovative form of finance: trust companies	• Unregulated financial institutions: hedge funds
• Stock market setting all-time highs	• Companies reporting record earnings
• A limited role for government	• Absence of many safety buffers
• Markets swing from great optimism to great pessimism	• Dow 14,164 to 6,500 in 16 months

VISUAL 1, CONTINUED
PANDEMONIUM IN THE MARKETS

DIFFERENCES

1907

- J.P. Morgan, a private citizen, orchestrated the bailout
- The Panic lasted for six weeks, though the economy didn't return to pre-Panic levels until 1909
- Many banks were closed and many depositors lost their savings
- The nation was on the gold standard and the supply of money was fixed
- The San Francisco earthquake was a catalyst for the Panic
- The climate toward business was hostile prior to crisis

2007

- The Federal Reserve and Treasury Department organize the reaction
- The event has been unfurling for more than three years
- Many banks closed and folded into healthier banks, but depositors did not lose any of their savings
- The nation uses Federal Reserve notes, creating a flexible money supply
- Hurricane Katrina was generally benign as a catalyst
- The climate toward business was friendly prior to crisis

TEACHING FINANCIAL CRISES © COUNCIL FOR ECONOMIC EDUCATION, NEW YORK, NY

HOW ECONOMIC PERFORMANCE FROM 2007-2009 COMPARES TO OTHER PERIODS IN U.S. HISTORY

LESSON 2

HOW ECONOMIC PERFORMANCE FROM 2007-2009 COMPARES TO OTHER PERIODS IN U.S. HISTORY

LESSON DESCRIPTION

The students examine information and data about six **recessions** in the United States. In small groups, they use the information to make short presentations about the recessions, highlighting data on economic performance during the time periods, and then they present this information to the class. The students discuss similarities and differences between the various events and guess which years they correspond to.

INTRODUCTION

Modern successful economies experience steady economic growth enabling the vast majority of citizens and workers to participate in rising standards of living. Those economies also go through periods where growth slows, sometimes stops, and even reverses itself. Primary contributing factors in determining the trends in rates of growth are the level and rate of change in technology; the amount of investment in tools, machines, computers, infrastructure, and buildings; and the skill and experience levels of the economy's labor. It is more difficult to pinpoint a given set of factors that cause economies to grow faster for short periods of time and then to slow and eventually turn down.

We often use the term **business cycles** to summarize that process of faster growth followed by dips in **real GDP** and employment levels. The short-run fluctuations are not cycles in a regular, periodic sense; sometimes they occur only a few months apart; other times, they have a decade of healthy, expanding economic growth in between. The causes of cycles are many and varied. The downturns are difficult to predict; they are almost impossible to prevent, or at least we have not figured out how to do so yet. However, the time between recessions has increased; therefore, the number of recessions has decreased in the past 30 years compared to the rest of the last century. Most observers would say that we are much better at under-

standing and managing monetary policy, which is the primary factor in explaining our fortunate moderation.

In this lesson, we examine six periods of economic fluctuations, from the Great Depression to the recent crisis of 2007-2009. All the periods discussed here have similarities, but different causes, and are slowdowns of varying degrees. They all fit the general definition of a recession, which is not a technical one by any means. In fact, there is some art in defining when a recession starts and when one ends. For example, we did not declare the beginning date until December 2008. We did not declare the end date of June 2009 until September 2010.

The National Bureau of Economic Research (NBER) defines beginning and ending dates of recessions. It looks at a wide variety of data but focuses on levels of employment and production in all parts of the economy. It believes that economic conditions have to have changed over much of the country, that the downturn has to last more than a few months, and that it has to be a significant decline. Obviously "much of the country," "more than a few months," and "significant" leave much room for debate and discussion. Given the definition, it should be clear why we are not able to declare that we are in a recession until we have been in one for "more than a few months."

Economic growth over time is crucial to enhancements in economic well-being. However, the fluctuations along the way mean that individuals lose jobs, incomes decline, profits decline and become losses, and businesses and individuals struggle under difficult circumstances. The more we know about economic fluctuations, the better able we will be to expand the time between recessions, limit their severity, minimize their costs to all, and perhaps eventually even prevent them.

CONCEPTS

- Business cycles
- Depression
- Real gross domestic product
- Inflation
- Macroeconomic indicators
- Money supply
- Recession
- Unemployment
- Unemployment rate

OBJECTIVES

Students will:

1. Develop and make presentations about the Great Depression and the recessions of 1973-1975, 1981-1982, 1990-1991, 2001 and 2007-2009.

2. Compare six recessions in U.S. economic history and explain the similarities and differences.

3. Explain with data how economic performance during these periods was affected.

CONTENT STANDARDS

- Fluctuations in a nation's overall levels of income, employment, and prices are determined by the interaction of spending and production decisions made by all households, firms, government agencies, and others in the economy. Recessions occur when overall levels of income and employment decline.

- Unemployment imposes costs on individuals and the overall economy. Inflation, both expected and unexpected, also imposes costs on individuals and the overall economy. Unemployment increases during recessions and decreases during recoveries.

TIME REQUIRED

Two class periods, plus student library time

MATERIALS

- Activity 1: Recessions in U.S. History (one copy of one of the periods in economic history for each student)

- Visual 1: Business Cycles (transparency)

- Visual 2: U.S. Real GDP (transparency)

- Visual 3: U.S. Unemployment Rate (transparency)

- Visual 4: Data on Economic Performance for Reference (optional transparency) (See procedure 7B)

PROCEDURE

1. Explain that this lesson will ask the students to examine the events that caused recessions in recent history, to consider economic data related to these periods in economic history and to compare these time periods to one another.

2. Write the term recession on the board. Ask: What is a recession? What recessions have you studied in school?

   *Answers will vary. Students will likely know about the very recent recession and the Great Depression. They will also likely know that recessions are times when the economy is weak and that the **unemployment rate** is elevated.*

3. Explain that a recession is determined by a group of economists at the National Bureau of Economic Research (NBER). Consider showing the NBER's website, which dates recessions back to the 1850s (http://www.nber.org/cycles/cyclesmain.html).

   Explain that the NBER considers a recession a significant decline in economic activity spread across the economy, lasting more than a few months, normally visible in **macroeconomic indicators** such as real GDP, real income, employment, industrial production, and wholesale-retail sales.

4. Explain that recessions are measured from the peak of economic activity to the trough while an expansion is measured from

trough to peak. Use Visual 1: Business Cycles to make this point. Also, show the students the historical data in Visual 2: U.S. Real GDP. Discuss how real GDP and **unemployment** (Visual 3: U.S. Unemployment Rate) tend to behave during recessions. You may need to review how GDP and the unemployment rate are calculated. You may use the NBER website to demonstrate how long recent recessions have been in months and how long the economy expanded between recessions.

Note that there have been 14 recessions since 1929, including two during the Great Depression and the current recession, which began in December 2007. We focus on six of those time periods as these are among the most serious and have a wide variety of causes.

5. Explain that many recessions can be explained by analyzing aggregate demand and aggregate supply shifts. AP Economics students will already understand these concepts; however, students in other courses will likely need some instruction on these ideas. Explain that aggregate demand is the total quantity of goods and services demanded at each price level and that aggregate supply is the total quantity of goods and services supplied at each price level. Have the students consider factors that might shift these curves and explain that the equilibrium in this model determines the economy's real GDP.

6. Tell the students that they will each be on a team responsible for studying one period in economic history. Randomly distribute the sections of Activity 1 to students (giving each student one historical period). Tell the students that there are six periods in economic history that they will be investigating. Allow time for the students to read the information that you've given them.

7. Tell the students to find others that have the same information they have and form groups (if you have a large class consider forming two groups for each historical period so that you have 12 groups). Instruct each group to develop a presentation informing others about the period in economic history that they've been assigned. The students should use the information on the activity to begin with; however, they will need to conduct further research in the library or on the Internet. Each presentation should include:

a. A summary of the causes of the recession.

b. A presentation of relevant economic data on the recession (some interesting economic data are provided for reference in optional Visual 4). You may use these data as a guide for what the students should collect, give the students these data and ask them to find more about the relevant time period, or use this information to determine whether the data the students collect are accurate.

c. Length and severity of the recession.

d. Pop culture information and other interesting facts about the time period.

8. Ask the students not to reveal the years of their recession during the presentation as the groups will later guess the time period. Instead of students using years to display the economic data in their presentations, suggest that they use phrases such as *peak unemployment rate = X percent in second year of the recession*. Give the students enough time to create these presentations. You may want to perform the instruction parts of this lesson in one class period and assign the student presentations at the next.

9. Ask each group to select a spokesperson to present to the class. The student should make the presentation without disclosing the dates or time period of the recession. After each presentation, write the key facts about the recession on the board and leave them up. Have the students guess the time period in U.S. history of each recession (other than their own); reveal the actual dates after they guess.

10. Discuss the following questions:

a. The unemployment rate and **gross domestic product** are important statistics. What other measures might be important to understanding the health of the economy?

Students may mention employment, the inflation rate, industrial production, stock prices, income, or many other measures.

b. What similarities and differences did you observe regarding the various recessions?

Accept many answers. Answers are likely to include that some recessions are attributed to the price of oil, others to a decline in the housing sector, others to monetary policy mistakes; and the Great Depression had its roots in orders for durable goods and Federal Reserve policy. (There is a continuing debate about the importance of each of a number of contributors to the Great Depression.) Further, recessions differed in length and severity, as evidenced by duration, peak unemployment rate, and decline in real GDP. Students may wish to explore why the peak unemployment rates are often reached after the end of a recession and continue to be high for some time thereafter.

c. What actions have the Federal Reserve and U.S. government taken to combat the most recent recession?

*The Fed has, in many ways, acted oppositely from how it did during the Great Depression. The Fed has created and used a variety of new monetary policy tools aimed at providing liquidity and/or reducing risk in the financial marketplace. It supported some large failing banks and financial institutions, cut interest rates (expanded the **money supply**) and even rescued some financial firms.*

d. How did the supply of oil from the Middle East affect two of the recessions?

During the 1981-1982 and 1973-1975 recessions, the supply of oil from the Middle East was restricted. This decrease in the supply of oil raised the price of oil and the price of many goods produced in the United States. This led to an increase in inflation and decline in spending, often described as stagflation.

e. Why might the Great Depression have ended around the time World War II began?

Wars can have a substantial effect on an economy. Due to the production required to fight the war, supply the troops, and develop military equipment, wars are frequently times of strong economic growth. Many argue that World War II production led to the end of the Great Depression. After World War I the economy struggled to revert to peace-time production without military demand and with an influx of war veterans who needed jobs.

CLOSURE

Review the definition of a recession and how the unemployment rate and growth rate of real GDP are frequently used to determine the severity of such economic downturns. Review the six periods of economic history studied in this lesson and, in particular, what makes them similar and different. Stress the role of housing in the current recession, the supply of oil in the 1970s and 1980s downturns, and the role of the Federal Reserve in the Great Depression and the most recent recession.

ASSESSMENT

Multiple-choice questions

1. A recession is best defined as a period during which:

a. The percentage of the population employed is expanding.

*b. Employment, output and income all decline.

c. The price level is declining.

d. More resources are used.

2. Stagflation refers to:

   a. A period of strong economic growth and high inflation.

   b. A period of strong economic growth and low inflation.

   *c. A period of slow economic growth with high inflation.

   d. A period of slow economic growth and low inflation.

3. Recessions are measured from the:

   *a. Peak of economic activity to the trough.

   b. Trough of economic activity to the peak.

   c. Peak of economic activity to the next peak.

   d. Trough of economic activity to the next trough.

4. During the 2007-2009 recession, real GDP declined by approximately:

   a. 15 percent.

   b. 11 percent.

   c. 7 percent.

   *d. 4 percent.

Constructed-response questions

1. Compare and contrast the current economic downturn with those in the past.

   The current downturn has been characterized by slow economic growth and high unemployment, as have many in recent history. Unlike the slowdowns of the 1970s and 1980s the current recession began in the housing market and was not related to oil prices. Inflation has also stayed under control in this downturn. Levels of unemployment have not come close to the levels seen during the Great Depression.

2. How has the Federal Reserve behaved differently during the recent recession compared with its conduct throughout the Great Depression?

During the recent downturn, the Fed has cut interest rates to near zero percent and supported U.S. banks and financial institutions in an effort to prevent their failure. During the Great Depression, the Fed's actions were nearly the opposite. The Fed allowed the money supply to decline sharply and bank failures to become widespread.

Activity 1
Recessions in U.S. History

1. The Financial Crisis of 2007-2009

What happened? The subprime mortgage crisis led to the collapse of the housing market in the U.S. Falling prices of housing-related financial assets contributed to a global financial crisis. The crisis led to the failure or collapse of many of the U.S.'s largest financial institutions, including Bear Stearns, Fannie Mae, Freddie Mac, Lehman Brothers and AIG, as well as the automobile industry. The government responded with an unprecedented $700 billion bank bailout and $787 billion fiscal stimulus package. By June 2009, the recession ended. Real GDP began to increase in the third quarter of 2009 (1.6 percent, annual rate) and continued in the fourth quarter (5.0 percent, annual rate). As is often the case at the end of a recession, unemployment continued to be a problem at between 9 and 10 percent.

2. The Recession of 2001

What happened? During the 1990s, the U.S. experienced the longest period of continuous growth in American history. The collapse of the speculative dot-com stock bubble brought this period of growth to an end while accounting scandals and fraud at Enron and other companies caused further problems. Increases in interest rates also contributed. Despite these major shocks, the recession was brief and shallow.

3. The Recession of 1990-1991

What happened? After a long economic expansion in the 1980s, inflation began to increase and the Federal Reserve responded by raising interest rates from 1986 to 1989. This slowed growth, but the 1990 oil price shock (due to the Gulf War), the debt accumulation of the 1980s, ongoing concern from the savings and loan crisis, and growing consumer pessimism combined with the weakened economy to produce a brief recession. This recession contributed to the defeat of President George H.W. Bush and the election of President Bill Clinton.

4. The Recession of 1981-1982

What happened? The Iranian Revolution sharply increased the price of oil around the world, causing the 1979 energy crisis. The new regime in power in Iran, which exported oil at inconsistent intervals and at a lower volume, forced prices up. Tight monetary policy in the U.S. was adopted to control inflation. The Fed feared a possible spiraling of inflation that was carried over from the 1970s and adopted policies that fell to sharply higher interest rates.

In 1982, business bankruptcies rose 50 percent over the previous year. Farmers were especially hard hit, as agricultural exports declined, crop prices fell, and interest rates rose. Although this slowdown in economic activity hurt the nation it also finally ended the long battle with inflation the country had been fighting since the 1970s.

ACTIVITY 1, CONTINUED
RECESSIONS IN U.S. HISTORY

5. The Recession of 1973-1975

What happened? During this period, there was economic stagnation in much of the Western world, putting an end to the general post-World War II economic boom. It differed from many previous recessions—it was characterized by a stagnant economy (causing high unemployment) and coincided with high inflation. The phenomenon was labeled stagflation.

Among the causes were the Vietnam War and the 1973 oil crisis. The 1973 oil crisis began when members of Organization of Petroleum Exporting Countries (OPEC) proclaimed an oil embargo. This caused the 1973 "oil price shock," which severely slowed the production of goods and services in the U.S.

According to the National Bureau of Economic Research, the recession in the United States lasted from November 1973 to March 1975. Although the economy expanded in the years following, inflation remained extremely high for the rest of the decade.

During this recession, the real GDP of the U.S. fell 3.2 percent. Although the recession ended in March 1975, the unemployment rate remained high for several months. In May 1975, the rate reached its peak for the cycle at 9 percent.

6. The Great Depression (1929-1938)

What happened? The Great Depression of 1929-1938 began with falling demand for durable and investment goods followed by a slowdown in business activity. A stock market crash occurred in October 1929, reducing the value of many Americans' assets and their willingness to spend money. Unemployment continued to rise. In March 1933, more than a quarter of the labor force was out of work. The primary cause of this continued decline was more than 9,000 bank failures between 1929 and 1933, which led to a significant reduction in the money supply.

Although the Federal Reserve System had been established in 1913 in part to prevent bank failures, it chose not to act as the lender of last resort during this period. The Federal Reserve also raised interest rates in late 1931, which further discouraged business borrowing and expansion. A combination of President Roosevelt's New Deal and government spending on World War II eventually led to the end of this dark period in American history.

Visual 1
Business Cycles

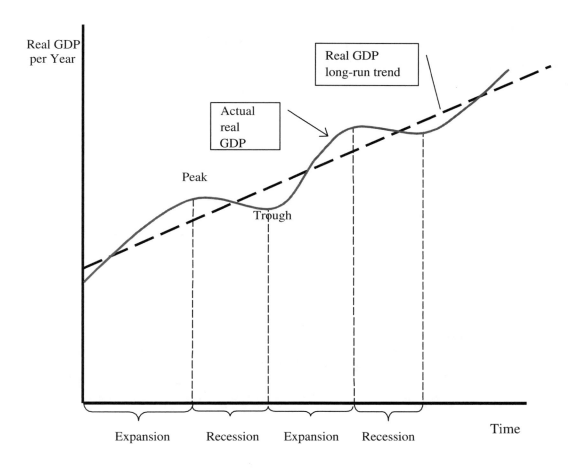

VISUAL 2
U.S. REAL GDP

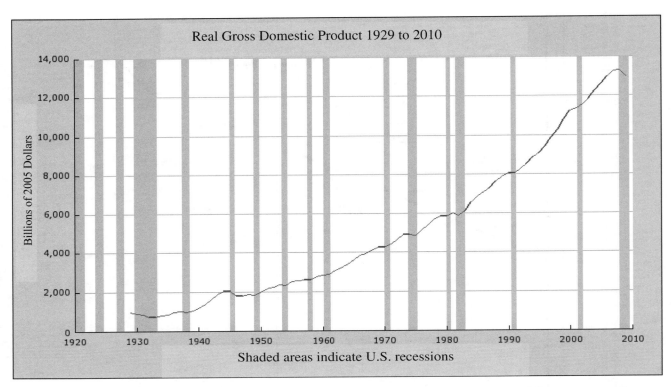

Source: Data from the Bureau of Economic Analysis, U.S. Department of Commerce, www.bea.gov

Visual 3
U.S. Unemployment Rate

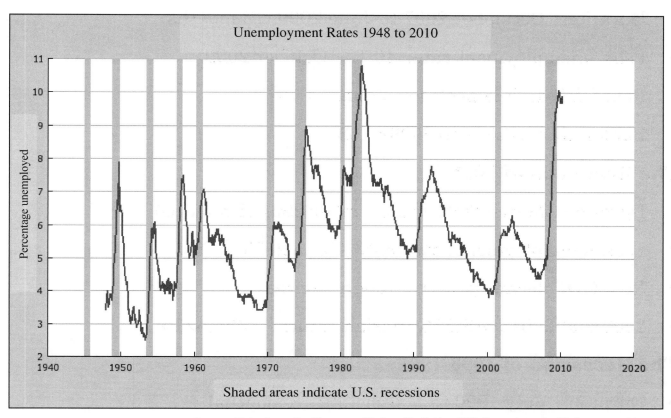

Unemployment Rates 1948 to 2010

Shaded areas indicate U.S. recessions

Source: Data from the Bureau of Labor Statistics, U.S. Department of Labor, www.bls.gov

VISUAL 4
DATA ON ECONOMIC PERFORMANCE FOR REFERENCE

The Financial Crisis of 2007-2009

- Duration: December 2007 to June 2009 (18 months)

- Peak unemployment rate: 10.1% (October 2009)

- Real GDP decline peak to trough: -4.1%

- Bank failures (2007 to 2009): 168

The Recession of 2001

- Duration: March 2001 to November 2001 (8 months)

- Peak unemployment rate: 6.3% (June 2003)

- Real GDP decline peak to trough: -0.3%

- 2000 and 2001 NASDAQ market return: -40%, -21%

The Recession of 1990-1991

- Duration: July 1990 to March 1991 (8 months)

- Peak unemployment rate: 7.8% (June 1992)

- Real GDP decline peak to trough: -1.4%

The Recession of 1981-1982

- Duration: July 1981 to November 1982 (16 months)

- Peak unemployment rate: 10.8% (November 1982)

- Real GDP decline peak to trough: -2.7%

- 1981 inflation rate (consumer price index): 8.9%

Visual 4, Continued
Data on Economic Performance for Reference

The Recession of 1973 -1975

- Duration: November 1973 to March 1975 (16 months)

- Peak unemployment rate: 9.0% (May 1975)

- Real GDP decline peak to trough: -3.2%

- 1974 inflation rate (consumer price index): 11%

The Great Depression (1929-1938)

- Duration: 1929-1933 (43 months) and 1937-1938 (13 months)

- Peak unemployment rate: 25.0% (1933)

- Real GDP decline peak to trough: -30% (1929-1933) and -3.4% (1937-1938)

- Bank failures: 9,106 (1930-1933) and 102 (1937-1938)

Data sources: Peak unemployment and inflation rates are from the United States Bureau of Labor Statistics (www.bls.gov). GDP data come from the Bureau of Economic Analysis (www.bea.gov). Bank failure data come from the Federal Deposit Insurance Corporation (www.fdic.gov).

MANIAS, BUBBLES, AND PANICS IN WORLD HISTORY

LESSON 3
MANIAS, BUBBLES, AND PANICS IN WORLD HISTORY

LESSON DESCRIPTION

This lesson addresses the psychology surrounding speculative manias, often referred to as **bubbles**. The class will be introduced to some of the theories behind bubbles and apply those concepts to the recent housing bubble. Students will then be introduced to five bubble events in world history: Tulipmania, the South Sea Bubble, the Roaring Twenties Stock Bubble, Japan's Bubble Economy, and the Dot-com Bubble.

Students will participate in an activity to analyze the features of the five bubbles to find similarities. Each bubble era will be assigned a number (1-5) and each student a corresponding number (1-5). The like-numbered students will meet and analyze the basic issues. Then new groups will be formed. The students will acquire information about their bubble from one of the essays in the lesson package and arrange the similarities of these events.

INTRODUCTION

Economic analysis assumes that men and women are rational beings who will respond logically to incentives. Yet, economic history is filled with tales of utter madness and mass hysteria in the pursuit of profits. Even though these cases are well documented, we tend to believe that every new experience will be different than all the rest. Spectacular instances of this irrational response have been happening about once a century. But in contemporary times, they are happening with greater frequency.

A once-ignored economist has gained attention recently because he spent most of his career writing about flawed human experiences in finance. Hyman Minsky described a typical bubble event in these phases:

Displacement. A crisis usually begins with an outside shock to the economic system such as war, a new invention, a political event, a surprising financial success, a

change in monetary policy in the aftermath of financial instability, or anything that alters the economic outlook and offers profit opportunities [**incentives**].

Boom. The optimism from this change leads to a rapid rise in **prices** of a physical or financial asset as investors and speculators attempt to earn profits.

Euphoria. Lenders offer more credit, sometimes at lower costs, which motivates people to take investment risks first increasing demand, then prices, then profits, then investment, and the cycle repeats. New financial instruments are often created. Firms and households see others making money and they mimic their behavior [**market psychology**]. At this point, even the most marginal investors are drawn in and rational decision-making succumbs to manic behavior. The bubble is inflating.

Profit-taking. Prices have risen to a point where a few insiders begin to take their profits and price increases begin to level off. At this point, large investors often realize that they may be overextended and are taking undue risk.

Panic. The failure of a large institution, the realization of a swindle, or an increase in the supply of the asset brings everyone back to their senses. People start selling in an orderly fashion but the market quickly deteriorates into chaos. People scramble to sell while they still have the potential for profit.

A sixth phase has been proposed by some:

Bailout. If a central bank exists, it may begin to expand the money supply to salvage the most essential financial institutions. The rationale for an economic role for government is that individuals and institutions other than those directly involved and perhaps the entire economy may pay some or most of the costs of the bubble cycle. Economists describe this as a **negative**

externality. The anticipation of a bailout may indirectly add to the problem because people may take greater risks if they are confident that a safety net is in place. This disregard for the full consequences of market actions is known as a **moral hazard**.

A more famous economist, John Kenneth Galbraith, suggested two factors that add to the bubble mentality:

"Investors have a short financial memory (or ignorance of history) that makes them oblivious to previous financial disasters."

"Investors have a tendency to attribute greater intelligence to individuals, the more income or assets they control."

Because acquiring wealth is so difficult for most people, we often have an unbounded admiration for those who succeed. We assume that they must know what they are doing and will signal to the world when it is time to change course.

CONCEPTS

- Asymmetric information
- Bubble
- Incentives
- Prices
- Speculation
- Market psychology
- Negative externalities
- Moral hazard

OBJECTIVES

Students will:

1. Explore the reasons why bubbles occur in market economies and the elements of human nature that make bubbles inevitable.

2. Identify the events surrounding five famous bubbles in world history.

3. Name and describe the common elements that run through all financial bubbles.

CONTENT STANDARDS

- People usually respond predictably to positive and negative incentives.

- A market exists when buyers and sellers interact. This interaction determines market prices and thereby allocates scarce goods and services.

- Prices send signals and provide incentives to buyers and sellers. When supply or demand changes, market prices adjust, affecting incentives.

TIME REQUIRED

Two class periods

MATERIALS

- Activity 1: Bubbles in World History (one copy per student)

- Activity 2: The Common Elements of Speculative Events (one copy per student)

- Visual 1: Bubble Quotes (transparency)

- Handout 1: Excerpt from "Why Wall Street Always Blows It" by Henry Blodget in *The Atlantic* (December 2008) (one copy per student). The link to the complete article can be found at http://www.theatlantic.com/doc/200812/blodget-wall-street

- Handout 2: Essay 1: Tulipmania (one copy to each student in assigned group)

- Handout 3: Essay 2: The South Sea Bubble (one copy to each student in assigned group)

- Handout 4: Essay 3: The Roaring Twenties Stock Bubble (one copy to each student in assigned group)

- Handout 5: Essay 4: Japan's Bubble Economy (one copy to each student in assigned group)

- Handout 6: Essay 5: The Dot-com Bubble (one copy to each student in assigned group)

- A method to show the film found at this location: http://www.library.hbs.edu/hc/historicalreturns/fb/movie.html

PROCEDURE

1. Distribute a copy of Handout 1: Excerpt from "Why Wall Street Always Blows It" by Henry Blodget in *The Atlantic* (December 2008) to each student and have them read it at their desks.

2. Use the article as a backdrop for a discussion on why bubbles inevitably happen. The scenario that the author spins is an especially good model of the behavior. Consider presenting and discussing the five stages of a bubble that are described in the introduction to this lesson. Ask students the following questions:

   a. What was the event that created the climate for **speculation** in the housing market?

   Possible answers might be the pursuit of "safer" investments after the dot-com bubble burst, the illusion that housing prices always rise, and the broad availability of cheap credit.

   b. Why did the country fall so quickly for another speculative fascination?

   Possible answers might be the reduction of interest rates, the encouragement of home ownership by the White House, the financial innovations that expanded access to credit, the apparent willingness of Wall Street to bet heavily on housing, and the fact that some of our neighbors were getting rich and we were not.

   c. Why do investors ignore the warnings, such as Alan Greenspan's "irrational exuberance" remark in 1996 about rapid increases in financial asset prices or the strong signals sent by other economists?

   Possible answers might be the general belief that "this time is different," the fear that you will be the person who has the proverbial door of opportunity slammed in your face, the contradiction of rising values despite the alarms, and the fact that typically the doomsayers are far outnumbered by the optimists.

   d. What caused the realization that this time was no different than any other?

   Possible answers might be the rising interest rates, the increasing supply of housing, the growing number of mortgage defaults, and the failure of very high profile financial institutions, such as Lehman Brothers and Bear Stearns.

   e. Why is it likely that another speculative boom awaits us?

   Possible answers might be that human nature seems to lead us down a path to euphoria, the natural pursuit of self-interest may inevitably create a speculative atmosphere, our eagerness to earn profit we see others earning, and designing and enforcing effective regulation is a very difficult challenge.

3. At this point, tell the students that they will now analyze the events surrounding speculative bubbles in world history. Break the class up into five groups of equal size and have them move their desks into circles for discussion. Assign each group a number 1-5 and tell the students that they will keep that number throughout the activity. Assign the five essays (Handouts 2-6), and give a copy to each student in the corresponding group. In addition, give all of the students a copy of Activity 1: Bubbles in World History.

   In their "home" groups, have the students read and explore the elements of the particular speculative period they have been assigned. Instruct groups to formulate answers to the four questions in the first two rows of Activity 1.

   a. When did the bubble begin and when did it end?

   b. What was the cause of the bubble and what caused the bubble to burst?

   c. What was life like during the bubble?

   d. What happened after the bubble?

   Answers will vary but should include the following: Tulipmania began in the 1630s; the South Sea Bubble in the 1710s; the

Roaring Twenties Stock Bubble in the 1920s; Japan's Bubble Economy in the late 1980s; and the Dot-com Bubble in the 1990s into the early 2000s. All lasted most of a decade. The causes differ depending upon the exact nature of the target of speculation. All included rapidly rising incomes and wealth followed by speculative financial periods. Life during the bubbles was filled with frenetic, ultimately unsustainable buying of financial assets. The periods ended with prices of financial assets reaching all-time highs and buyers becoming skeptical of the realism of the high prices, followed by collapses of financial asset prices. After the bubbles, economic slowdowns were common. In some cases, the breaking of the bubbles was a major contributing factor to the slowdowns; in others, such as the 1920s and 1990s, the collapse of the bubbles and the slowing economies had common causes and contributed to one other.

4. When that phase of Activity 1 is finished, create specialist groups with at least one individual from each of the original groups involved so all five bubbles are represented. Ask the specialists to share their story with the new group and, once all of the details of the five events are revealed, have students work toward completing the bottom row of Activity 1 by finding a set of common elements during and after each of the events.

   Possible answers: a significant external event preceded the bubble; the money supply was expanding and credit was increasingly available; a new opportunity became available followed by a great deal of investment enthusiasm; an absence of effective government regulation over the proceedings; reckless investments and uncontrollable envy; people displaying their new-found wealth conspicuously; a rapid rise and fall of prices; remorse and disbelief when the episode ends; and efforts by government to enact strong measures to correct market flaws.

5. Once the specialist groups have completed the common element section of Activity 1,

have students return to their home groups. Distribute a copy of Activity 2: The Common Elements of Speculative Events to all students and have the groups use the information they gathered in the specialist groups to respond to the questions.

   a. What role does credit typically play in the beginning of speculative events?

   b. What role does the government often play during the development of speculative events?

   c. What typically fuels the rapid increase in prices during speculative events?

   d. Why is it often said during speculative events that "this time is different?"

   e. What typically occurs at the beginning of the end of speculative events?

   f. What do people invariably say about the speculative events in the aftermath?

   Possible answers to the Activity 2 questions: (a) credit was plentiful and interest rates were low; (b) the government lowered barriers and encouraged the behavior; (c) investors see others doing well and want to jump on the bandwagon, there's an urgency to get in regardless of the late stage and this keeps driving up prices; (d) there's a sense of euphoria and profitable investors are labeled geniuses, the culture of irrationality leads to people ignoring the signals and even holding doomsayers in contempt; (e) some people begin to take profits and sell, which leads to a negative momentum, fraud may be exposed and confidence in the market evaporates; and (f) there is complete disbelief that this could happen, there is commitment to fixing the problem, and the cleansing of the system and new regulations may emerge.

6. Once the students have completed Activity 2, show the Harvard Business School video clip found at http://www.library.hbs.edu/hc/

historicalreturns/fb/movie.html. It takes about four minutes and establishes numerous connections between the South Sea Bubble and the Dot-com Bubble and will serve as a review of the themes of this lesson.

CLOSURE

Display Visual 1 and have the students respond to the statements. Ask them if they've witnessed the behavior and envy described in the first quote. Does it mean that we really do not want friends to do well financially?

Remind students of the scenario described in the opening reading, "Why Wall Street Always Blows It," how no one in the neighborhood wanted to miss the party and if you were not heavily immersed in real estate there was something wrong with you. Remind the students of all of the television space dedicated to shows about renovating, decorating, and flipping residential property.

Ask students to reflect on the second statement, how housing prices could go nowhere but up. Finally, ask them about the likelihood of their own manic behavior. Could they ever get caught up in a frenetic whirlwind like the ones they have studied? Are they sure they would be able to resist when everyone around them was earning profits? Why is it likely they would participate?

ASSESSMENT

Constructed-response questions

1. In 1720 and 1999, investors envisioned "new worlds" ahead of them and they were hungry for pieces of them. Describe the world the South Sea investors visualized prompting such blind faith in the ventures they were supporting. When dot-com investors were buying initial public offerings of shares of stock as quickly as they were announced and bidding up prices, what did they believe the Internet and the World Wide Web would mean to their future?

    Both investments were in the great unknown—a mysterious land halfway around the world and a mysterious alternative universe in cyberspace. In both cases, investors felt that these uncharted places were new markets to be conquered and that civilization would be far better off. The 18th century expectation was that the new world would offer cheap resources, new products, cheap labor, and abundant wealth. The late 20th century expectation was that cyberspace would create huge changes in productivity and new products.

    The new frontiers and the new technology would both generate significant profits and those who invested at the beginning would capture much of the profits. Prices of shares of stocks in the new ventures would increase dramatically as the potential in both instances was realized. As a few new companies were extremely successful, investors looked for the next great idea. Prospects were dramatically overestimated and the enthusiasm bordered on manic.

2. What role do expectations of prices play in the bubble process?

    An increase in demand, for whatever initial reason, will cause a rise in prices. If that increase in prices creates an impression that prices will continue to increase in the future, expectations of those higher prices will increase demand now. As a result, prices rise. If this increase further changes expectations, demand rises once more and prices increase again. It is the change in expectations that triggers the bubble expansion.

    The opposite occurs on the downside—the breaking of the bubble. If enough people expect prices to fall in the future, they will sell now. The increase in selling will lower prices and if that sell-off is sufficiently large, expectations of further lower prices will be reinforced. The downward path will continue—perhaps initially quite rationally, but ultimately only because people expect the changes.

3. Name the five steps in the process of a bubble being formed and then breaking. Can you explain the connections between the steps?

The steps are: a new product, innovation, event, or policy is created or happens; a boom, as people react to take advantage of the change; euphoria, as expectations of further price changes take over; profit-taking on the part of some bright, fortunate, and thoughtful individuals; and finally, panic as people begin to sell to protect their investments.

The innovation creates the perception or reality of new profit potential. That potential leads to some investors making decisions to support the efforts. If there are sufficient reasons, and prices of the investments are rising, expectations of further increases actually cause increases in purchases and the subsequent rise in prices. If the price increases are large enough, some individuals will begin to realize their profits and leave the market. That alone may not be sufficient to cause a panic. But the initial profit-taking combined with a surprise event that causes many to question may lead to panic selling and the breaking of the bubble.

ACTIVITY 1
BUBBLES IN WORLD HISTORY

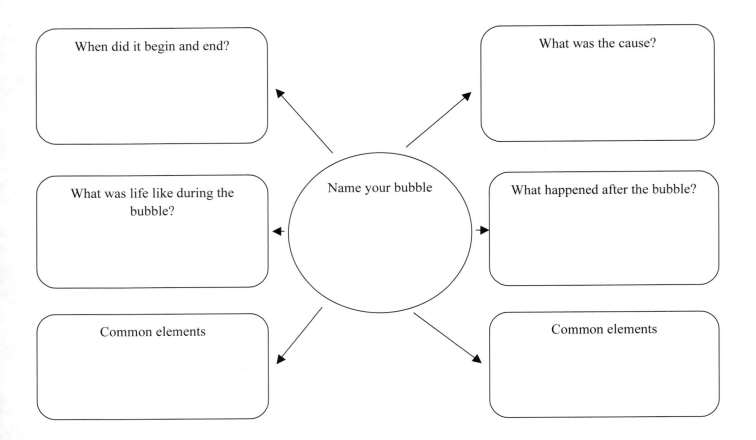

ACTIVITY 2
THE COMMON ELEMENTS OF SPECULATIVE EVENTS

In your home group, draw from the information you gathered from other bubble periods to answer the questions below.

A.   What role does credit typically play in the beginning of speculative events?

B.   What role does the government often play during the development of speculative events?

C.   What typically fuels the rapid increase in prices during speculative events?

D.   Why is it often said during speculative events that "this time it's different?"

E.   What typically occurs at the beginning of the end of speculative events?

F.   What do people invariably say about the speculative events in the aftermath?

VISUAL 1
BUBBLE QUOTES

"There is nothing as disturbing to one's well-being and judgment as to see a friend get rich."

Charles P. Kindleberger

"The four most expensive words in the English language are, *this time it's different.*"

attributed to Sir John Templeton

HANDOUT 1
EXCERPT FROM "WHY WALL STREET ALWAYS BLOWS IT" BY HENRY BLODGET IN *THE ATLANTIC* (DECEMBER 2008)

To understand why bubble participants make the decisions they do, let's roll back the clock to 2002. The stock market crash has crushed our portfolios and left us feeling vulnerable, foolish, and poor. We're not wiped out, thankfully, but we're chastened, and we're certainly not going to go blow our extra money on Cisco Systems again. So where should we put it? What's safe? How about a house?

House prices, we are told by our helpful neighborhood real-estate agent, almost never go down. This sounds right, and they certainly didn't go down in the stock-market crash. In fact, for as long as we can remember—about 10 years, in most cases—house prices haven't gone down. (Wait, maybe there was a slight dip, after the 1987 stock-market crash, but looming larger in our memories is what's happened since; everyone we know who's bought a house since the early 1990s has made gobs of money.)

We consider following our agent's advice, but then we decide against it. House prices have doubled since the mid-1990s; we're not going to get burned again by buying at the top. So we decide to just stay in our rent-stabilized rabbit warren and wait for house prices to collapse.

Unfortunately, they don't. A year later, they've risen at least another 10 percent. By 2006, we're walking past neighborhood houses that we could have bought for about half as much four years ago; we wave to happy new neighbors who are already deep in the money. One neighbor has "unlocked the value in his house" by taking out a cheap home-equity loan, and he's using the proceeds to build a swimming pool. He is also doing well, along with two visionary friends, by buying and flipping other houses—so well, in fact, that he's considering quitting his job and becoming a full-time real-estate developer. After four years of resistance, we finally concede—houses might be a good investment after all—and call our neighborhood real-estate agent. She's jammed (and driving a new BMW), but she agrees to fit us in.

We see five houses: two were on the market two years ago for 30 percent less (we just can't handle the pain of that); two are dumps; and the fifth, which we love, is listed at a positively ridiculous price. The agent tells us to hurry—if we don't bid now, we'll lose the house. But we're still hesitant: last week, we read an article in which some economist was predicting a housing crash, and that made us nervous. (Our agent counters that Greenspan says the housing market's in good shape, and he isn't known as "The Maestro" for nothing.)

When we get home, we call our neighborhood mortgage broker, who gives us a surprisingly reasonable quote—with a surprisingly small down payment. It's a new kind of loan, he says, called an adjustable-rate mortgage, which is the same kind our neighbor has. The payments will "reset" in three years, but, as the mortgage broker suggests, we'll probably have moved up to a bigger house by then. We discuss the house during dinner and breakfast. We review our finances to make sure we can afford it. Then, the next afternoon, we call the agent to place a bid. And the house is already gone—at 10 percent above the asking price.

By the spring of 2007, we've finally caught up to the market reality, and our luck finally changes: We make an instant, aggressive bid on a huge house, with almost no money down. And we get it! We're finally members of the ownership society.

You know the rest. Eighteen months later, our down payment has been wiped out and we owe more on the house than it's worth. We're still able to make the payments, but our mortgage rate is about to reset. And we've already heard rumors about coming layoffs at our jobs. How on Earth did we get into this mess?

HANDOUT 1, CONTINUED
EXCERPT FROM "WHY WALL STREET ALWAYS BLOWS IT" BY HENRY BLODGET IN *THE ATLANTIC* (DECEMBER 2008)

The exact answer is different in every case, of course. But let's round up the usual suspects:

- The predatory mortgage broker? Well, we're certainly not happy with him, given that he sold us a loan that is now a ticking time bomb. But we did ask him to show us a range of options, and he didn't make us pick this one. We picked it because it had the lowest payment.

- Our real-estate agent? We're not speaking to her anymore, either (and we're secretly stoked that her BMW just got repossessed), but again, she didn't lie to us. She just kept saying that houses are usually a good investment. And she is, after all, a saleswoman; that was never very hard to figure out.

- Wall Street fat cats? Boy, do we hate those guys, especially now that our tax dollars are bailing them out. But we didn't complain when our lender asked for such a small down payment without bothering to check how much money we made. At the time, we thought that was pretty great.

- The SEC? [the U.S. Securities and Exchange Commission] We're furious that our government let this happen to us, and we're sure someone is to blame. We're not really sure who that someone is, though. Whoever is responsible for making sure that something like this never happens to us, we guess.

- Alan "The Maestro" Greenspan? We're annoyed at him too. If he hadn't been out there saying everything was fine, we might have believed that economist who said it wasn't.

- Bad advice? Yes, we got bad advice. Our real-estate agent. That mortgage guy. Our neighbor. Greenspan. The media. They all gave us horrendous advice. We should have just waited for the market to crash. But everyone said it was different this time.

Still, except in cases involving outright fraud—a small minority—the buck stops with us. Not knowing that the market would crash isn't an excuse. No one knew the market would crash, even the analysts who predicted that it would. (Just as important, no one knew when prices would go down, or how fast.) And for years, most of the skeptics looked—and felt—like fools.

Everyone else on that list above bears some responsibility too. But in the case I have described, it would be hard to say that any of them acted criminally. Or irrationally. Or even irresponsibly. In fact, almost everyone on that list acted just the way you would expect them to act under the circumstances.

Source: http://www.theatlantic.com/doc/200812/blodget-wall-street

HANDOUT 2
ESSAY 1: TULIPMANIA

Conditions in the Dutch Republic in the 1630s were ripe for an outburst of speculative activity. There was a great deal of optimism in the economy emanating from a booming textile trade and the ending of the Spanish military threat. The legislature moved into a comfortable new building in 1631 and the East India Company was profitably developing its investments in Batavia (known today as Jakarta in Indonesia). The prices of shares of stock in that company rose faster than at any other time in the century. House prices were booming, generating a rush to construct larger, nicer houses. The Dutch enjoyed the highest incomes in Europe and were becoming a nation of consumers. The tulip became an ostentatious object of their affection.

Tulips were first brought to Europe in the mid-sixteenth century from Turkey and introduced to the Dutch in 1573. Initially confined to the gardens of the most affluent, they quickly became the symbol of wealth and the obsession of those who pursued them. They would eventually become the focus of rampant speculation. A sign of things to come occurred in 1624 when a striking sample of the Semper Augustus strain fetched the breath-taking price of 1,200 guilders, a sum sufficient to purchase a small Amsterdam townhouse.

Tulips (the word's origin was from the Turkish for turban) were ripe for speculation because of their unpredictable nature. It's understood today that the infinite variations in color were the result of a non-lethal virus common during this time, but to traders in the 1630s they represented a thrilling gamble. A plain breeder bulb could emerge as the most precious of samples generating a virtual tulip lottery. Public shares of companies cultivating the flower became wildly popular but most of the irrationality focused on bulb speculation. Tulip trading's association with status attracted opportunists from all classes. Weavers, spinners, cobblers, bakers, grocers, and peasants all staked their financial futures on the fortune wheel of bulbs. The nature of tulip trading changed as traffic increased. Private negotiations were common, but more frequently auctions occurred in the meeting rooms of inns where raucous bidding sessions (fueled by wine, beer, spirits, and sumptuous buffets) carried on into the night. Profits earned in the evening were quickly spent on new coaches, horses, and haute couture the next day. People who said the prices could not possibly go higher watched with chagrin as their friends and relatives made enormous profits. A market in tulip futures developed where investors paid for the promised delivery of a bulb in the spring by signing a personal credit note. To put things in perspective, at the height of the frenzy in 1636, the average annual wage in Holland was between 200 and 400 guilders. Bulbs were fetching prices in the thousands of guilders. It was calculated that the 2,500 guilders paid for one bulb could instead have bought 27 tons of wheat, 50 tons of rye, four fat oxen, eight fat pigs, 12 fat sheep, two hogsheads of wine, four tons of beer, two tons of butter, three tons of cheese, a bed with linen, a wardrobe of clothes, and a silver beaker. People started to barter their personal belongings including land, jewels, and furniture to obtain the bulbs that they expected would make them wealthier.

HANDOUT 2, CONTINUED
ESSAY 1: TULIPMANIA

On February 3, 1637, the tulip market suddenly crashed. Most of the bulbs promised and the credit statements wagered never materialized. When word got out that there were no more buyers, prices collapsed. For the individuals who had mortgaged their homes and exchanged their livestock for a lottery dream, the effects were catastrophic. Many tried to get their windfalls back through litigation of broken contracts. Finally, in May of 1638, a government commission declared that tulip contracts could be annulled on payment of 3.5 percent of the agreed price. Traders with foresight picked up numerous bargain bulbs at this juncture and claimed tidy profits when prices recovered to pre-mania prices within a few years. Tulipmania quickly turned to tulip aversion as people had difficulty casting their eyes upon the object of this tumult. After the collapse of the mania, the Dutch authorities went on a campaign of cleansing society of the wickedness and folly that had consumed it. These actions were an attempt to once and for all expunge the human affinity for irrational exuberance.

Sources:
Edward Chancellor, *Devil Take the Hindmost*, Plume Books, 1999.
Charles P. Kindleberger, *Manias, Panics, and Crashes: A History of Financial Crises* 4th ed., Wiley Books, 2000.
Burton G. Malkiel, *A Random Walk Down Wall Street* 8th Ed., Norton, 2003.
Donald Rapp, *Bubbles, Booms, and Busts*, Copernicus Books, 2009.
http://web.rollins.edu/~jsiry/Tulipmania.html, Dr. Joseph Siry, UCSB.

HANDOUT 3
ESSAY 2: THE SOUTH SEA BUBBLE

At the time of the South Sea Bubble, a long period of British prosperity had resulted in swollen savings accounts and few places to invest them. The government did its part to encourage investment by eliminating taxes on dividends and allowing stock to be one of the few forms of property that women could possess in their own right. The War of the Spanish Succession left Britain in debt by 10 million pounds. In 1711, Britain proposed a deal to a financial institution, the South Sea Company, whereby Britain's debt would be financed in return for 6 percent interest. Britain added another benefit to sweeten the deal: exclusive trading rights in the South Seas. The South Seas meant Africa, the East and West Indies, South America, and Asia.

The South Sea Company quickly agreed because of the prospects of trade with wealthy South American colonies. The company planned on developing a monopoly in the slave trade. Additionally, it was thought that the Mexicans and South Americans would eagerly trade their gold and jewels for the wool and fleece clothing of the British. The South Sea Company issued stock to finance operations and gain investors. Speculators quickly saw what they perceived as value in the monopoly of the South Seas. Shares were snatched up from the start, resulting in a second issuance. Investors seemed to have no reluctance despite the company having a highly inexperienced management team at the helm. Their sights were set on stratospheric profits. The South Sea Company was a combination of politics, commerce, and finance. None of its governors or directors had any experience in trade with the New World, but John Blunt, who wrote the charter and was the company's dominant director, had been a scribe and then director of the Sword Blade Bank. He and his cohort had a fine understanding of financial manipulation. They also understood the art of public appearance and rented an imposing building in London. They furnished it with trappings of success. The South Sea Company was really a financial institution that used its monopoly primarily as a means of attracting investors. Some slave-trade voyages were made but these produced little profit. When Britain and Spain officially went to war again in 1718, the immediate prospects for any benefits from trade with South America were dashed. What mattered to speculators, however, were future prospects, and here it was argued that incredible prosperity lay ahead and profits would be realized when open hostilities came to an end.

In 1719, the South Sea directors made a proposal to assume the entire public debt of the British government generated during the second war. A large number of bribes were paid to politicians to sway the vote, often in fictitious holdings of stock. The government agreed in April 1720 and the Company immediately started to drive up the price of the stock through artificial means; these largely took the form of new subscriptions combined with the circulation of new trade-with-Spain stories designed to give the impression that the stock could only go higher.

South Sea stock rose steadily, prompting the sudden appearance of all kinds of joint-stock companies hoping to cash in on the speculation mania. New ventures materialized, all with a "New World" flavor. People could now invest in land in what would become Mississippi, walnut imports from what would be Virginia, or the improvement of Greenland fisheries. Raising sums of money from selling stock became quite simple. The height of sheer mania was illustrated through a business enterprise described as "A company for carrying on an undertaking of great advantage, but nobody to know what it is" (Mackay):

> [the prospectus stated] that the required capital was half a million, in five thousand shares of 100 pounds each, deposit 2 pounds per share. Each subscriber, paying his [or her] deposit, was entitled to 100 pounds per annum per share. How this immense profit was to be obtained, [the Proposer] did not condescend to inform [the buyers] at that time, but promised that in a month full particulars should be duly announced, and a call made for the remaining 98 pounds of the subscription. Next morning, at nine o'clock, this great man opened an office in Cornhill. Crowds of people beset his door, and when he

HANDOUT 3, CONTINUED
ESSAY 2: THE SOUTH SEA BUBBLE

shut up at three o'clock, he found that no less than one thousand shares had been subscribed for, and the deposits paid. He was thus, in five hours, the winner of 2000 pounds. He was philosophical enough to be contented with his venture, and set off the same evening for the Continent. He was never heard of again. (Mackay, pp. 55-56)

"In order to pay out profits, the South Sea Company needed both to raise more capital and to have the price of its stock moving continuously upward," wrote the economist and MIT professor emeritus Charles P. Kindleberger in his classic work *Manias, Panics, and Crashes: A History of Financial Crises.* "And it needed both increases at an accelerating rate, as in a chain letter or a Ponzi scheme."

The company repeatedly raised cash through new issues of stock as its price spiraled upward in the summer of 1720. Not even the South Sea Company was capable of handling the demands of all the buyers. Investors searched myopically for the next ground-floor opportunity. At the height of absurdity, there were nearly 100 different projects proposed to investors. Opportunities included importing large numbers of donkeys from Spain, a venture to make fresh water out of salt water, developing plywood out of sawdust, extracting silver from lead, producing a wheel of perpetual motion, and extracting sunlight from cucumbers. For a while it seemed the public would buy anything. Ultimately, the stock company scams were bad for South Sea business. South Sea stock had been at 175 pounds at the end of February, 380 at the end of March, and around 520 by the end of May. It peaked at the end of June at over 1,000 pounds. With legitimacy seriously in doubt and widespread rumors of sell-offs, the bubble began to deflate. By mid-August the bankruptcy listings in the *London Gazette* reached an all-time high, an indication of suffering by people who bought on credit or margin. Thousands of fortunes were lost, both large and small. The directors attempted to generage more speculation, but they failed.

The full collapse came by the end of September when the stock stood at 135 pounds. A committee was formed to investigate the South Sea Company; by early 1721 it uncovered widespread corruption and fraud among the directors, company officials and their friends in government. Unfortunately, some of the key players had already fled the country with the incriminating records in their possession. The South Sea Bubble affected the fortunes of many and remained in the consciousness of the Western world for the rest of the 18th century, not unlike our cultural memory of the 1929 Wall Street crash.

Sources:
http://myweb.dal.ca/dmcneil/bubble/bubble.html David McNeil, Dalhousie University.
http://www.library.hbs.edu/hc/historicalreturns/fb/movie.html, Harvard Business School, Baker Library Historical Collection.
http://web.rollins.edu/~jsiry/South_Sea-Bubble.html, Dr. Joseph Siry, UCSB.
Edward Chancellor, *Devil Take the Hindmost*, Plume Books, 1999.
Charles P. Kindleberger, *Manias, Panics, and Crashes*: A History of Financial Crises 4th ed., Wiley Books, 2000.
Charles MacKay, *Extraordinary Popular Delusions and the Madness of Crowds*, with a foreword by Andrew Tobias. Harmony Books, 1980.

HANDOUT 4
ESSAY 3: THE ROARING TWENTIES STOCK BUBBLE

The 1920s was absolutely going to be the decade of difference. Rarely before had the perfect elements of promise fallen so gracefully into place. The end of World War I brought a significant recession in 1919-1921 as the economy slowly reverted to civilian life. By 1922, the engines were fired up and the country experienced an average rate of growth of 5.5 percent for the remainder of the decade. The economy was driven by new investment opportunities in three new areas: electric power, telephones, and automobiles. Investment expanded to related areas like road building, service stations, and oil refining. The proliferation of the car promoted the development of suburbs and the first commuters. Homebuilding began to boom and, with it, housing prices. Another technology that attracted a great deal of investment interest was the radio. Although it would not become commercially viable until later, it caught the fancy of many stock traders. The trans-Atlantic travels of Charles Lindbergh and the film crews that captured his magic moments generated excitement in the aviation and motion picture industries. It was widely perceived to be the dawning of a new age of prosperity.

The financial powers fueling this growth were sensing an unprecedented confidence. The creation of a central bank, the Federal Reserve in 1913, was perceived to be the solution for wild business cycles. The booms and busts that had occurred in the past would now be easily managed in the future by the powers of the Fed to manipulate the money supply. On the public relations front, the White House was touting the new paradigm as "Coolidge prosperity," which included a softening of anti-trust legislation, extension of free trade, low inflation, and a stream of pro-business and pro-growth propaganda.

As is often the case, the fruits of this prosperity were not equitably distributed. While the rich got richer, the working class did not. The pro-business sway of the Republican administrations during the decade resulted in impediments to the progress made by labor since the Gilded Age. Discouraged and often intimidated from organizing, many workers saw their real wages decline. The evaporation of purchasing power created a dearth of consumers for the growing inventories. But demand was vitalized by the creation of a broad new program of consumer credit—the installment system. By the end of the decade, about one in eight consumer purchases of all kinds were made with credit.

Affording credit to investors stimulated an explosion of brokerages as more people found it possible to reach for their dreams. The Federal Reserve accommodated the surge of borrowers by lowering interest rates in 1925 and not raising them until 1928. The continuously rising market and the profits generated from buying on margin were too enticing for many to ignore.

Share prices for a wide array of equities exploded in the latter half of the decade. General Motors shares increased ten-fold between 1925 and 1928. The radio industry was dominated by Radio Corporation of America, both the leading manufacturer and broadcaster in the nation. Its share prices rose from a low of $1.50 in 1921 to $85.50 in early 1928. Prices on average on the New York Stock Exchange increased a whopping two and a half times between March 1926 and October 1929. These years were punctuated by the proverbial madness that infects crowds.

Meanwhile, the strains of this go-go economy were beginning to be felt. Share prices were rising at a pace three times the rate of growth of corporate earnings, the increase in interest rates had began to quell consumption, installment loans had reached their limits as real wages continued to decline, a severe decline in commodity prices dramatically affected the fortunes of farmers who comprised a major segment of the population, and growth slowed as many consumers now had the houses, cars, and radios they needed. Unfortunately, most of the speculators ignored the dissonance and kept on buying. In the autumn of 1929, Yale economist Irving Fisher declared that "stock prices have reached what looks like a

HANDOUT 4, CONTINUED
ESSAY 3: THE ROARING TWENTIES STOCK BUBBLE

permanent high plateau." A few weeks after his remarks the Dow Jones Industrial Average had declined by more than a third. By July 1932, the Dow Jones closed at 41.88, a 90 percent decline from the point at which Fisher spoke.

As is always the case, the platitudes about the new era of permanent prosperity were wrong. Banks shuttered their doors by the thousands, the nation's real GNP fell 60 percent from its 1929 levels, and by 1932, 25 percent of the nation's workforce was unemployed. The greatest stock speculative bubble to date had burst and was followed by the greatest depression to date.

Sources:
Edward Chancellor, *Devil Take the Hindmost*, Plume Books, 1999.
Charles P. Kindleberger, *Manias, Panics, and Crashes: A History of Financial Crises* 4th ed., Wiley Books, 2000.
Burton G. Malkiel, *A Random Walk Down Wall Street* 8th ed., Norton, 2003.

HANDOUT 5
ESSAY 4: JAPAN'S BUBBLE ECONOMY

The period between 1985 and 1990 was a time of unprecedented affluence in Japan. But it was also a period of unparalleled corruption, extravagance and waste for this island nation. When the bubble burst, the Japanese economy regressed to depths from which the country has yet to fully recover from.

Japan's economy boomed in the late 1950s and through the 1960s. The Nikkei stock market index, which started at 100 in May 1949, was at 5,000 in the early '70s and at 10,000 by 1984. Innovation and technological progress dramatically improved productivity, resulting in a surge of economic growth with little inflation. The government engaged in deregulation to encourage further investment, but it also added to speculation in stocks and real estate. Japan was hitting peak economic performance in manufacturing. The world couldn't get enough of Japanese cars or electronics. Money poured into Japan. The Japanese people benefited from their nation's growth and personal savings rates reached an all-time high.

In September 1985, a meeting was held at the Plaza Hotel in New York City hosted by the U.S. and attended by trade representatives of Japan and three other countries. An agreement was signed calling for the depreciation of the dollar against the yen with the intended outcome being less-expensive U.S. exports and a lower U.S. trade deficit. The vast amount of saving in Japan had contributed to lower interest rates. The Japanese central bank further lowered interest rates as concern about possible falling exports arose.

Japanese banks began freely lending to corporations and individuals; much of the credit was funneled into real estate. When the land increased in value, even more loans were used to speculate in real estate and in the stock market. A rapid cycle was created, resulting in excessively overvalued real estate and stocks. During the second half of the 1980s, the Tokyo Stock Exchange's compass seemed permanently stuck on north. Between 1986 and 1991, Japan's assets expanded by roughly the equivalent of France's gross domestic product, then $956 billion. Very little government intervention was even suggested as asset values skyrocketed.

Life inside Japan during these years was surreal. A nation historically recognized for its frugality now saw life as one extravagant party. Land prices made headlines around the world. At the start of the 1990s, a square meter of prime urban real estate cost as much as $300,000. Homes were so expensive in land-scarce Japan that families took out multigenerational loans. The property that housed the Imperial Palace in downtown Tokyo was believed to be worth as much as the entire state of California. It was also a period of increased international travel with Japanese consumers scouring the world for Louis Vuitton, Armani, and fine wine. Some of the most conspicuous art sales in history were made, most notably several multi-million dollar runs on Van Gogh's paintings. Banks continued to lend heavily, with land as collateral. No one, apparently, questioned the wisdom of this, despite Japan's aggregate property value reaching levels four to five times the aggregate property value in the U.S. — and Japan is smaller than California.

The strong yen made it very inexpensive for Japanese investors to purchase American assets. Famous American landmarks were being snatched up by speculators. New York's Rockefeller Center and California's Pebble Beach golf course were among the iconic landmarks purchased by Japanese investors.

In late 1990, a wave of rationality washed over the country as the Japanese were unable to finance the rise in asset prices any longer. An international recession and increased competition in autos and electronics slowed the growth in Japanese exports. Some weak banks failed. Many began to recognize that interest rates were too low and that stock and land prices were unrealistically high.

HANDOUT 5, CONTINUED
ESSAY 4: JAPAN'S BUBBLE ECONOMY

The real estate and stock markets collapsed. The Tokyo Stock Exchange lost more than two trillion dollars of value by December 1990. Economic growth stalled and newspapers were filled with stories of businesses going bankrupt. Japanese investors began unloading their foreign assets for pennies on the dollar. Exposure of corrupt deals involving senior leadership at some of the more venerable banks doused any remaining optimism. Residential lending firms collapsed and banks were forced to merge and consolidate their bad loans. The government attempted to resuscitate the economy with big public works projects, but nothing seemed to work. The next 10 years came to be known as Japan's "Lost Decade" as the nation struggled to emerge from a lengthy trough. Consumers went back to their extraordinarily austere traditions, vowing never again to abandon the country's moral, social, and cultural values. As is so common, the nation had become intoxicated by its good fortune and believed that this time was different. Those assigned to guarding the gate missed the signs and reacted far too late. The recoil response was as dramatic as the flight of fancy and the Japanese economy came back to earth with remarkable speed.

Sources:
Eric Johnston, "Japan's Bubble Economy", *Japan Times Online*, January 6, 2009.
Edward Chancellor, *Devil Take the Hindmost*, Plume Books, 1999.
Charles P. Kindleberger, *Manias, Panics, and Crashes: A History of Financial Crises* 4th ed., Wiley Books, 2000.
Donald Rapp, *Bubbles, Booms, and Busts*, Copernicus Books, 2009.

HANDOUT 6
ESSAY 5: THE DOT-COM BUBBLE

Wrigley Launches "Internet Bubble" Gum®

Chicago, Ill. (SatireWire.com) — *The world's biggest chewing gum maker today unveiled Wrigley's Internet Bubble Gum®, the "irrationally overpriced gum" that produces an "unsustainably large" bubble. The gum, which went on sale this morning at $14 a pack, reached an intraday high of $84 a pack, but ended the day at just 25 cents. As a result, Wrigley announced it will reevaluate its ingredients model, and lay off one-third of its employees.*

Public awareness of the existence of something called the Internet did not exist prior to the 1990s. A boom period quickly followed with everyone sizing up the value of this tool to business and society. As is often the case, many people perceived limitless opportunities and saw no downside to the potential of the World Wide Web. The obsession of getting in on the ground floor of what could be a "once in a century" opportunity was too compelling. From 1995 to the beginning of 2001, the mania surrounding the development of the dot-coms was real. Entrepreneurs, financiers, and casual investors imagined themselves at the dawn of a new paradigm and they expected to profit beyond their wildest dreams.

The sounds of a successful dial-up connection on Netscape and the declaration "You've Got Mail" on AOL were becoming increasingly familiar and companies recognized this as an unchartered gateway to expanding their customer base. As a result, droves of Internet start-ups sprouted everywhere in an attempt to capture this audience and master the medium. Many of these companies arrived under the illusion that if you build it, paying customers will come. Thousands of companies were formed to be a one-stop shop for all needs: virtually every site wanted to have an auction section, and there seemed to be as many search engines as people searching. In addition, there was the army of writers to create the content filling all of these locales.

Some of the more notable premiers and highlights were:

- Amazon, 1994
- Craigslist, 1995
- Yahoo, MSN, and eBay, 1995
- eToys, 1997
- Boo.com, Flooz.com, Go.com, Kozmo.com, and Pets.com, 1998
- Google, founded in 1998
- Gov.Works.com, Kibu.com, Webvan.com, MVP.com, 1999
- AOL acquired Time Warner in 2000
- Super Bowl XXXIV in January 2000 featured 17 dot-com companies that each paid over two million dollars for a 30-second spot

Many of these technology companies were selling stock in initial public offerings (IPOs). Some initial shareholders became overnight millionaires as other investors jumped on board to purchase the stocks in the weeks following the IPOs. A perfect illustration was in the initial offering of Netscape, an early rival to AOL. In 1995, five million shares were offered for sale at an opening price of $28. The stock rose as high as $74 on the first day before closing at $58. Between 1992 and 1996, the market valuation of AOL increased from $70 million to $6.5 billion. The hype over the new economy was met with a broad expansion of new investors in the stock market. Americans poured money into equities and especially dot-coms.

The growth of 401(k) retirement plans and the overwhelming contributions into the stock market were like gasoline on the fire. In a year and a half starting in 1995, the Dow Jones Industrial Average rose 45 percent and the NASDAQ Composite 65 percent. By the summer of 1996, there were over 800,000 online

HANDOUT 6, CONTINUED
ESSAY 5: THE DOT-COM BUBBLE

stock trading accounts in the United States. A few doomsayers cautioned about an overheated market, but they were scoffed at by the euphoric herd that felt that this was actually the moment when man had it all figured out.

Washington did its part to fan the flames. Both Bill Clinton and Al Gore touted the "information superhighway" as the bridge to the future. Alan Greenspan, the Chairman of the Federal Reserve, kept interest rates low, spoke frequently on the benefits of technology, and failed to rein in the speculative nature of the market.

By 2000, the bubble began to show signs of weakness. In March of that year, the NASDAQ index peaked at 5,000 (an astounding number considering it is less than half that 10 years later). It became clear that many of the fledgling companies could not continue with no revenues, only costs, and thus no profits. The money generated by the IPOs was the only revenue for many. Very few of these companies would ever turn a profit in their brief existence. A handful of the pioneers survived, but the vast majority of hopefuls spent much more than their initial revenues.

The NASDAQ lost 19 percent and the Internet sector index lost 32 percent over three days in the spring of 2000. Without a doubt, the Internet changed the world, but while investors and entrepreneurs were measuring what they called "eyeballs" (the number of people looking at web pages), many forgot basic business fundamentals: revenues, costs, and profits.

Sources:
Burton G. Malkiel, *A Random Walk Down Wall Street* 8th ed., Norton, 2003.
Donald Rapp, *Bubbles, Booms, and Busts*, Copernicus Books, 2009.
http://www.pbs.org/wgbh/pages/frontline/shows/dotcon/
http://ac360.blogs.cnn.com/2009/11/24/the-dot-com-bubble-how-to-lose-5-trillion/, David Gerwitz,
　　Editor-in-Chief, Zatz Publishing.

LESSON 4
THE JAPAN COMPARISON

LESSON 4
THE JAPAN COMPARISON

LESSON DESCRIPTION

In this lesson, students play the role of economic advisors to the U.S. president. They learn about Japan's "Lost Decade," and then they compare economic data and policies to analyze the potential future of the U.S. economy.

INTRODUCTION

The financial crisis of 2007–2009 is often compared to the Great Depression, but a more accurate comparison may be with Japan's Lost Decade (1991–2000). Both the United States and Japan experienced speculative bubbles in equity and real estate markets. The increases in housing and land values were unprecedented in both countries. The bubbles eventually burst, Japan's in 1990-1991 and the United States' in 2007. Housing prices fell almost as dramatically as they rose. The real estate crises were so large that they spilled over into the financial sectors as banks and other investors suffered huge losses. Credit markets failed to function as panic spread throughout major financial institutions. Even healthy companies were unable to secure sufficient credit.

The financial crises in both countries spilled over into the larger economy, causing recessions. Real **gross domestic product** (GDP) growth rates became negative, **unemployment** rose, inflation rates fell, and stock prices plummeted. The governments in both countries responded to the crises with traditional monetary and **fiscal policies** to try to turn the economies around. New policies targeting the failing financial industries were also attempted.

Although Japan's crisis is referred to as the Lost Decade, Japan's economy was still underperforming at the time this lesson was written. The U.S. crisis is currently only about three years old. Therefore, given the similarities between the two crises, a comparison of the two situations should be very helpful in predicting whether the United States will also suffer through a prolonged economic slump. We can learn from the Japanese experience and deal more effectively with the problems we face.

CONCEPTS

- Gross domestic product
- Unemployment
- Inflation
- Deflation
- Monetary policy
- Fiscal policy

OBJECTIVES

Students will:

1. Describe Japan's Lost Decade.

2. Compare economic performance between Japan's Lost Decade and the United States' financial crisis of 2007-2009.

3. Predict future economic conditions in the United States using Japan's economic performance during the Lost Decade.

CONTENT STANDARDS

- People usually respond predictably to positive and negative incentives.

- Interest rates, adjusted for inflation, rise and fall to balance the amount saved with the amount borrowed, which affects the allocation of scarce resources between present and future uses.

- Fluctuations in a nation's overall levels of income, employment, and prices are determined by the interaction of spending and production decisions made by all households, firms, government agencies, and others in the economy. Recessions occur when overall levels of income and employment decline.

- Federal government budgetary policy and the Federal Reserve System's monetary policy influence the overall levels of employment, output, and prices.

TIME REQUIRED

Two class periods

MATERIALS

- Activity 1: Japan's Lost Decade (one copy per student)

- Activity 2: Comparing and Contrasting the Japanese and U.S. Financial Crises Using Data (one copy per student)

- Activity 3: Comparison of Government Interventions in the Japan and United States Financial Crises (one copy per student)

- Activity 4: Advising the President (one copy per student)

- Visual 1: Comparison of Japan and U.S. Home Prices (transparency)

- Visual 2: Comparison of Japan and U.S. Real GDP Growth Rates (transparency)

- Visual 3: Comparison of Japan and U.S. Unemployment Rates (transparency)

- Visual 4: Comparison of Japan and U.S. Inflation Rates (transparency)

- Visual 5: Comparison of Japan and U.S. Stock Markets (transparency)

- Visual 6: Comparison of Japan and U.S. Monetary Policies (transparency)

- Visual 7: Comparison of Government Interventions in the Japan and United States Financial Crises (transparency)

PROCEDURE

1. Tell students that they have been asked to join the President's Council of Economic Advisors to help analyze the current state of the U. S. economy and to make predictions about its future direction.

   Divide students into six groups. Each group will act as a separate Council of Economic Advisors.

2. Hand out Activity 1: Japan's Lost Decade. Ask each of the groups of economic advisors to prepare statements on each of the questions. Briefly discuss the answers to the

questions either in a class-wide discussion or after presentations on each question or part of a question by each group.

a. What caused the speculative bubble in housing and stock prices?

   There was a strong demand for Japanese exports and low interest rates during the early 1990s. Japanese exports resulted in large amounts of foreign currency coming into the country and low interest rates made borrowing money easy and cheap. Significant amounts were used to purchase both stocks and land. As a result, prices of both increased.

b. What caused the bubble to burst?

   The Japanese government feared that prices of stocks and land (homes) were not justified by fundamental economic indicators and therefore were not sustainable in the long run. This is referred to as a bubble. The government decided to "pop the bubble" by increasing interest rates. This eliminated one of the major factors pushing up prices.

c. What did the Japanese government do in the early 1990s to try and bring the economy out of the recession? Was it successful?

   The government used both monetary and fiscal policy to try to turn the economy around. The discount rate fell from 6 percent at the beginning of the decade to zero by 1999. The government also spent nearly $2.1 trillion on public works projects in 1992 and 1993 and incurred a deficit equal to 4 percent of all economic activity during the decade. In addition to traditional monetary and fiscal policy, the government also intervened by putting money directly into the banking system.

   These policies were not successful. Although the economy appeared to be recovering in 1994 and 1995, it quickly slipped back into a recession. Real GDP growth remained low for the remainder of the decade.

d. What controversies were there over the government response to the economic downturn?

Some people thought that the government had to bail out the banks in order to ensure that the financial system did not collapse. Others believed that the bailouts created "zombie banks" that were so unhealthy that they should be allowed to fail. There were also disagreements about fiscal policy. Some believed that there was too much stimulus, some too little. Some believed that government expenditures were the appropriate fiscal response; others would have preferred tax cuts. There was also widespread disagreement about what the stimulus was spent on.

e. Prices in Japan declined from 1994 through 2009, with the exception of 1997. If high inflation is a problem for an economy, is **deflation** good? Use the following two examples to help in answering this question.

Example 1. Assume you are a corn farmer. Corn is currently selling for $5 a bushel. You can produce a bushel of corn for $4.75. Therefore you plant your crops in April with the expectation of harvesting and selling your corn in August. But what if the country is suffering from deflation? By the time you have harvested your crop, the selling price of corn is $4.60. Instead of making a profit of $0.25 a bushel, you have lost $0.15 a bushel. Now it is spring again, what will you do? The country is still in deflation, so that the costs of seed, fertilizer and workers have fallen, and you estimate that you can produce a bushel of corn for only $4.30 a bushel. Will you plant corn this year?

You may decide not to plant corn this year or next year. Businesses produce goods in order to make a profit and you must be able to sell your goods and services for more than they cost in order to do so. Deflation makes this very diffi-

cult. In this case, you are able to purchase the inputs necessary to grow corn for less than the previous year, but the price you receive may also be falling. Therefore deflation creates a disincentive for firms to produce, which could lead to a deeper recession or even depression. Rising prices may create problems for an economy, but falling prices can be just as destructive or worse.

Example 2. Assume you are in the market for a new automobile. Your current car still works fine, but you have been eyeing a new model. The car has not changed, but because the country is facing deflation, the price has fallen from $32,000 to $30,000. In addition, economists predict that the country will continue to be in a deflationary cycle for at least the next three years, with prices falling an average of 10 percent per year. Will you purchase the car this year?

Maybe not. As long as your current car is still working, you have an incentive to postpone your purchase because you expect the price to continue to fall. If consumers stop shopping in anticipation of lower prices, firms will stop producing and lay off workers. Therefore deflation can contribute to a fall in real GDP and an increase in unemployment. The fall in output and employment may lead to further decreases in prices and a destructive cycle.

3. Tell students that now that they know a little about the Japanese Lost Decade, they are going to compare Japanese data from this time period with U.S. data to determine similarities between the Lost Decade and the financial crisis of 2007-2009 and what we can learn from the Japanese experience.

Reading the graphs may be a little tricky, as the data from different time periods in Japan and the United States are on the same graph. Data for the United States starts in 1997 and in 1982 for Japan. This results in the alignment of the two data series at the peak of both of their real estate markets (1991 in Japan and 2006 for the United States.) That is year 10 on the graphs.

Assign one of the six parts of the Activity 2 graphs to each of the Councils of Economic Advisors. Ask students to look at the assigned graph and prepare answers to the questions that follow. The objective is to determine how similar the two crises are and what the United States might expect if trends continue. This will help the councils come up with policy recommendations for the United States.

Have each of the Councils of Economic Advisors sit at the front of the room in order to present their findings to the president (the teacher). Show Visuals 1-6 and have members of each of the councils discuss the answers about the economic data they were assigned.

Ask each council to describe the data illustrated on their graph. They are also asked to interpret the data and make predictions about the future of the economic statistics (e.g., future changes in home prices) in the United States given the data from Japan. There are no right answers to these questions. The goal is to develop good critical thinking skills. The teacher should play the role of president and help direct student responses. All students should be encouraged to ask questions of each of the councils as they present their findings.

Part 1. A. Briefly describe the trends in housing prices in both countries after hitting the peak. In what ways are the trends similar? In what ways are the trends different?

Both countries suffered significant decreases in housing prices. The United States exhibited a sharper decline in prices in the first two years of the crisis than did Japan. The fall in prices leveled off in the United States in 2009. Prices in Japan continued to fall at a constant rate for over a decade after the bubble burst.

B. Using this information, predict what you expect will happen to housing prices in the United States over the next five to 10 years.

One possible answer is that housing prices will continue to decline as they did in Japan. Another possible answer is that housing prices have already started to stabilize and that this might mean that housing prices may stay relatively unchanged over the next few years. A third possible response is that the United States might learn from the Japanese experience and therefore undertake policies that prevent housing prices from continuing to fall over the next five to 10 years.

C. Does the Japanese experience lead you to be optimistic or pessimistic about the future of housing prices in the U.S.?

The data from Japan are not encouraging. The summary of the Lost Decade states that the Japanese government undertook a number of monetary and fiscal policies in order to turn the economy around. Although the U.S. may determine that the Japanese policies were not aggressive enough or that they were the wrong policies, the Japanese experience does not create optimism.

Part 2. A. Briefly describe the trend in the Japanese economy, as measured by the growth rate of real GDP after the housing bubble burst.

Growth in the Japanese economy actually started falling prior to the peak in the real estate market. Real GDP grew at a 2.7 percent rate in 1991, down from 6.2 percent the prior year. After the bubble burst, growth in real GDP continued to fall. In 1993, the economy actually shrank as the real GDP growth rate became negative. But the economy rebounded with the rate of change in real GDP going up for three consecutive years. The recovery was not sustained as real GDP growth rates fell, returning into negative numbers by 1998. The Japanese economy has been on a roller coaster since then, with real GDP growth rates above 2 percent in 1996, 2000, and 2003-2006, and negative growth rates for 1993, 1998, 2001, and 2008.

B. One of the president's aides says that if the U.S. crisis follows the pattern of Japan, the worst is over and we should expect to see the economy grow again. How would you comment?

The data indicate that Japan enjoyed a rebound in the economy just three years after the real estate bubble burst, but that this did not last. The economy failed to sustain this growth and fell back into a recession. So the short-run trend in Japan suggests that the U.S. economy may begin to grow again, but we should be cautious. The Japanese experience shows that the U.S. economy could end up falling into an even deeper recession.

Part 3. A. Comment on the graph showing the unemployment rate in the two countries. How are the trends similar? How are they different?

The Japanese unemployment rate increased steadily for 11 straight years following the decline in housing prices. The United States also saw its unemployment rate increase following the bursting of the housing bubble, but at a much faster pace. Japan saw its unemployment rate rise from 2.1 percent to 2.9 percent between 1990 and 1993, while the U.S. unemployment rate more than doubled from 4.4 percent in 2006 to 10 percent in 2009. At its worst in 2001, the unemployment rate in Japan hit 5.4 percent, 11 years after the Lost Decade began. This is slightly more than half the rate found in the United States after only the first three years of the financial crisis.

Students should also recognize that historically the unemployment rate in Japan has been less than that in the United

States. Put in perspective, the increase from 2.1 percent to 5.4 percent in Japan would equate to an increase from 4.4 percent to 11.3 percent in the United States.

B. Members of Congress are worried about unemployment in the long run. What does the Japanese comparison suggest for the United States? Do you think the United States needs to be concerned about unemployment?

The comparison suggests that the unemployment rate could continue to increase for a number of years. The rapid increase in the U.S. rate over such a short time, in conjunction with the Japanese experience, indicates that the United States should be very concerned about future unemployment rates.

Part 4. A. Briefly describe the trend in inflation in Japan. Compare this with the inflation rate in the United States following the real estate market crash.

Inflation rates fell dramatically in Japan. By 1994 Japan was in a deflationary mode with general prices decreasing. Prices increased slightly in 1997, before sinking again in 1998. Since then Japan has suffered from deflation. The United States has seen a significant decline in the rate of inflation since the housing market peaked. Prices decreased in some months. The average price level at the end of 2008 was equal to the average price level at the end of 2007.

B. As an economic advisor to the president, why might the Japanese experience with inflation be a concern to you? Predict what you would expect to happen to real GDP in the United States if deflation were to take hold.

Japan has suffered from deflation for all but one year between 1994 and 2008. If deflation were to take hold in the United States, it would be reasonable to expect real GDP to decline as consumers put off purchases and firms reduce production because of the difficulty of earning profits when prices are falling.

Part 5. A. Comment on the trend in stock prices in the two countries prior to the peak in home prices.

The trend in stock prices was very different in the two countries leading up to the peak in home prices. The Nikkei stock market (Japan) had fallen almost 50 percent (from 40,000 to around 20,000) prior to the real estate bubble bursting. In the United States, the housing market and the S&P 500 (U.S.) peaked at roughly the same time.

B. Comment on the trend in stock prices in the two countries after the peak in home prices.

Stock prices generally fell in both Japan and the United States after the real estate market bubble burst.

C. Does the recent increase in stock prices in the United States shown in the graph make you confident about the future of the economy?

Students may answer this question in a couple of ways. Some might answer that if increases in the stock market are an indicator that businesses have become profitable again, it is a good signal about the future. In fact, the stock market is an example of a leading economic indicator. On the other hand, the data from Japan suggest the recovery might be short-lived. This is similar to the trend seen in the real GDP growth rate data.

Part 6. A. Briefly describe the trends in **monetary policy** in the United States and Japan. How are the policy responses similar? How are they different?

Both Japan and the United States responded to their respective financial crises by lowering interest rates. The United States appears to have been more aggressive, reducing interest rates to nearly zero more quickly than Japan did.

B. What does the graph suggest about interest rates in the United States in the future?

There are two features of this graph that students should be aware of. First, the data from Japan suggest that interest rates are likely to be kept low for a significant amount of time. Second, there isn't room for further reductions in either country. Interest rates are effectively at zero. If these rates are not low enough to stimulate investment, the government will have to rely on policies other than traditional monetary policy.

4. After the Councils of Economic Advisors have made their reports, reconfigure the councils. The new councils should include one member of each of the previous councils. This will result in each council having an expert on each of the economic statistics. (This will probably result in fewer than six councils, but this is not important for this part of the lesson.) Hand out Activity 3: Comparison of Government Interventions in Japan and United States Financial Crises to students. Tell them that this is a chart showing some of the government interventions that the Japanese and U.S. governments undertook in dealing with their financial crises.

Assign each of the councils one of the statements and ask each council to present their views. Display Visual 7 during the discussion.

Which of the following statements can reasonably be supported by the information that you have observed? Explain why.

a. Both Japan and the United States employed monetary and fiscal policy in attempts to stabilize their economies.

This is true. The chart includes dates for changes in discount rates in Japan and cuts in the federal funds rate in the United States (monetary policy). It also includes dates for stimulus packages (fiscal policy) in the two countries.

b. The United States acted more quickly than Japan in trying to address its economic problems.

There is justification for this statement. While both countries reacted quickly in initially cutting interest rates (seven months from peak for the United States and nine months from peak for Japan), the United States was much quicker in attempting to stimulate the economy through fiscal policy (12 months vs. 22 months) and by directly intervening in financial firms (19-20 months vs. 89 months). The U.S. also exhausted traditional monetary policy faster by reducing short-term interest rates to zero only 22 months into the crisis; it took the Bank of Japan 100 months to reduce rates to zero.

c. Banks were healthier during the financial crisis in Japan than in the United States.

Although it took longer for banks to fail and for the Japanese government to directly inject money into the banks, there doesn't appear to be evidence to support the claim that banks were healthier in Japan. The summary of the Lost Decade at the beginning of this lesson also suggested that many banks survived only because of government bailouts, leading to the term "zombie banks" to describe them.

d. Both Japan and the United States no longer have the ability to use traditional monetary policy as a means of improving the economy.

The chart indicates that both the United States and Japan have reduced short-term interest rates to zero. Therefore it is reasonable to state that the Federal Reserve in the United States and the Bank of Japan no longer have the ability to cut interest rates in order to stabilize the economy.

5. Hand out Activity 4: Advising the President. Ask each Council of Economic Advisors to develop recommendations on the two issues. Have each council choose one member for a roundtable debate on the two issues. (Councils should choose a different member for each of the issues.)

a. The U.S. government suffered a budget deficit of $1.4 trillion in 2009. This equaled 9.9 percent of GDP, the highest since WWII. Should the U.S. govern-

ment start taking immediate action to reduce the deficit? Why?

Possible arguments:

Yes, the deficit is too large and will eventually hurt the economy by driving up interest rates. The forecast future debt was already a problem because of the expected increased Social Security and Medicare costs when the baby boomers retire.

No, Japan raised taxes prematurely and sent the economy into a second downturn. The unemployment rate is still too high. The economy needs to be stronger before we worry about the deficit.

b. What do you think is the biggest lesson that the United States can learn from Japan's Lost Decade?

Possible responses:

The financial crisis of 2007-2009 could have serious consequences for the U.S. economy for many years to come.

We need to continue trying to strengthen the economy to prevent another downturn.

Traditional economic tools (monetary and fiscal policy) do not always work the way we hope they will.

CLOSURE

Summarize the lesson by asking the following questions:

1. What was a main cause of the Lost Decade and the financial crisis of 2007-2009?

The bursting of a real estate bubble, with resulting effects throughout the rest of the economy.

2. Why is it called the Lost Decade?

From 1990 through at least 2001, Japan suffered from a poor economy. Slow economic growth, rising unemployment, falling stock prices and deflation contributed to and were evidence of poor economic performance for more than a decade.

3. What types of policies did the two coun-

tries use in an attempt to turn the economy around?

Lower interest rates, economic stimulus packages, and injection of funds directly into banks.

4. Predict what the U.S. economy will be like in 2015 or 2020.

   If the U.S. economy follows the path that Japan's economy did, we will be faced with many years of poor economic performance. The outcome depends upon whether consumers and businesses regain confidence, what policies the U.S. government proposes, and how other world events unfold.

5. What were the major economic problems facing the United States in 2010?

   High unemployment, slow-growing economy (real GDP), fear of deflation, and large and rising federal budget deficits.

Explain to students that there are similarities between the Lost Decade and the financial crisis of 2007-2009. Data for important economic variables, such as real GDP growth, inflation and the stock market, are similar. The governments have also used many of the same policy tools, including monetary policy, fiscal policy and direct intervention in individual banks. This does not mean that the U.S. economy from 2010 and beyond will continue to mirror the Japanese economy during its crisis. By understanding the similarities between the two situations and by analyzing the Lost Decade, the United States may be able to avoid a protracted economic downturn.

ASSESSMENT

Multiple-choice questions

1. What was the primary cause of both the Lost Decade and the financial crisis of 2007–2009?

   a. Economic uncertainty due to terrorism.

   b. The inability to compete with China's expanding economy.

   *c. Unsustainable prices in real estate markets.

   d. High oil prices.

2. Which statement concerning economic data for Japan and the United States is correct?

   *a. The U.S. unemployment rate in 2010 is higher than Japan's at any time during the Lost Decade in Japan.

   b. The fall in housing prices caused inflation rates to rise in both Japan and the United States.

   c. The Japanese real estate market collapsed before the Japanese stock market.

   d. Japan's real GDP failed to grow at more than 2 percent in any year during the Lost Decade.

3. Which of the following statements about Japan's and the United States' policies to fight financial crises is correct?

   a. Japan first cut its discount rate in September 2007.

   b. The U.S. has passed more stimulus packages than Japan.

   c. The U.S. directly injected money into banks, Japan did not.

   *d. Both the U.S. and Japan used monetary policy within one year of the peak of real estate prices.

Constructed-response question

Mark Twain is credited with saying, "The past does not repeat itself, but it rhymes." Write an essay relating the Lost Decade and the financial crisis of 2007–2009 to this quote.

The quote suggests that although the past and the present are not identical, many similarities exist. The Lost Decade in Japan and the financial crisis of 2007-2009 certainly reinforce this. Essays should describe the "rhymes" between the Lost Decade and the financial crisis in the U.S., including similarities in economic data and general public policy responses. But the financial crisis of 2007–2009 is not a repeat of the Lost Decade, or even of the first three years of the Japanese crisis. Students should identify differences in unemployment rates, and the timing of government intervention as illustrations of this.

ACTIVITY 1
JAPAN'S LOST DECADE

Congratulations. You have been asked to join the President's Council of Economic Advisors. It has been a little over three years since the housing price bubble burst sending first real estate markets, then credit markets, and finally the overall economy into a tailspin. Although the crisis has been compared to the Great Depression, many economists believe our current situation has more in common with Japan's Lost Decade of 1991–2000.

Your first job is to learn about the Lost Decade. Read the following summary of the economy in Japan during this time. In subsequent activities, you will be asked to compare and contrast economic conditions during the Lost Decade and the financial crisis of 2007-2009. Next, you will use this information to identify potential problems facing the United States.

Japan's Lost Decade History

The Japanese economy was booming in the late 1980s. Strong demand for Japanese exports and extremely low interest rates fueled a speculative surge in both the stock and real estate markets. Fearing that real estate prices were not sustainable, the Japanese government burst the bubble by significantly increasing interest rates in 1989 and 1990. This led to a rapid decline in both land and equity prices.

Much of the boom in stocks and real estate was supported by debt, so the collapse in prices led to a credit crisis. Banks suffered massive losses as they were faced with rising default rates on loans. The government injected large sums of money into banks to keep them from failing. This was very controversial. On the one hand, many claimed that these banks were "too big to fail" and that letting them go bankrupt would have serious ripple effects that would harm the overall economy. On the other hand, critics claimed that the bailout plan gave birth to "zombie banks," institutions that could not survive without continual government support. They believed that until these unprofitable banks were allowed to fail, the credit crisis would continue.

Eventually the problems in the real estate market and banking industry spilled over into the entire economy. The Japanese economy entered a recession with the growth rate of real GDP falling from 6.2 percent in 1990 to only 1.0 percent in 1992. The government responded to the downturn using both monetary and fiscal policy. The Finance Ministry used monetary policy, lowering the discount rate in the middle of 1991. Between 1991 and 1993, the discount rate fell from 6 percent to 1.75 percent. By the end of the decade, the discount rate approached zero. Growth averaged 1.1 percent for the decade, and the 1990s ended with two years of decline in real GDP.

Japan also attempted to use fiscal policy to bolster the economy between 1992 and 1993 with a stimulus package equal to 6 percent of GDP. By 1995, the Japanese had spent nearly $2.1 trillion on public projects, mostly road and bridge construction, in an attempt to jump-start the economy. Many people were critical of the Japanese stimulus plan. Some argued that the government spent too much money, while others believed that the government stopped spending too soon. Some argued that the money was wasted on useless infrastructure projects and that they would have received more benefit if the money had been spent on education and social services. Others argued that the economy would have benefited more if the government had reduced taxes and allowed people to decide what to do with the money.

The economy started to rebound in 1994, with real GDP rising by 1.9 percent and 2.6 percent in 1995 and 1996, respectively. But this proved to be a false recovery. The economic stimulus plans were creating huge budget deficits. The deficits equaled 4 percent of real GDP for the decade of the 1990s. The Japanese government increased taxes to reduce the deficits and by 1997 real GDP growth was again at zero.

ACTIVITY 1, CONTINUED
JAPAN'S LOST DECADE

Despite driving the discount rate down to 0.5 percent in 1995, Japan was still suffering from deflation. Between 1994 and 2009, prices declined each year, with the exception of 1997 when the GDP deflator rose by a modest 0.9 percent. Not only were low interest rates unsuccessful at defeating deflation, they did not have a significant impact on increasing the amount of borrowing taking place. Investment spending continued to lag, which helped keep the country in recession until 2003–2004, when Japan finally had back-to-back years of modest real GDP growth (rates well above 2 percent).

Late in 1997, Japan experienced the failure of some of its largest financial institutions. By the spring of 1998, the government began injecting an additional 1.8 trillion yen into more than 20 banks. In early 1999, the Finance Ministry lowered the discount rate to essentially zero.

Questions

A. What caused the speculative bubble in housing and stock prices?

B. What caused the bubble to burst?

C. What did the Japanese government do in the early 1990s to try to bring the economy out of the recession? Was it successful?

D. What controversies were there over the government response to the economic downturn?

E. Prices in Japan declined from 1994 through 2009, with the exception of 1997. If high inflation is a problem for an economy, is deflation good? Use the following two examples to help in answering this question.

Example 1. Assume you are a corn farmer. Corn is currently selling for $5 a bushel. You can produce a bushel of corn for $4.75. Therefore you plant your crops in April with the expectation of harvesting and selling your corn in August. But what if the country is suffering from

ACTIVITY 1, CONTINUED
JAPAN'S LOST DECADE

deflation? By the time you have harvested your crop, the selling price of corn is $4.60. Instead of making a profit of $0.25 a bushel, you have lost $0.15 a bushel. Now it is spring again, what will you do? The country is still in deflation, so that the costs of seed, fertilizer and workers have fallen and you estimate that you can produce a bushel of corn for only $4.30 a bushel. Will you plant corn this year?

Example 2. Assume you are in the market for a new automobile. Your current car still works fine, but you have been eyeing a new model. The car has not changed, but because the country is facing deflation, the price has fallen from $32,000 to $30,000. In addition, economists predict that the country will continue to be in a deflationary cycle for at least the next three years, with prices falling an average of 10 percent per year. Will you purchase the car this year?

ACTIVITY 2
COMPARING AND CONTRASTING THE JAPANESE AND U.S. FINANCIAL CRISES USING DATA

Below are a number of graphs comparing Japan and the United States. Each graph plots a given variable, such as unemployment or real GDP growth rates. The first data point for Japan is for the year 1982. The first data point for the United States is for 1997. This aligns the two data series such that the year housing prices peaked are at the same point on the horizontal or x axis. This is 1991 for Japan and 2006 for the United States.

Part 1. Change in Home Prices

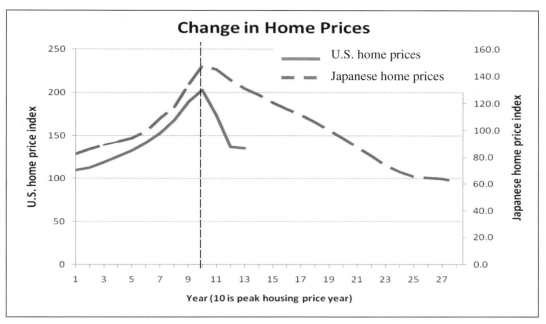

Source: Data from Case-Shiller Home Price Index, www.irrationalexuberance.com, and Bank of Japan, www.boj.or.jp/en

1. The graph shows housing prices trended similarly in both Japan and the United States leading up to the peak.

A. Briefly describe the trends in housing prices in both countries after hitting the peak. In what ways are the trends similar? In what ways are the trends different?

B. Using this information, predict what you expect will happen to housing prices in the United States over the next five to 10 years.

C. Does the Japanese experience lead you to be optimistic or pessimistic about the future of housing prices in the U.S.?

ACTIVITY 2, CONTINUED
COMPARING AND CONTRASTING THE JAPANESE AND U.S. FINANCIAL CRISES USING DATA

Part 2. Real GDP Growth Rates

Source: Data from the Bureau of Economic Analysis, U.S. Department of Commerce, www.bea.gov, and Bank of Japan, www.boj.or.jp/en

2. The graph shows the growth rate in real GDP for Japan and the United States.

A. Briefly describe the trend in the Japanese economy, as measured by the growth rate of real GDP, after the housing bubble burst.

B. One of the president's aides says that if the U.S. crisis follows the pattern of Japan, the worst is over and we should expect to see the economy grow again. How would you comment?

ACTIVITY 2, CONTINUED
COMPARING AND CONTRASTING THE JAPANESE AND U.S. FINANCIAL CRISES USING DATA

Part 3. Unemployment rates

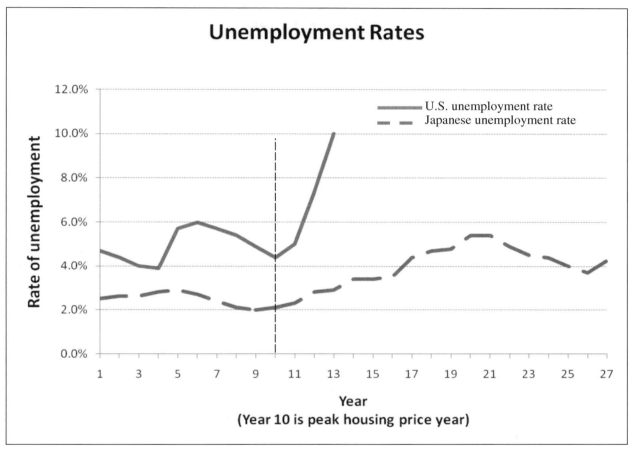

Source: Data from Bureau of Labor Statistics, U.S. Department of Labor, www.bls.gov, and Bank of Japan, www.boj.or.jp/en

3. The graph shows the unemployment rate in Japan and the United States. The vertical line represents the year each country reached its real estate price peak.

A. Comment on the graph showing the unemployment rate in the two countries. How are the trends similar? How are they different?

B. Members of Congress are worried about unemployment in the long run. What does the Japanese comparison suggest for the United States? Do you think the United States needs to be concerned about unemployment?

ACTIVITY 2, CONTINUED
COMPARING AND CONTRASTING THE JAPANESE AND U.S. FINANCIAL CRISES USING DATA

Part 4. Inflation rates

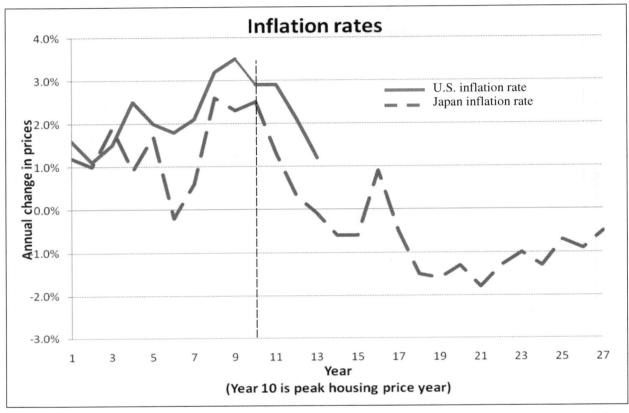

Source: Data from Bureau of Labor Statistics, U.S. Department of Labor, www.bls.gov, and Bank of Japan, www.boj.or.jp/en

4. The graph shows the inflation rate in Japan and the United States as measured by changes in the GDP deflator.

A. Briefly describe the trend in inflation in Japan. Compare this with the inflation rate in the United States following the real estate market crash.

B. As an economic advisor to the president, why might the Japanese experience with inflation be a concern to you? Predict what you would expect to happen to real GDP in the United States if deflation were to take hold.

ACTIVITY 2, CONTINUED
COMPARING AND CONTRASTING THE JAPANESE AND U.S. FINANCIAL CRISES USING DATA

Part 5. Changes in the stock markets

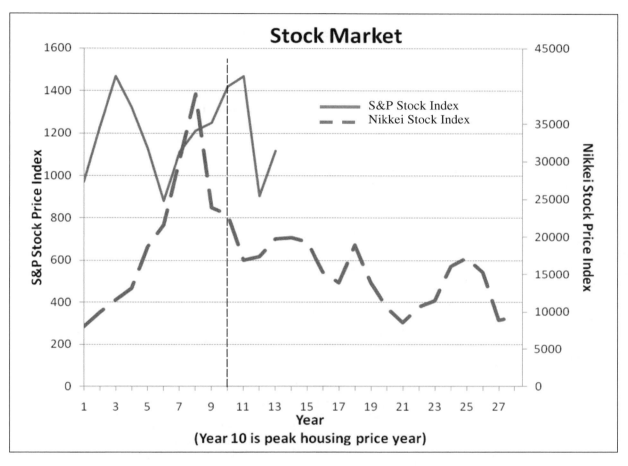

Source: Data from the Board of Governors of the Federal Reserve System, www.federalreserve.gov, and Bank of Japan, www.boj.or.jp/en

5. The graph shows stock market prices for Japan and the United States.

A. Comment on the trend in stock prices in the two countries prior to the peak in home prices.

B. Comment on the trend in stock prices in the two countries after the peak in home prices.

C. Does the recent increase in stock prices in the United States shown in the graph make you confident about the future of the economy?

ACTIVITY 2, CONTINUED
COMPARING AND CONTRASTING THE JAPANESE AND U.S. FINANCIAL CRISES USING DATA

Part 6. Monetary policy

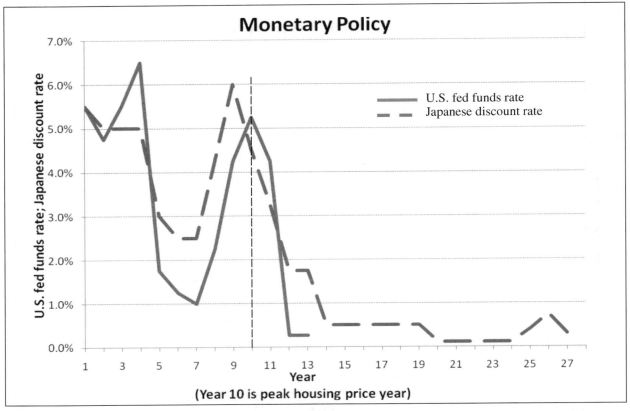

Source: Data from the Board of Governors of the Federal Reserve System, www.federalreserve.gov, and Bank of Japan, www.boj.or.jp/en

6. The graph illustrates the monetary policies of Japan and the United States. Japan's discount rate and the U.S. federal funds rate are shown above.

A. Briefly describe the trends in monetary policy in the United States and Japan. How are the policy responses similar? How are they different?

B. What does the graph suggest about interest rates in the United States in the future?

ACTIVITY 3
COMPARISON OF GOVERNMENT INTERVENTIONS IN JAPAN AND UNITED STATES FINANCIAL CRISES

Japan			United States		
Date	Months from peak	Event	Date	Months from peak	Event
1991	-	Land prices reach peak	2006	-	Home prices reach peak
7/1991	9	First cut in discount rate	9/2007	7	First cut in fed funds rate
8/1992	22	First stimulus (additional stimulus packages in '93, '94, '95, '98 and '99)	2/2008	12	Bush signs Economic Stimulus Act
11/1997	85	Four major financial institutions fail	9/2008	19	Government takes control of Fannie Mae and Freddie Mac. Lehman Brothers bankruptcy. AIG bailout
3/1998	89	Government injects 1.8 trillion yen (equal to $13.5 billion U.S. dollars; less than 0.5% of Japan's GDP) into banks. (secondary injection in 3/99)	10/2008	20	Troubled Asset Relief Program (TARP) – purchase of stock in major banks $700 billion (equal to 70 trillion yen; almost 5 percent of U.S. GDP)
2/1999	100	Discount rate approaches zero	12/2008	22	Federal funds target rate of 0 to .25
			2/2009	24	$787 billion stimulus package

Source: Adapted from chart 1, www.boj.or.jp/en/type/press/koen07/ko0905a.htm

Which of the following statements can reasonably be supported by the information above? Explain why.

A. Both Japan and the United States employed monetary and fiscal policy in attempts to stabilize their economies.

B. The United States acted more quickly than Japan in trying to address their economic problems.

C. Banks were healthier during the financial crisis in Japan than in the United States.

D. Both Japan and the United States no longer have the ability to use traditional monetary policy as a means of improving the economy.

ACTIVITY 4
ADVISING THE PRESIDENT

The Council of Economic Advisors has spent a great deal of time learning about the similarities and differences between Japan's Lost Decade and the financial crisis of 2007-2009 in the United States. The president would like some recommendations from the Council concerning the following issues:

1. The U.S. government suffered a budget deficit of $1.4 trillion in 2009. This equaled 9.9 percent of GDP, the highest since WWII. Should the U.S. government start taking immediate action to reduce the deficit? Why?

2. What do you think is the biggest lesson that the United States can learn from Japan's Lost Decade?

VISUAL 1
COMPARISON OF JAPAN AND U.S. HOME PRICES

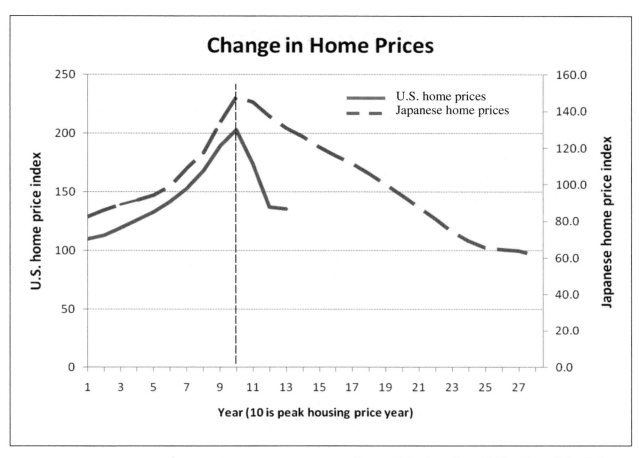

Change in Home Prices

Legend:
- U.S. home prices
- Japanese home prices

Year (10 is peak housing price year)

Source: Data from Case-Shiller Home Price Index, www.irrationalexuberance.com, and Bank of Japan, www.boj.or.jp/en

2
COMPARISON OF JAPAN AND U.S. REAL GDP GROWTH RATES

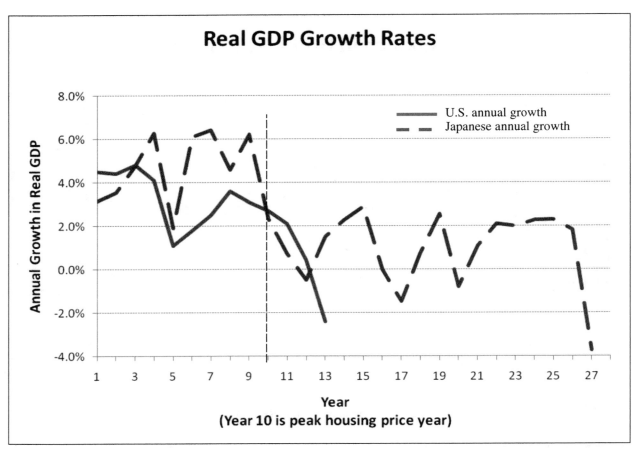

Source: Data from the Bureau of Economic Analysis, U.S. Department of Commerce, www.bea.gov, and Bank of Japan, www.boj.or.jp/en

VISUAL 3
COMPARISON OF JAPAN AND U.S. UNEMPLOYMENT RATES

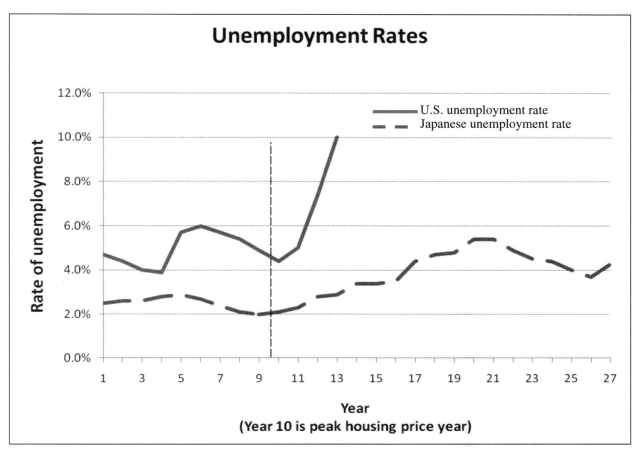

Source: Data from Bureau of Labor Statistics, U.S. Department of Labor, www.bls.gov, and Bank of Japan, www.boj.or.jp/en

VISUAL 4
COMPARISON OF JAPAN AND U.S. INFLATION RATES

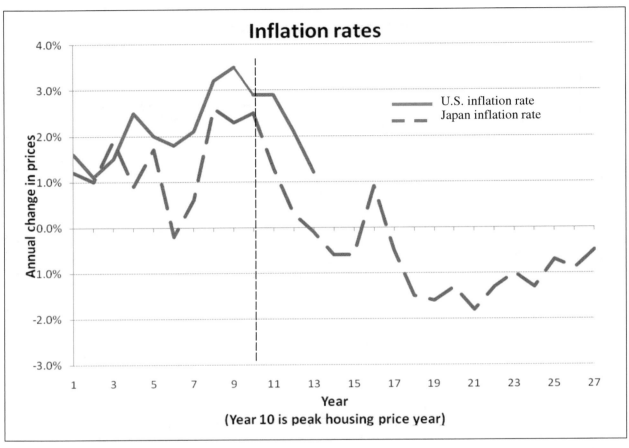

Source: Data from Bureau of Labor Statistics, U.S.
Department of Labor, www.bls.gov, and Bank of
Japan, www.boj.or.jp/en

VISUAL 5
COMPARISON OF JAPAN AND U.S. STOCK MARKETS

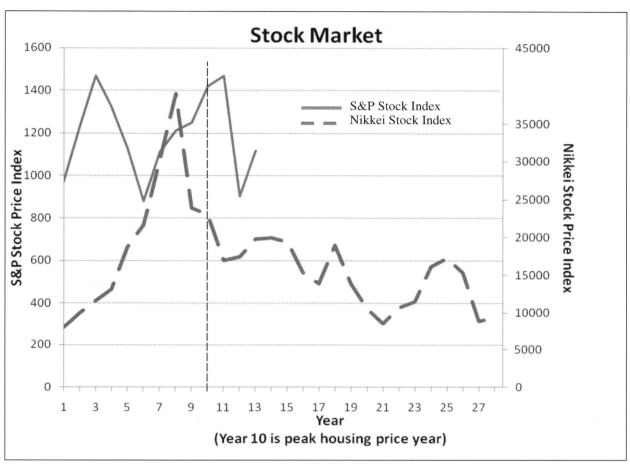

Source: Data from the Board of Governors of the
Federal Reserve System, www.federalreserve.gov, and
Bank of Japan, www.boj.or.jp/en

VISUAL 6
COMPARISON OF JAPAN AND U.S. MONETARY POLICIES

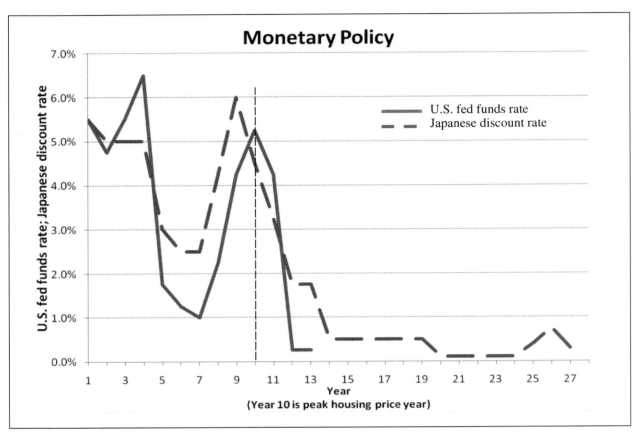

Source: Data from the Board of Governors of the
Federal Reserve System, www.federalreserve.gov, and
Bank of Japan, www.boj.or.jp/en

VISUAL 7

COMPARISON OF GOVERNMENT INTERVENTIONS IN THE JAPAN AND UNITED STATES FINANCIAL CRISES

Japan			United States		
Date	Months from peak	Event	Date	Months from peak	Event
1991	-	Land prices reach peak	2006	-	Home prices reach peak
7/1991	9	First cut in discount rate	9/2007	7	First cut in fed funds rate
8/1992	22	First stimulus (additional stimulus packages in '93, '94, '95, '98 and '99)	2/2008	12	Bush signs Economic Stimulus Act
11/1997	85	Four major financial institutions fail	9/2008	19	Government takes control of Fannie Mae and Freddie Mac. Lehman Brothers bankruptcy. AIG bailout
3/1998	89	Government injects 1.8 trillion yen (equal to $13.5 billion U.S. dollars; less than 0.5% of Japan's GDP) into banks. (secondary injection in 3/99)	10/2008	20	Troubled Asset Relief Program (TARP) – purchase of stock in major banks $700 billion (equal to 70 trillion yen; almost 5 percent of U.S. GDP)
2/1999	100	Discount rate approaches zero	12/2008	22	Federal funds target rate of 0 to .25
			2/2009	24	$787 billion stimulus package

Source: Adapted from chart 1, www.boj.or.jp/en/type/press/koen07/ko0905a.htm

MONETARY POLICY IN THE RECENT FINANCIAL CRISIS

LESSON 5
MONETARY POLICY IN THE RECENT FINANCIAL CRISIS

LESSON DESCRIPTION

Actions are taken by the Board of Governors of the Federal Reserve System (the Fed) to create a stable macroeconomy. Part 1 of the lesson places the student in the role of an economic analyst diagnosing the economy by viewing 2007-2009 data regarding the Consumer Price Index (CPI), unemployment, and real GDP growth. Students are likely to conclude from their analysis that **monetary policy** tools were needed to correct for the crisis. In Part 2 of the lesson, students will be introduced to tools historically available to the Fed as well as to new tools created by the Fed. Student teams will serve as members of the Board of Governors and make monetary policy decisions by choosing from among traditional and new tools. Students will evaluate the action by the Fed to pay interest on required and excess reserves held by banks and observe and analyze the effects of the monetary expansion on the Fed's balance sheet.

For advanced students, three extension opportunities with supporting materials are provided.

INTRODUCTION

Controlling the supply of money circulating in the economy is the responsibility of an independent central bank known as the Fed, established by Congress with the Federal Reserve Act and signed by President Woodrow Wilson in 1913. The Fed is sometimes referred to as a "fourth branch of government" because of the power it has to control monetary policy and, in turn, the health and wealth of our nation.

The captain at the helm during the financial crisis is a former economics professor from Princeton University, Ben Bernanke, whose dissertation research for his doctorate from MIT focused on monetary policy mistakes made by the Fed during the Great Depression. Named *Time* magazine's Person of the Year in 2009, he was described as "the most important player guiding the world's most important economy. His creative leadership helped ensure that 2009 was a period of weak recovery rather than cata-strophic depression, and he still wields unrivaled power over our money, our jobs, our savings and our national future."

Perhaps Bernanke's "creative leadership" was the use of new monetary policy tools. Collectively, the alphabet-soup-sounding tools such as the TALF, PDCF, and TSLF, comprise the Fed's new recipe for dealing with turmoil in credit markets. These complex tools were created to accomplish the broad goals of lengthening the maturity of loans, broadening the assets accepted as collateral in policy operations, and extending credit to more institutions than has been customary.

CONCEPTS

- Recession
- Inflation
- The Federal Reserve System
- Monetary policy
- Traditional monetary policy tools
- New monetary policy tools
- Reserve requirement
- Discount rate
- Open market operations
- Federal funds rate

OBJECTIVES

Students will:

1. Analyze economic data from 2007-2009 regarding **inflation**, national and state unemployment, and real GDP growth.

2. Identify the traditional monetary tools used by the Fed and how these tools were used during the financial crisis.

3. Identify the new monetary tools used by the Fed and how these tools were used during the financial crisis.

4. Explain the effect of the Fed's actions on the money supply.

CONTENT STANDARDS

- Fluctuations in a nation's overall levels of income, employment, and prices are determined by the interaction of spending and production decisions made by all households, firms, government agencies, and others in the economy. Recessions occur when overall levels of income and employment decline.

- Unemployment imposes costs on individuals and the overall economy. Inflation, both expected and unexpected, also imposes costs on individuals and the overall economy. Unemployment increases during recessions and decreases during recoveries.

- Federal government budgetary policy and the Federal Reserve System's monetary policy influence the overall levels of employment, output, and prices.

TIME REQUIRED

Two or three class periods (more time if using optional extensions)

MATERIALS

- Activity 1: You Are an Economic Analyst: Diagnosing the Economy (one copy per student)

- Activity 2: You Are a Governor: Making Monetary Policy (one copy per student)

- Visual 1: What You Will Learn from This Lesson (transparency)

- Visual 2: Traditional Tools of the Fed (transparency)

- Visual 3: Traditional Plus New Tools of the Fed (transparency)

- Visual 4: Excess Bank Reserves (transparency)

- Visual 5: The Fed's Balance Sheet (transparency)

- Extension Visual 6: Is the Fed a Public or Private Institution?

- Extension Visual 7: Balancing the Responsibilities of the Fed

- Handout 1: CPI 2007-2010 (one copy per student or provide as a visual)

- Handout 2: Unemployment Rates Monthly and Annually 2007-2010 (one copy per student or provide as a visual)

- Handout 3: State Unemployment Rates 2007-2009 (one copy per student or provide as a visual)

- Handout 4: Percentage Change in Real GDP 2007-2010 (one copy per student or provide as a visual)

- Handout 5: Excerpt from "Banks Promise Loans But Hoard Cash" by Liz Moyer in *Forbes* (February 2009)

- Extension Handout 6: New Tools Defined by the Fed

- Extension Handout 7: Bernanke's Views on the 2007-2009 Crisis

PROCEDURE

1. Display Visual 1: What You Will Learn from This Lesson. Review the lesson objectives with the students.

Part A. Financial Crisis Data Collection

2. Distribute Handout 1: CPI 2007–2010 (or provide as a visual) and ask the following question:

   a. What is the CPI?

   The Bureau of Labor Statistics monitors the prices of over 90,000 goods and services that consumers purchase, from houses to haircuts. These prices are summarized by the Consumer Price Index. If the index rises, prices have increased, and if it continues to rise, we are experiencing inflation.

3. Distribute Handout 2: Unemployment Rates 2007-2010 (or provide this as a visual) and ask the following question:

   a. What criteria are required by the Bureau of Labor Statistics to categorize a person as unemployed?

   Persons in the labor force are those who are age 16 and older and actively seeking work. If these workers in the labor force cannot find a job, they are considered unemployed. Persons who work part time are considered employed even though they may desire a full-time job. Persons who have become discouraged about finding a job and have stopped looking for work are not in the labor force and are therefore not categorized as unemployed.

4. Distribute Handout 3: State Unemployment Rates 2007-2009 (or provide as a visual) and ask the following questions:

   a. What states realized a rate that tripled during the financial crisis?

      Alabama, Florida, and Idaho.

   b. What state suffered from the highest unemployment rate at the end of 2009?

      Michigan.

   c. What states enjoyed "full" employment at the end of 2009? Hint: by definition, full employment occurs when 4-5 percent of the workforce is unemployed.

      Nebraska, North Dakota, and South Dakota.

   d. Teachers should ask their students about their own state and discuss why unemployment may be higher or lower than the national average and why the change may have been greater or less.

      Answers will vary.

      The unemployment column includes data from approximately one year prior to the beginning of the recession to convey conditions before the slowdown in the economy.

5. Distribute Handout 4: Percentage Change in Real GDP 2007-2010 (or provide as a visual), review the following economic concepts and ask the following questions:

   a. What happens when overall spending is greater than production?

      Inflationary pressures will be created if

the economy is at or near full employment; increased production and employment, if the economy is producing less than its full-employment level of output.*

   b. What happens when overall spending is less than production?

      There is a reduction in production and employment. Deflationary pressures are possible.

   c. What is the definition of **recession**?

      The National Bureau of Economic Research determines whether a recession is occuring. It defines a recession as a period during which there is a significant decline in economic activity spread across the economy and lasting more than a few months. A common business-news definition of a recession is "two declining quarters of GDP;" however, that is not true of all recessions. Recessions exhibit falling output and falling employment that are significant and last for more than a few months.

   d. What is the definition of "deflation?" (Although at the time of this writing the economy is not suffering from deflation, it is of concern because it may lead to further recessionary pressures.)

      A general decline in prices. Deflation occurs when the annual inflation rate falls below zero percent. To combat deflation, the Fed can institute monetary policy to stimulate spending.

   e. Which three quarters had the greatest declines in real gross domestic product?

      The third and fourth quarters of 2008 and the first quarter of 2009.

   f. Which components experienced the largest declines in those periods?

Consumption declined in all three quarters, but the decreases in investment spending were particularly large. Within investment, residential and non-residential investment declines were significant. There were large declines in exports in the last quarter of 2008 and the first quarter of 2009. Counterbalancing those decreases were declines in imports

6. Distribute Activity 1: You are an Economic Analyst: Diagnosing the Economy.

   a. Tell students that they will use Handouts 1–4 (or visuals) to continue analyzing the financial crisis of 2007-2009.

b. Direct the students to Column 2, which provides definitions to key economic terms. Note that the unemployment definitions continue into Column 3.

c. Direct the students to Column 3, which provides the ranges for the ideal CPI, unemployment rates, and real GDP that typically characterize macroeconomic stability.

d. Instruct the students to follow the directions on the activity handout. They will complete a three-part analysis.

Answers to Activity 1:

Part A

Economic Component	Economic Component Defined	Ideal Range	2007	2008	2009	Change
Handout 1 Consumer Price Index (CPI)	Bureau of Labor Statistics (BLS) measures the change in prices of consumer goods and services.	1-3%	*2.8% annual*	*3.8% annual*	*-0.4% annual*	*Increased rate of inflation from 2007 to 2008 and then prices falling slightly from 2008 to 2009*
Handout 2 National Unemployment	The BLS counts the number of persons who are in the labor force (age 16 and older and actively seeking work) and do not have a job.	"Full" employment: 4-5% of the labor force is unemployed	*4.6% Jan* *5.0% Dec* *4.6% annual*	*5.0% Jan* *7.4% Dec* *5.8% annual*	*7.7% Jan* *10.0% Dec* *9.3% annual*	*Increasing unemployment*
Handout 3 State Unemployment (Select YOUR state and any second state)	National percentages in excess of 5% are often due to changes in the business cycle (cyclical unemployment). State unemployment higher than 5% is likely due to specific local conditions.	4-5%	*Your state: Second state: #s vary*	*Your state: Second state: #s vary*	*Your state: Second state: #s vary*	*Your state: Second state: #s vary*
Handout 4 Real GDP	Real GDP is the total value (adjusted for changing prices) of the final goods and services produced by a nation in a given year.	2-3% growth rate in real GDP	*1st quarter 0.9%* *2nd quarter 3.2%* *3rd quarter 2.3%* *4th quarter 2.9%* *1.9% annual*	*1st quarter -0.7%* *2nd quarter 0.6%* *3rd quarter -4.0%* *4th quarter -6.8%* *0.0% annual*	*1st quarter -4.9%* *2nd quarter -0.7%* *3rd quarter 1.6%* *4th quarter 5.0%* *-2.6% annual*	*Significant declines since 2007, improving 2nd half 2009*

Part B

Gross private domestic investment experienced the largest decline, -50.5% in the first quarter of 2009. Within this component, nonresidential structures declined 43.6%, with residential investment a close second, declining 38.2%.

Part C

Inflation does not seem to be a concern for the Fed at the time but it could become one in the future. Teachers may want to quote Ben Bernanke in a speech he delivered on December 7, 2009. Bernanke said, "Unprecedented balance sheet expansion and near-zero overnight interest rates raise our third frequently asked question: Will the Federal Reserve's actions to combat the crisis lead to higher inflation down the road? The answer is no; the Federal Reserve is committed to keeping inflation low and will be able to do so."

The annual rate of unemployment and a majority of state unemployment rates are high at any rate above the natural rate of unemployment or full employment (a rate of 4 percent-5 percent). This additional unemployment is primarily cyclical unemployment that is due to the overall slowing of the economy. A portion of individual state unemployment beyond the national levels may be due to increased structural unemployment caused by changing industry patterns within the economy.

Declines in real GDP from 2007-2009 are significant with gross private domestic investment (investment spending by businesses, specifically on new nonresidential structures and residential housing structures), suffering the most significant decline. Spending by consumers, government, and net exports was fairly stable compared to gross private domestic investment by businesses. Consumer spending on durable goods and exports and imports changed significantly in a few quarters.

Part B. Action Needed by the Fed: Traditional Tools and New Tools

7. Display Visual 2: Traditional Tools of the Fed. Remind students that the Fed is sometimes compared to a mechanic repairing an engine, a carpenter rebuilding a house, a physician healing a sick patient, or a plumber installing new lines. Although students may already be familiar with the traditional tools, a review of the tools may be needed. Remind students that these tools can be used to change the money supply, credit availability, and interest rates in response to expected economic conditions. Broadly speaking, in the event of inflation, the Fed adopts a tight money policy that decreases the supply of money circulating in an economy. In the

event of recession, unemployment, slow growth in GDP, or depression, the Fed adopts an easy money policy that increases the supply of money circulating in an economy.

8. Display Visual 3: Traditional Plus New Tools of the Fed. Review these categories with the students. The traditional tools are shown in the upper left-hand corner of Visual 3. The categories of the new tools are in line with the broad goals that the Fed and Bernanke sought to accomplish, including lengthening the maturity of loans, broadening the assets accepted as collateral, and extending credit to more institutions than was customary.

The new tools adopted during the 2007-2009 crisis were designed to go beyond traditional monetary policy. All of these tools were created to help provide liquidity to traditional banks and other financial institutions, mitigating their reluctance to make loans and financial investments.

The first group of new tools is shown in the upper right-hand corner of Visual 3. These tools were meant to provide short-term liquidity to banks and other financial institutions. In addition, efforts were extended to foreign central banks to ensure sufficient dollars for their financial institutions.

The second group of new tools in the lower left-hand corner of Visual 3 directly provided liquidity to borrowers and investors in specific credit markets. (Descriptions of each of the new tools designed to increase short-term liquidity and those intended to provide liquidity directly to key credit markets are included in Extension Handout 6.) Almost all of these new tools had ended by July 2010. Only the TALF in the key credit markets was still functioning.

The final group of new tools in the lower right-hand corner of Visual 3 expanded traditional **open market operations** to longer-term securities by purchasing government-sponsored enterprise (GSE) debt and longer-term U.S. Treasury securities. The GSEs were Fannie Mae and Freddie Mac, government-sponsored private companies that purchased mortgage-backed securities with the goal of providing more funds to housing markets. The longer-term U.S. Treasury securities purchases were meant to increase liquidity in that market and to bring down longer-term interest rates.

9. Tell students they are going to create their own **monetary policy**. Teachers will divide the class into teams and refer to the teams as the Fed's Board of Governors. Remind them that there are seven mem-

bers of the Board of Governors who are nominated by the president and confirmed by the Senate for one 14-year term. The Board of Governors, along with five of the presidents of the 12 regional Federal Reserve Banks, make up the Federal Open Market Committee (FOMC), which is responsible for conducting monetary policy.

10. Distribute Activity 2: You Are a Governor: Making Monetary Policy. Direct students to follow the directions provided on the activity handout. Ask each student to mark the correct answers.

11. Review the answers with the students. (Answers are shaded below.)

Part 1:

Traditional Tools	Make your Decision. Would your Governors...	
Reserve Requirement	⬆	⬇
Discount Rate	⬆	⬇
Open Market Operations	Buy	Sell
• Federal Funds Rate	⬆	⬇

Part 2:

Specific Goals of New Tools	Make your Decision. In Which Direction? Would your Governors...
Change the due dates when banks and other financial institutions pay back loans to the Fed	Shorten or lengthen the due dates (maturity)
Change the type of assets accepted as collateral in policy monetary policy operations	Broaden or narrow the assets accepted
Lend money directly to financial institutions	Restrict or extend credit (or provide credit to more institutions than was customary)
Purchase more short-term or long-term financial assets	Buy short-term or long-term financial assets

Part C. Results of the Fed's Monetary Policy

12. Ask students whether the new programs suggest that the Fed was implementing a tight money policy or an easy money policy.

    The Fed implemented an easy money policy.

    Ask students to consider what effect this increase in the money supply will have on the price of money (interest rates) that banks charge consumers and businesses on loans.

    Interest rates will decline.

13. Display Visual 4: Excess Bank Reserves, which shows the increased volume of bank excess reserves. Ask students to speculate about the following question: Why are the banks not lending the excess reserves? Should we be concerned or is this normal monetary policy?

    Monetary policy in times of extreme financial stress may not be as effective as it normally would be. If banks and financial institutions are extremely worried about the future they will not make as many loans or financial investments as they would in better times. Thus, excess reserves increase dramatically as shown in Visual 4. The article in Handout 5 will shed some light on the issues.

14. Distribute Handout 5: An Excerpt from "Banks Promise Loans but Hoard Cash" by Liz Moyer in *Forbes* (February 2009). For the full article, link to

    http://www.forbes.com/2009/02/03/
    bankingfederal-reserve-business-
    wall-street-0203_loans.html

    Tell students that there are two other new tools not listed on Visual 3. These two tools continue to be used as of June 2010. The first, which will almost definitely continue to be used in the future, is that the Federal Reserve began paying banks interest on both required reserves and the excess reserves on October 3, 2008, as part of the Economic Stabilization Act of 2008.

Lead a discussion on the reading that includes the question posed above about the volume of excess reserves as well as the following:

a. Once the interest began being paid, did the excess reserves increase or decrease?

   Increase.

b. What are the problems associated with not lending out the money?

   A credit crunch occurs when banks are less inclined to lend out money to businesses and consumers. No lending means no investment in the economy by businesses and no job creation. Unemployment and slow growth in real GDP continue to plague the economy.

c. Why are banks reluctant to lend money?

   *Banks are being paid an interest rate by the Fed that might encourage banks to keep excess reserves. However, that interest rate is equal to the target **federal funds rate** and is unlikely to have a significant effect. The purpose of the new tool is to lower the effective tax on banks from losing interest on required reserves and to set a lower bound for the federal funds rate. No bank will lend other banks reserves at an interest that is below the rate paid by the Fed. The primary reason for the dramatic increase in reserves must be that banks are reluctant to make loans given the experience with high foreclosure rates and the seriousness of the recession and the financial crisis.*

   The second other new tool, established in early 2010, is labeled the Term Deposit Facility (TDF). It allows banks to make longer term deposits with the Fed and is meant to serve as a means of slowing the expansion of the money supply when loans begin to be made in large quantities once again. The Fed will be able to offer an alternative to making new loans if it believes the money supply is rising too rapidly. Evidence as to this tool's effectiveness will not be available for some time.

15. Display Visual 5: The Fed's Balance Sheet. Ask students the significance of the data presented.

The Fed's monetary policy strategy to provide a foundation for an easy money policy has been accomplished. The graph correctly depicts a comment Bernanke made during a speech before the Economic Club of Washington, D.C., on December 7, 2009, when he described the growth in the Federal Reserve's assets "...from less than $900 billion before the crisis began to about $2.2 trillion today." During that time period, the money supply as measured by the narrow definition of (M1) increased 24 percent and the broader money supply (M2) increased by 15 percent. The growth in the money supply was significantly less than the growth in the Federal Reserve's assets. That increase in assets should have resulted in a multiple expansion of the amount of money.

Certainly, the growth in the money supply was substantial enough to provide opportunities to make it easier and cheaper for consumers and businesses to borrow money, buy more goods, open more factories, and hire more workers in the future. One criticism of monetary policy in general, however, is that under recessionary conditions, it may be like "pushing a string." Low interest rates must be taken advantage of and loans must be made if spending is to increase and growth to be realized.

CLOSURE

Review the main points of the lesson by again displaying Visual 1: What You Will Learn from This Lesson. Ask students to:

1. Evaluate the 2007-2010 economic data regarding inflation, national and state unemployment, and GDP growth.

   See Handouts 1-4 for answers.

2. Identify the traditional monetary tools used by the Fed and how these tools were used during the financial crisis.

   See Visual 2.

3. Identify the new monetary tools used by the Fed and explain why they were used.

   See Visual 3.

4. Explain why the Fed's actions had an effect on the money supply and whether or not that effect was as large as might be expected.

   See Visuals 4 and 5 to begin.

ASSESSMENT

Multiple-choice questions

1. All of following could correctly describe the financial crisis of 2007-2009 except:

   *a. Accelerating inflation

   b. Slow growth in GDP

   c. Nonresidential investment spending declined

   d. Rising unemployment rates in most states

2. Which of the following monetary policy tools was created during the 2007-2009 crisis to increase liquidity in the financial markets?

   a. Discount rate

   b. Open market operations

   c. Reserve requirement

   *d. Purchase of money market fund assets

3. The Fed responded to the crisis of 2007-2009 by implementing all of the following monetary policy actions except:

   a. Making loans to depository institutions through the Primary Credit Facility

   *b. Providing fewer reserves to banks through open-market operations

   c. Extending the maturity of loans made to banks using the Term Auction Facility

   d. Swapping a preferred class of Treasury

securities in the open market through the Term Security Lending Facility

Constructed-response questions

1. When Ben Bernanke was named Person of the Year by *Time* magazine in 2009, author Michael Grunwald described the chairman as "the most important player guiding the world's most important economy. His creative leadership helped ensure that 2009 was a period of weak recovery rather than catastrophic depression, and he still wields unrivaled power over our money, our jobs, our savings and our national future." Do you agree with Grunwald's assessment of Bernanke?

Answers will vary. Students and teachers may want to read Time's double issue (December 28, 2009-January 4, 2010) for further elaboration.

2. How important do you think it is for the Fed to maintain its independence within the federal government?

Answers will vary but students should recognize both the unique structure and the unique responsibilities that the Fed has been given through legislation passed by elected members of Congress. The Fed's status as an independent institution run by nonelected officials suggests that it can focus on the responsibilities of price stability and economic growth while being insulated from short-term political pressures that invariably haunt fiscal policy decisions. Keeping money creation under the auspices of the Fed and the spending authority under the auspices of Congress provides a vital separation of power that serves to avoid periods of hyperinflation like those that plagued Latin America in the 1990s and Zimbabwe throughout much of the past decade.

3. (Optional, use with Extension 7.) Ben Bernanke's dissertation for his doctorate in economics from M.I.T. focused on the Fed's purposeful decision not to inject liquidity and credit into the markets in the 1930s, thereby heightening the depths of the Great Depression. How do you think

Bernanke's awareness of these decisions influenced his handling of the 2007-2009 crisis?

Answers will vary, but students should present the argument that cites the Fed's balance sheet presented in Visual 5: The Fed's Balance Sheet as evidence of the extent to which he sought to bolster the economy and avert economic calamity.

EXTENSIONS

Extension Part 1: Background on the Federal Reserve System

16. For teachers who would like to present students with background on the Fed, direct the students to Extension Visual 6: Is the Fed a Public or Private Institution? Ask the following questions:

a. Is the Fed a public or private institution?

The Fed is both a public and a private institution and, as such, is considered quasi-governmental. It is a central bank created by Congress yet is considered independent of politics as it performs its responsibilities. Evidence of its public and private underpinnings is provided in the visual.

b. What are the benefits of being both public and private?

A private focus allows the Fed to make decisions that are more likely to be nonpolitical. Fiscal policy conducted by the president and Congress is subject to the reelection goals of politicians whereas monetary policy is conducted by nonelected officials. Teachers should introduce the ongoing debate among politicians and those at the Fed regarding whether the Fed should retain its independence. The Fed favors an independent position and politicians often favor greater Congressional oversight.

c. Ask students to interpret Bernanke's quote:

"In navigating through the crisis, the Federal Reserve has been greatly aided

by the regional structure established by the Congress when it created the Federal Reserve in 1913. The more than 270 business people, bankers, nonprofit executives, academics, and community, agricultural, and labor leaders who serve on the boards of the 12 Reserve Banks and their 24 branches provide valuable insights into current economic and financial conditions that statistics alone cannot. Thus, the structure of the Federal Reserve ensures that our policy-making is informed not just by a Washington perspective, or a Wall Street perspective, but also a Main Street perspective." (Economic Club of Washington, D.C., December 7, 2009)

Answers will vary, but students should have a sense that the Chairman, the Board of Governors, and members of the FOMC (Federal Open Market Committee) strive to make decisions that are in the best interests of the global economy, the overall U.S. economy, and millions of workers, consumers, and business owners.

17. Display Extension Visual 7: Balancing the Responsibilities of the Fed and ask the following questions:

    a. What were the responsibilities of the Fed in 1913?

        Provide price stability, preserve value of the dollar, prevent inflation.

    b. What responsibilities were added by the Humphrey-Hawkins Act in 1978?

        Added duty via the Humphrey-Hawkins Full Employment and Balanced Growth Act signed by President Jimmy Carter in 1978: provide full employment and economic growth.

    c. How might these responsibilities require balancing by the Fed?

        Because the Fed has the added responsibility of encouraging economic growth, during the 2007-2009 crisis it

had to employ all of its traditional tools as well as create new tools to avert a total downfall of the U.S. economy. Had the Fed, in the current crisis, been responsible for only price stability, which was not a critical issue, given the low inflation rates, there would not have been a policymaking role for the Fed to target economic growth.

Given both goals, there is often a trade-off between minimizing inflation and encouraging economic growth.

Extension Part 2: New Monetary Policy Tools

18. For teachers who want to present the extensive details of the new monetary policy tools, direct the students to Extension Handout 6: New Tools Defined by the Fed. This can be used in several ways. Given the amount of detail, including definitions, provided by the Fed, (http://www.federalreserve.gov/ monetarypolicy/default.htm), it may not be suitable as a handout for all students. Teachers who choose to distribute the handout should direct students to the first column, which lists the programs created by the Fed, and to the second column, which details the tasks each program is designed to fulfill. Teachers can display the two-page handout as a visual to highlight the number of facilities and programs that have been created by the Fed to remedy the crisis. Teachers can also use this handout to supplement their own understanding of these new tools.

While almost all of the new tools have been discontinued, they will likely be available for use if serious financial crises arise in the future. We will have learned a significant amount about their relative effectiveness.

Extension Part 3: Views of the Fed Chairman

19. Distribute Extension Handout 7: Bernanke's Views on the 2007-2009 Crisis (or provide as a visual). Divide the students into small groups and assign each group a query from column one. A member of each group can present Bernanke's

views during a teacher-led class discussion.

20. Direct the students to read and interpret the progression of viewpoints expressed by Ben Bernanke including a speech delivered in Wyoming in 2007, testimony before the House of Representatives in 2008, and a speech delivered at the London School of Economics in 2009:

"Housing, Housing Finance, and Monetary Policy" Speech at the Federal Reserve Bank of Kansas City's Economic Symposium, Jackson Hole, Wyoming, August 31, 2007. http://www.federal reserve.gov/newsevents/speech/bernanke 20070831a.htm

"The Economic Outlook" Bernanke Testimony before the Committee on the Budget, U.S. House of Representatives, January, 2008. http://www. federalreserve.gov/newsevents/ testimony/bernanke20080117a.htm

"The Crisis and the Policy Response" The Stamp Lecture, London School of Economics, London, England, January 13, 2009. http://www.federalreserve.gov/ newsevents/speech/bernanke20090113a.htm

ACTIVITY 1
YOU ARE AN ECONOMIC ANALYST: DIAGNOSING THE ECONOMY

Part A Data Collection: Complete the following chart by collecting data provided in Handouts 1-4. In the last column you are asked to determine whether the data indicate an *increase*, a *decrease*, or an *inconsequential change*.

Part B Economic Analysis: Select Handout 4. Of the four components of GDP, (C), (I), (G), (NX), find the component that experienced the largest quarterly decline. In which quarter was this? What component experienced this decline? What two subcomponents experienced the largest decline in this quarter? Support your answer with numbers.

Part C Economic Analysis: What conclusions can you draw regarding inflation, national unemployment, selected state unemployment, and growth in real GDP? Would you characterize U.S. economy as experiencing a recession? Present your answer in a detailed 75-100 word paragraph. Use the back if needed.

Economic Component	Economic Component Defined	Ideal Range	2007	2008	2009	Change
Handout 1 Consumer Price Index (CPI)	Bureau of Labor Statistics (BLS) measures the change in prices of consumer goods and services.	1-3%				
Handout 2 National Unemployment	The BLS counts the number of persons who are in the labor force (age 16 and older and actively seeking work) and do not have a job.	"Full" employment: 4-5% of the labor force is unemployed				
Handout 3 State Unemployment (Select YOUR state and any second state)	National percentages in excess of 5% are often due to changes in the business cycle (cyclical unemployment). State unemployment higher than 5% is likely due to specific local conditions.	4-5%				
Handout 4 Real GDP	Real GDP is the total value (adjusted for changing prices) of the final goods and services produced by a nation in a given year.	2-3% growth rate in real GDP				

ACTIVITY 2
YOU ARE A GOVERNOR: MAKING MONETARY POLICY

Part 1: Given the economic situation you analyzed in Activity 1, your Board of Governors must choose from among the traditional tools available to the Fed. Color in or circle the policy action your Board of Governors recommends. Explain your choice of goals to the class, compare your answers with the other Governors, and review your answers with the teacher.

Part 2: The financial crisis is so severe that the governors need to develop additional tools. Reassemble your Board of Governors and choose how you might use the new tools given the goals and the crisis of 2007-2009. Circle the direction your board is recommending, for example, shorten or lengthen. As above, explain your choice.

Traditional Tools	Make your Decision. Would your Governors...	Specific Goals of New Tools	Make your decision. In which direction? Would your Governors...
Reserve requirement	⇧ ⇩	Change the due dates when banks and other financial institutions pay back loans to the Fed	Shorten or lengthen the due dates (maturity)
Discount rate	⇧ ⇩		
Open market operations	Buy Sell	Change the type of assets accepted as collateral in monetary policy operations	Broaden or narrow the assets accepted
• Federal funds rate	⇧ ⇩	Lend money directly to financial institutions	Restrict or extend credit to more institutions than was customary
		Purchase more short-term or long-term financial assets	Buy short-term or long-term financial assets

VISUAL 1
WHAT YOU WILL LEARN FROM THIS LESSON

- How to draw conclusions from economic data from 2007-2009 regarding inflation, national and state unemployment, and real GDP growth.

- What the Fed's traditional monetary tools are and how they were used during the recent financial crisis.

- What new monetary tools the Fed employed during the recent financial crisis.

- How the Fed's actions affected (and are still affecting) the money supply.

VISUAL 2
TRADITIONAL TOOLS OF THE FED

Reserve requirements

- The percentage of checking deposits that the Fed requires banks to hold as reserves. Extra reserves can be loaned out.

- The Fed rarely alters these requirements.

- When the required reserve ratio is increased, the money supply contracts. When the required reserve ratio is decreased, the money supply expands.

Discount rate

- The interest rate the Fed charges banks for short-term loans.

- To conduct easy monetary policy, the Fed lowers the discount rate. To conduct more restrictive monetary policy, the Fed increases the discount rate

---

VISUAL 2, CONTINUED
TRADITIONAL TOOLS OF THE FED

Open market operations

- The Fed buys and sells existing Treasury securities on the open market.

- To conduct easy monetary policy, the Fed buys securities, which means that sellers end up with fewer securities and more money. To conduct more restrictive monetary policy, the Fed sells securities and buyers end up with more securities and less money.

A key indicator of monetary policy is the federal funds rate, which is the interest rate that banks charge other banks for overnight loans of reserves.

- When the Fed buys Treasury securities, banks end up with increased deposits and reserves. The supply of reserves will have increased and the federal funds rate will, therefore, decrease. If the Fed sells securities, reserves decrease and the federal funds rate increases.

VISUAL 3
TRADITIONAL PLUS NEW TOOLS OF THE FED

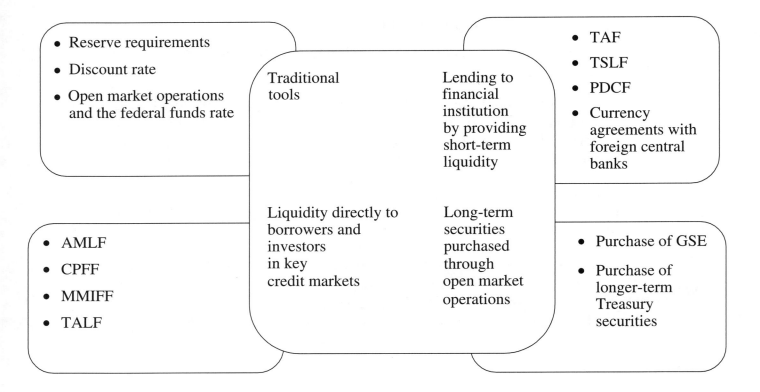

- Reserve requirements
- Discount rate
- Open market operations and the federal funds rate

Traditional tools

Lending to financial institution by providing short-term liquidity

- TAF
- TSLF
- PDCF
- Currency agreements with foreign central banks

- AMLF
- CPFF
- MMIFF
- TALF

Liquidity directly to borrowers and investors in key credit markets

Long-term securities purchased through open market operations

- Purchase of GSE
- Purchase of longer-term Treasury securities

VISUAL 4
EXCESS BANK RESERVES

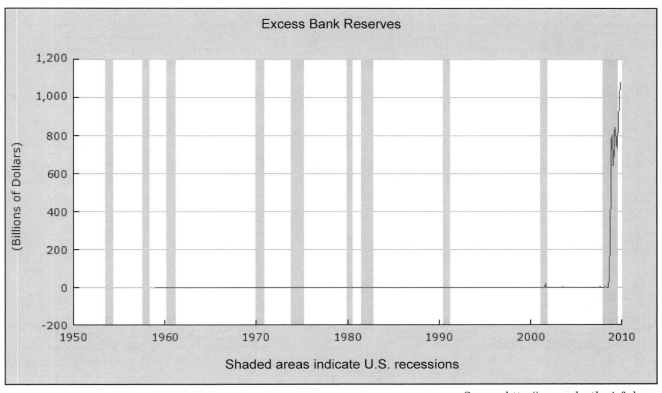

Source: http://research.stlouisfed.org

Visual 5
The Fed's Balance Sheet

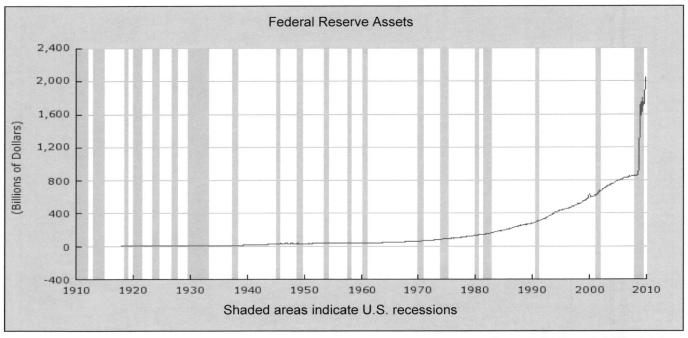

Federal Reserve Assets

Shaded areas indicate U.S. recessions

Source: http://research.stlouisfed.org

Question: The Fed's Balance Sheet (in billions of dollars)

What is the significance of these data? Be sure to respond to Ben Bernanke's comment from a speech before the Economic Club of Washington D.C., on December 7, 2009, when he described the growth in the Federal Reserve's assets as follows: "...from less than $900 billion before the crisis began to about $2.2 trillion today." Use the back of the sheet, if necessary.

EXTENSION VISUAL 6
IS THE FED A PUBLIC OR PRIVATE INSTITUTION?

Public	Private
Established by Congress with the signing of the Federal Reserve Act by President Woodrow Wilson in 1913.	The Federal Reserve System is privately owned by member banks.
The Board of Governors (Federal Reserve Board) is a federal government agency.	The 12 Reserve Banks are nonprofit.
Any income in excess of expenses and obligations is returned to the taxpayers. In 2008, the Fed returned $34.9 billion of its income to the taxpayers. In 2009, the Fed paid a record $46.1 billion in earnings to the Treasury.	Reserve Banks and the Board of Governors are subject to an audit by the GAO (General Accounting Office) but transactions with foreign central banks and open market operations are excluded from the GAO's audit.
There is a system of checks and balances within the Fed in that the public Board of Governors has oversight of the private Reserve Banks.	The private Reserve Banks are subject to regulation by the public Board of Governors.
The chairman of the Fed and members of the Board of Governors (Federal Reserve Board) are nominated by the President and subject to Senate approval. They receive limited 14-year terms with the Chairman reappointed for four-year terms (subject to Senate approval).	Each Reserve Bank has its own board of directors chosen from outside the bank by law.
Taxpayers pay the salary of the chairman and members of the Board of Governors. The monetary policymaking body of the Fed, the Federal Open Market Committee (FOMC), is composed of 12 members, seven from the public side (the Board of Governors, which includes the chairman of the Fed).	Reserve Banks pay the salary of the bank presidents, subject to approval by the Board of Directors. The monetary policymaking body of the Fed, the FOMC, is composed of 12 members. Five are from the private side: the president of the Federal Reserve Bank of New York and four of the remaining 11 Reserve Bank presidents, who serve one-year terms on a rotating basis.

EXTENSION VISUAL 7
BALANCING THE RESPONSIBILITIES OF THE FED

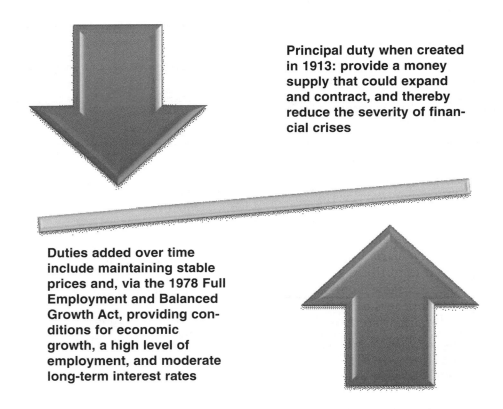

Principal duty when created in 1913: provide a money supply that could expand and contract, and thereby reduce the severity of financial crises

Duties added over time include maintaining stable prices and, via the 1978 Full Employment and Balanced Growth Act, providing conditions for economic growth, a high level of employment, and moderate long-term interest rates

"Our objective has not been to support specific financial institutions or markets for their own sake. Rather, recognizing that a healthy economy requires well-functioning financial markets, we have moved always with the single aim of promoting economic recovery and economic opportunity. In that respect, our means and goals have been fully consistent with the traditional functions of a central bank and with the mandate given to the Federal Reserve by the Congress to promote price stability and maximum employment." Fed Chairman Ben Bernanke at the Economic Club of Washington D.C., December 7, 2009.

HANDOUT 1
CPI 2007-2010

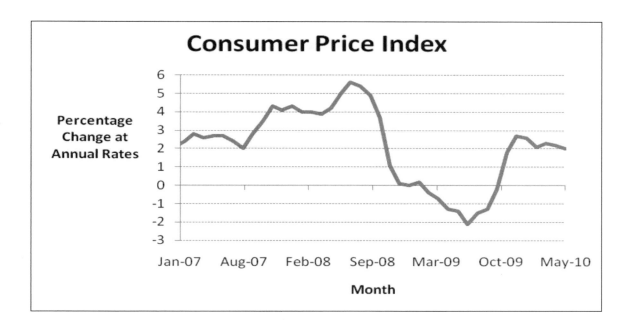

Year	Jan	Feb	Mar	Apr	May	Jun	Jul	Aug	Sep	Oct	Nov	Dec	Annual
2007	2.1	2.4	2.8	2.6	2.7	2.7	2.4	2.0	2.8	3.5	4.3	4.1	2.8
2008	4.3	4.0	4.0	3.9	4.2	5.0	5.6	5.4	4.9	3.7	1.1	0.1	3.8
2009	0.0	0.2	-0.4	-0.7	-1.3	-1.4	-2.1	-1.5	-1.3	-0.2	1.8	2.7	-0.4
2010	2.6	2.1	2.3	2.2	2.0								

Source: U.S. Bureau of Labor Statistics, June 2010

HANDOUT 2
UNEMPLOYMENT RATES MONTHLY AND ANNUALLY 2007-2010

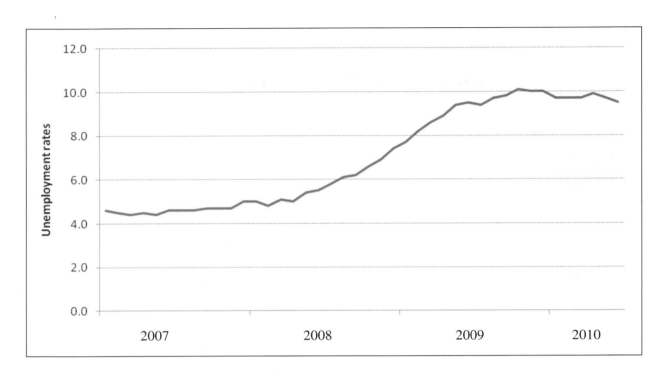

Year	Jan	Feb	Mar	Apr	May	Jun	Jul	Aug	Sep	Oct	Nov	Dec	Annual
2007	4.6	4.5	4.4	4.5	4.4	4.6	4.6	4.6	4.7	4.7	4.7	5.0	4.6
2008	5.0	4.8	5.1	5.0	5.4	5.5	5.8	6.1	6.2	6.6	6.9	7.4	5.8
2009	7.7	8.2	8.6	8.9	9.4	9.5	9.4	9.7	9.8	10.1	10.0	10.0	9.3
2010	9.7	9.7	9.7	9.9	9.7	9.5							

Source: U.S. Bureau of Labor Statistics, June 2010

HANDOUT 3
STATE UNEMPLOYMENT RATES 2007-2009

State	January 2007	December 2008	December 2009
Alabama	3.4	7.4	10.9
Alaska	6.1	6.9	8.6
Arizona	3.9	7.6	9.2
Arkansas	5.1	6.3	7.6
California	4.9	9.2	12.3
Colorado	3.8	6.2	7.3
Connecticut	4.4	6.7	8.8
Delaware	3.4	6.6	8.8
District of Columbia	5.4	8.1	11.9
Florida	3.5	8.2	11.7
Georgia	4.4	8.0	10.3
Hawaii	2.3	5.6	6.8
Idaho	2.7	6.4	9.1
Illinois	4.5	7.6	11.0
Indiana	4.6	8.1	9.7
Iowa	3.6	5.0	6.5
Kansas	4.1	5.3	6.5
Kentucky	5.7	8.5	10.6
Louisiana	3.9	5.5	7.3
Maine	4.5	6.8	8.1
Maryland	3.6	5.8	7.4
Massachusetts	4.6	6.7	9.3
Michigan	6.8	10.6	14.5
Minnesota	4.5	6.7	7.4
Mississippi	6.5	7.9	10.5
Missouri	4.7	7.6	9.6
Montana	3.2	5.4	6.7

State	January 2007	December 2008	December 2009
Nebraska	2.8	3.9	4.6
Nevada	4.4	9.1	13.0
New Hampshire	3.7	4.8	6.9
New Jersey	4.2	7.0	10.0
New Mexico	3.6	5.7	8.2
New York	4.3	6.7	8.9
North Carolina	4.6	8.5	10.9
North Dakota	3.1	3.8	4.3
Ohio	5.4	8.1	10.8
Oklahoma	4.1	4.6	6.8
Oregon	5.1	9.1	10.6
Pennsylvania	4.2	6.5	8.8
Rhode Island	4.9	9.3	12.7
South Carolina	5.9	9.4	12.4
South Dakota	3.0	3.9	4.7
Tennessee	4.7	8.5	10.7
Texas	4.4	6.1	8.2
Utah	2.5	5.1	6.6
Vermont	3.9	5.7	6.7
Virginia	2.9	5.2	6.8
Washington	4.6	6.9	9.2
West Virginia	4.2	5.3	9.0
Wisconsin	4.8	6.4	8.5
Wyoming	2.9	4.0	7.5

Source: Current Population Survey (CPS), Bureau of Labor Statistics, U.S. Department of Labor.

HANDOUT 4
PERCENTAGE CHANGE IN REAL GDP 2007-2010

	2007 III	2007 IV	2008 I	2008 II	2008 III	2008 IV	2009 I	2009 II	2009 III	2009 IV	2010 I	2010 II
Gross domestic product	2.3	2.9	-0.7	0.6	-4	-6.8	-4.9	-0.7	1.6	5	3.7	1.6
Personal consumption expenditures (c)	1.7	1.4	-0.8	0.1	-3.5	-3.3	-0.5	-1.6	2	0.9	1.9	2
Goods	2.4	1.1	-5.8	0.3	-7.7	-10.8	1.8	-1.5	7.2	1.7	5.7	3.6
Durable goods	3.8	2.4	-10.8	-2.9	-12	-22.3	4.8	-3.1	20.1	-1.1	8.8	6.9
Nondurable goods	1.7	.05	-3	2	-5.5	-4.9	0.4	-0.7	1.7	3.1	4.2	2.1
Services	1.4	1.5	1.9	0	-1.3	0.6	-1.6	-1.7	-0.5	0.5	0.1	1.2
Gross private domestic investment (I)	-2.9	-9.4	-9.4	-7.6	-12.5	-36.8	-42.2	-18.5	11.8	26.7	29.1	25
Fixed investment	-1.2	-4.8	6.2	-4.6	-11.9	-24.9	-35.4	-10.1	0.7	-1.3	3.3	19.5
Nonresidential	9.4	5.7	2	-1.6	-8.6	-22.7	-35.2	-7.5	-1.7	-1.4	7.8	17.6
Structures	24.3	7.4	-0.1	7.5	-3.6	-8.9	-41	-20.2	-12.4	-29.2	-17.8	0.4
Equipment and software	2.9	4.8	3	-6	-11.1	-29.5	-31.6	0.3	4.2	1.6	20.4	24.9
Residential	-24.1	-29.3	-27.9	-14	-22.6	-32.6	-36.2	-19.7	10.6	-0.8	-12.3	27.2
Net exports of goods and services (NX)												
Exports	15.8	11.6	5.7	13.2	-5	-21.9	-27.8	-1	12.2	24.4	11.4	9.1
Goods	12.8	9.9	9.6	14.5	-4.3	-26.6	-34.1	-3.7	18.7	31.7	14	12.2
Services	23	15.7	-2.8	10.2	-6.6	-9.8	-12.3	4.7	0.1	10.2	5.8	2.5
Imports	5	-10.6	-11.4	2.9	-0.1	-22.9	-35.3	-10.6	21.9	4.9	11.2	32.4
Goods	5.1	-11.8	-3.3	4.6	-1	-28.3	-38.9	-10.6	27.4	6.2	12	39.3
Services	4.4	-4	9.4	-6	5	11.7	-16.8	-10.9	1.5	-0.5	7.8	4.2
Government (G)	3.5	1.2	2.3	3.3	5.3	1.5	-3	6.1	1.6	-1.4	-1.6	4.3
Federal	9.6	1.1	6.9	7.8	14.2	8.1	-5	14.9	5.7	0	1.8	9.1
National defense	10.2	0	6.8	6.9	19.7	5.2	-8.4	16.8	9	-2.5	0.4	7.3
Nondefense	8.2	3.4	6.9	9.6	3	14.8	2.6	10.9	-0.9	5.6	5	12.9
State and local	0.2	1.3	-0.3	0.8	0.3	-2.4	-1.7	1	-1	-2.3	-3.8	1.2

Data are annual rates of change.

Source: Bureau of Economic Analysis, U.S. Department of Commerce, www.bea.gov

HANDOUT 5
EXCERPT FROM "BANKS PROMISE LOANS BUT HOARD CASH" BY LIZ MOYER IN *FORBES* (FEBRUARY 2009)

Bankers have done the equivalent of stuffing the mattress in the last few months, despite being prodded by the government to lend the hundreds of billions in cash being pumped into the banking system by the Federal Reserve and other regulators. They've been hoarding cash at the Federal Reserve, some $793 billion of excess reserves as of the end of January [2009], which is more than double the amount of money doled out or pledged to financial companies through the Treasury Department's $700 billion Troubled Asset Relief Program. The data support the anecdotal evidence that lawmakers on Capitol Hill have railed against: Banks are hoarding the bailout money, even as they promise to make more loans.

It highlights one of the biggest problems facing the financial system right now: balancing the [need to increase lending] and ignite the stalled economy with demands to shore up [financial firms'] balance sheets and insure survival during the riskiest lending environment in a generation. "They are nervous," says Mark Zandi of Moody's Economy.com.

Banks have to stash away a minimal level of reserves, but they can keep extra reserves. Last year at this time, excess reserves totaled $1.7 billion, according to Fed data. Back then, excess reserves were considered uneconomical, since banks could make more profits off lending the money to fellow banks overnight or to clients. But that all changed in October [2008], when the Fed started paying interest. Excess reserves went from $2 billion in August to $267 billion in October. As of the middle of January, they had mushroomed to $843 billion. Preliminary numbers for the end of January [2009] have them at $793 billion, currently accruing interest at 0.25%, the Fed's benchmark short-term rate.

Fed Chairman Ben Bernanke acknowledged the challenges with mounting excess reserves during a recent speech in London. "In practice, the federal funds rate has fallen somewhat below the interest rate on reserves in recent months, reflecting the very high volume of excess reserves, the inexperience of banks with the new regime and other factors," he said. Other Fed data show that while the amounts of loans and leases by commercial banks are up from December 2007, they have basically flat-lined in the last few months. In September [2008], loans and leases totaled $7 trillion, and in January [2009], they totaled $7 trillion. According to the latest Fed loan officer survey, demand for commercial and industrial loans dropped 60%, and banks reduced lines of credit available.

But citing a Fed statistic that consumer borrowing dropped $7.9 billion in November [2008], the biggest drop in 65 years, Citi [a financial firm] cautioned against big expectations for a lending glut. "Banks and other lenders have tightened access to credit and are conserving capital in order to absorb the losses that occur when borrowers default," the company said in its TARP update. "Citi will not and cannot take excessive risk with the capital the American public and other investors have entrusted to the company."

Source: http://www.forbes.com/2009/02/03/banking-federal-reserve-business-wall-street-0203_loans.html

EXTENSION HANDOUT 6
NEW TOOLS DEFINED BY THE FED

Liquidity Directly to Borrowers and Investors in Key Credit Markets 	**AMLF (Asset-Backed Commercial Paper Money Market Mutual Fund Liquidity Facility)** The Asset-Backed Commercial Paper Money Market Mutual Fund Liquidity Facility was a lending facility that provided funding to U.S. depository institutions and bank holding companies to finance their purchases of high-quality asset-backed commercial paper (ABCP) from money market mutual funds under certain conditions. The program was intended to assist money funds that hold such paper in meeting demands for redemptions by investors and to foster liquidity in the ABCP market and money markets more generally. **CPFF (Commercial Paper Funding Facility)** The Federal Reserve created the Commercial Paper Funding Facility (CPFF) to provide a liquidity backstop to U.S. issuers of commercial paper. The CPFF was intended to improve liquidity in short-term funding markets and thereby contribute to greater availability of credit for businesses and households. Under the CPFF, the Federal Reserve Bank of New York financed the purchase of highly rated unsecured and asset-backed commercial paper from eligible issuers via eligible primary dealers. **MMIFF (Money Market Investor Funding Facility)** expired on October 30, 2009. MMIFF was designed to provide liquidity to U.S. money market investors. Under the MMIFF, the Federal Reserve Bank of New York could provide senior secured funding to a series of special purpose vehicles to facilitate an industry-supported private-sector initiative to finance the purchase of eligible assets from eligible investors. **TALF (Term Asset-Backed Securities Loan Facility)** The Term Asset-Backed Securities Loan Facility (TALF) was a funding facility that was designed to help market participants meet the credit needs of households and small businesses by supporting the issuance of asset-backed securities (ABS) collateralized by loans of various types to consumers and businesses of all sizes. Under the TALF, the Federal Reserve Bank of New York (FRBNY) could lend up to $200 billion to holders of certain AAA-rated ABS backed by newly and recently originated consumer and small business loans. The FRBNY could have lent an amount equal to the market value of the ABS less a haircut and to be secured at all times by the ABS. The U.S. Treasury Department—under the Troubled Assets Relief Program (TARP) of the Emergency Economic Stabilization Act of 2008—provided $20 billion of credit protection to the FRBNY in connection with the TALF.
Lending to Financial Institutions by Providing Short-term Liquidity 	**TAF:** The Fed extended the maturity of loans made to depository institutions using the new Term Auction Facility. Under the Term Auction Facility (TAF), the Federal Reserve auctioned term funds to depository institutions. All depository institutions that were eligible to borrow under the primary credit program were eligible to participate in TAF auctions. All advances had to be fully collateralized. Each TAF auction was for a fixed amount, with the rate determined by the auction process (subject to a minimum bid rate). **TSLF (Term Securities Lending Facility)** The Term Securities Lending Facility (TSLF) was a weekly loan facility that promoted liquidity in Treasury and other collateral markets and thus fostered the functioning of financial markets more generally. The program offered Treasury securities held by the System Open Market Account for loan over a one-month term against other program-eligible general collateral. Securities loans were awarded to primary dealers based on a competitive single-price auction. **PDCF (Primary Dealer Credit Facility)** The Primary Dealer Credit Facility (PDCF) was an overnight loan facility that provided funding to primary dealers in exchange for a specified range of eligible collateral and was intended to foster the functioning of financial markets more generally.
Long-term Securities Purchased Through the Open Market 	"As a third set of instruments, the Federal Reserve has expanded its traditional tool of open market operations to support the functioning of credit markets through the purchase of longer-term securities for the Federal Reserve's portfolio. For example, on November 25, 2008, the Federal Reserve announced plans to purchase up to $100 billion in government-sponsored enterprise (GSE) debt and up to $500 billion in mortgage-backed securities. The Federal Reserve announced plans to purchase up to $300 billion of longer-term Treasury securities in addition to increasing its total purchases of GSE debt and mortgage-backed securities to up to $200 billion and $1.25 trillion, respectively." Ben Bernanke speech, January 13, 2009.

Defined by the Fed at: http://www.federalreserve.gov/monetarypolicy/default.ht

Defined by the Fed at: http://www.federalreserve.gov/monetarypolicy/default.htm

EXTENSION HANDOUT 7
BERNANKE'S VIEWS ON THE **2007-2009** CRISIS

Query	Views
How bad was it?	"…in the fall of [2008], the United States, indeed the world, confronted a financial crisis of a magnitude unseen for generations. Concerted actions by the Federal Reserve and other policymakers here and abroad helped avoid the worst outcomes. Nevertheless, the turmoil dealt a severe blow to our economy from which we have only recently begun to recover." *At the Economic Club of Washington, D.C., December 7, 2009*
Is inflation on the horizon?	"The Committee's aggressive monetary easing was not without risks. During the early phase of rate reductions, some observers expressed concern that these policy actions would stoke inflation. These concerns intensified as inflation reached high levels in mid-2008, mostly reflecting a surge in the prices of oil and other commodities. The Committee takes its responsibility to ensure price stability extremely seriously, and throughout this period it remained closely attuned to developments in inflation and inflation expectations." *At the Stamp Lecture, London School of Economics, London, England, January 13, 2009*
Should the Fed's balance sheet cause concern?	"Indeed, our balance sheet is already beginning to adjust, because improving financial conditions are leading to substantially reduced use of our lending facilities. The balance sheet will also shrink over time as the mortgage-backed securities and other assets we hold mature or are prepaid. However, even if our balance sheet stays large for a while, we will be able to raise our target short-term interest rate—which is the rate at which banks lend to each other overnight—and thus tighten financial conditions appropriately."*At the Economic Club of Washington, D.C., December 7, 2009*
What does the future hold?	"…the economy confronts some formidable headwinds that seem likely to keep the pace of expansion moderate. Despite the general improvement in financial conditions, credit remains tight for many borrowers, particularly bank-dependent borrowers such as households and small businesses. And the job market, though no longer contracting at the pace we saw in 2008 and earlier this year, remains weak. Household spending is unlikely to grow rapidly when people remain worried about job security and have limited access to credit."*At the Economic Club of Washington, D.C., December 7, 2009*
What is the role of the Fed?	"Monetary policy makers are public servants and have a responsibility to give a rationale for decisions." *At the Cato Institute 25th Annual Monetary Conference, Washington, D.C., November 14, 2007* "We have come a long way in our battle against the financial and economic crisis, but there is a long way to go. Now more than ever, America needs a strong, nonpolitical and independent central bank with the tools to promote financial stability and to help steer our economy to recovery without inflation." *November 29, 2009, The Washington Post*

THE ROLE OF HOUSING IN THE FINANCIAL CRISIS OF 2007-2009

LESSON 6
THE ROLE OF HOUSING IN THE FINANCIAL CRISIS OF 2007-2009

LESSON DESCRIPTION

Students begin by examining data on the rise and fall of home prices and use **supply and demand** to analyze potential causes of the price changes. Then students learn about changes in the mortgage industry and identify the incentive effects of these changes. Students take part in a demonstration of the effects of **securitization** on investing in the housing market. Finally students calculate the costs and benefits of engaging in leveraging.

INTRODUCTION

The financial crisis of 2007-2009 has its origins in the housing market. Beginning in the late-1990s, housing prices started increasing at rates significantly higher than the historical average. The housing market continued at a torrid pace until 2006 when rising mortgage rates, increasing numbers of foreclosures, a glut of new houses, and changing expectations helped pop the housing bubble. Prices started to fall rapidly in 2007. Changes in the mortgage industry, most prominently the securitization of mortgage loans and the advent of **subprime mortgages** caused the housing crisis to intensify and eventually led to the financial crisis. Credit markets froze and well-known financial institutions collapsed as investors in mortgage-backed and related securities suffered massive losses.

CONCEPTS

- Supply and demand
- Subprime mortgages
- Securitization
- Mortgage-backed securities
- Leverage

OBJECTIVES

Students will:

1. Use supply and demand curves to explain trends in housing prices.

2. Identify the incentive effects in changes in mortgages.

3. Explain how securitization can both spread individual risk and increase the level of systemic risk.

4. Understand how leveraging magnifies both potential profits and potential losses.

CONTENT STANDARDS

- People usually respond predictably to positive and negative incentives.

- A market exists when buyers and sellers interact. This interaction determines market prices and thereby allocates scarce goods and services.

- Prices send signals and provide incentives to buyers and sellers. When supply or demand changes, market prices adjust, affecting incentives.

- Fluctuations in a nation's overall levels of income, employment, and prices are determined by the interaction of spending and production decisions made by all households, firms government agencies, and others in the economy. Recessions occur when overall levels of income and employment decline.

- Federal government budgetary policy and the Federal Reserve System's monetary policy influence the overall levels of employment, output, and prices.

TIME REQUIRED

Two class periods

MATERIALS

- Activity 1: Housing Prices (one copy per student)

- Activity 2: Taking Out a Mortgage (one copy per student)

- Activity 3: The Rise in Housing Prices (one copy per student)

- Activity 4: The Fall in Housing Prices (one copy per student)

- Activity 5: Leveraging (one copy per student)

- Activity 6: Events Linking Housing Prices to the Financial Crisis (one copy per student or transparency)

- Visual 1: Housing Prices (transparency)

- Visual 2: Taking Out a Mortgage (transparency)

- Visual 3a: The Rise in Housing Prices (transparency)

- Visual 3b: Potential Causes of Rising Housing Prices (transparency)

- Visual 4: Changes in Ownership of Mortgages (transparency)

- Visual 5a: Mortgage Investments (transparency)

- Visual 5b: Mortgage-backed Security (transparency)

- Five pieces of different colored 8½" x 11" paper

- Pair of scissors

- One die

PROCEDURE

1. Tell students that the financial crisis of 2007-2009 had its beginnings in the housing market. You may first want to explain to students that the housing price index reflects the real price of housing, which means that housing prices have been adjusted for inflation. The Case-Shiller Price Index represents an average of housing prices throughout the country. The index equals 100 for the price of housing in 1890, over 120 years ago. The price index for 2007 is approximately 174. Therefore, housing prices, adjusted for inflation, rose 74 percent between 1890 and 2007.

   Hand out copies of Activity 1: Housing Prices, and ask students to answer the questions. Show Visual 1: Housing Prices and briefly discuss the answers.

a. Describe the general trend in real home prices from 1950 through 1997.

The index of home prices increased slightly over the 47-year period. There were two periods of sizeable increases in home prices, one from 1978 to 1980, and another around 1990. But prices eventually returned to their original level. The Case-Shiller index equaled 106 in 1950 and an almost identical 110 in 1997. (Exact numbers are available at www.irrationalexuberance.com.)

b. Describe the general trend in real home prices from 1997 through 2006.

Home prices rose significantly between 1997 and 2006. The Case-Shiller index was 110 in 1997 and 206 in 2006. Therefore, real home prices nearly doubled during this time.

c. Describe the general trend in real home prices from 2006 through 2009.

The index of home prices fell dramatically, from a high of 206 in 2006 to 141 during 2009. This represents a 33 percent decline.

d. Predict what the value of the real home price index would have been in 2009 if the general trend in prices had continued at the 1950 to 1997 pace.

Answers should vary between 105 and 120. As noted above, the index increased only slightly between 1950 and 1997, from 106 to 110. Therefore, assuming the index increased at the same slow rate, real home prices would have gone up only a couple of percentage points during the following 10 years. This can be estimated using a ruler to draw a straight line through the price index at 1950 and 1997. Alternatively, students could estimate using their eyes and the knowledge that housing prices remained fairly unchanged from 1950 to 1997.

Use this opportunity to make sure students see how extraordinary the time period from 1997 through 2006 was in the housing market. From 1950 to

1997 housing prices adjusted for inflation did not change significantly. According to www.irrationalexuberance.com, real housing prices remained relatively constant over most of the last hundred years.

Note that the index is adjusted for overall inflation and for changes in sizes and quality of housing. In other words, it tells us what is happening to the prices of identical houses over time after the effects of inflation.

e. What might be some reasons for the observed trend in real home prices from 1997 through 2006?

Depending upon how much knowledge students have about economics or have read or heard about the housing crisis, the following answers concerning the rapid increase in housing prices may be forthcoming:

Increases in population, increases in income, easy credit, rise in building costs, social contagion (the expectation that housing prices will continue going up), changed and perhaps unethical behavior by banks and mortgage brokers, and poor decisions by buyers.

f. What might be some reasons for the observed trend in real home prices from 2006 through 2009?

Again, depending upon the level of interest in current events, students may answer the following with respect to the fall in housing prices: people unable to pay mortgages, increase in foreclosures, increases in homes built by developers, changes in expectations, more scrutiny of potential borrowers by mortgage lenders, and fallout from the recession.

2. Hand out Activity 2: Taking Out a Mortgage, and have students read the characteristics of prime and subprime mortgages. Explain to students that these are generalizations, but are indicative of changes that took place in the mortgage industry during the 1990s and 2000s. Also

tell students some loans are often called subprime mortgages because the borrower does not meet the same standards (credit, down payment, income) that someone taking out a prime mortgage does. Show Visual 2: Taking Out a Mortgage and discuss the answers.

a. The U.S. government made increased home ownership by lower income groups a public policy goal. Which type of mortgage, prime or subprime, would be more likely to result in the government's goal? Why?

Subprime mortgages would be more likely to increase home ownership among individuals with lower incomes. Oftentimes these households do not have sufficient income to save for a down payment. They are also more likely to have credit problems that would disqualify them for a prime mortgage.

b. If someone defaults on a mortgage, why is it better for the bank if the borrower had put down a 20 percent down payment as opposed to no down payment?

If someone defaults and they have put a down payment of 20 percent, it is more likely that the bank will get all of its money back, even if it has to sell the house for less than the original price. Assume someone pays $100,000 for a house and they put $20,000 as a down payment. This requires them to borrow $80,000 from the bank.

Now assume the person loses their job and they are no longer able to make their mortgage payment. If the bank ends up foreclosing on the house, it only needs to sell the house for $80,000 in order to get its original investment back. If the person had put no money down and taken out a $100,000 loan, the bank would have to sell the house for at least that much in order to break even. Therefore, a larger down payment increases the likelihood that the bank will get its money back if the house goes into foreclosure.

c. Compare the level of risk to banks and financial institutions between prime and subprime mortgages. Who do you think is more likely to become delinquent on their mortgage payment and face foreclosure? Someone with a prime mortgage or a subprime mortgage? Why?

Subprime mortgages pose a greater risk to banks and financial institutions than prime mortgages. Subprime mortgages are more likely to be late or to default. This is because 1) the lack of documentation means that some people that do not have the resources to consistently repay their loans nonetheless receive mortgages, 2) some people may initially be able to afford the mortgage payments but after the teaser rates end and the lenders reset the interest rate, the increase in monthly payments may be more than the borrower can handle, and 3) with little or no down payment, the borrower has less incentive to keep up with payments once things get difficult.

In addition, if the bank does take ownership of the house, it must resell it for the full amount of the mortgage in order to avoid a loss.

[Note: Adjustable rate mortgages reset interest rates for two reasons. One, there will normally be a reset at the end of the teaser rate period. Two, rates reset if the benchmark interest rate changes. An example: Assume that a mortgage has an adjustable interest rate that is equal to the interest rate on one-year Treasury bill plus 3 percent. If the current T-bill rate is 1.5 percent, then the adjustable rate mortgage would have an interest rate of 4.5 percent. But the mortgage may have a "teaser rate" of 1 percent for the first two years. This means that at the end of the second year, the interest rate on the mortgage would increase from 1 percent to 4.5 percent assuming nothing else changed. But if the bench-

mark (in this case, the interest rate on the one-year Treasury bill) changed, it would also cause the interest rate on the mortgage to reset. Therefore if the T-bill rate rises from 1.5 percent to 2.5 percent during the third year of the mortgage, the adjustable rate mortgage would reset from 4.5 percent to 5.5 percent.]

d. During the run-up in housing prices, banks and mortgage brokers significantly increased the number of subprime mortgages. Why might banks be willing to take on more risky loans during times of increasing prices?

When housing prices are continually going up, the risk to banks and other investors in residential housing is minimal. Even if a homeowner defaults on the loan, the bank could easily resell the property for a higher price than the amount of the mortgage. So even if no down payment was made, the bank can end up ahead. Therefore, as long as it appears that housing prices will continue to rise, there is little risk associated with subprime mortgages.

Assume a bank has issued a subprime mortgage for a house worth $100,000. With no down payment, the loan amount is the full value of the house, or $100,000. If the homeowner defaults on the mortgage, the bank must sell it. If housing prices are rising at a rate of 10 percent per year, the bank does not have to worry too much about selling the house at a loss and not getting all of its funds back. In this case, it would be able to sell the house for $110,000, $10,000 more than the value of the mortgage.

In addition, it is less likely that as many borrowers will default when the interest rate adjusts. A new loan based on the new value will likely permit borrowers to qualify for a lower interest rate.

[Note: Some individuals who had good credit records and healthy, steady incomes took subprime loans in order to purchase a house that was somewhat more expensive than they could afford. They may have done so under the assumption that the house price would increase quickly and allow them to refinance when the adjustable rates changed.]

3. Now tell students that they are going to analyze possible reasons for the increase in housing prices between 1997 and 2006. Hand out copies of Activity 3: The Rise in Housing Prices. Remind students that prices are determined in markets and that housing prices are the result of the forces of **supply and demand**. Tell them to use the graph in helping answer the questions. Display Visual 3a: The Rise in Housing Prices, and discuss the answers to questions A through F in Activity 3. You may want to emphasize the correct answer for each by drawing the correct new curve for each part.

a. Between 1997 and 2006, housing prices increased dramatically. Would an increase or decrease in demand cause this? Is this illustrated by a rightward or leftward shift of the curve?

An increase, or rightward shift, in the demand curve would cause prices to increase.

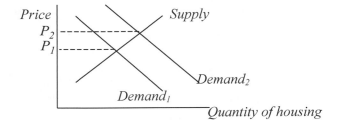

b. Between 1997 and 2006 housing prices increased dramatically. Would an increase or decrease in supply cause this? Is this illustrated by a rightward or leftward shift of the curve?

A decrease or leftward shift in the supply curve would cause prices to increase.

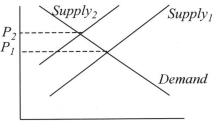

c. Between 2007 and 2009 housing prices fell dramatically. Would an increase or decrease in demand cause this? Is this illustrated by a rightward or leftward shift of the curve?

A decrease or leftward shift in the demand curve would cause the price of housing to fall.

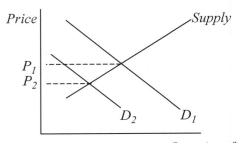

d. Between 2007 and 2009 housing prices fell dramatically. Would an increase or decrease in supply cause this? Is this illustrated by a rightward or leftward shift of the curve?

An increase or rightward shift of the supply curve would cause the price of housing to fall.

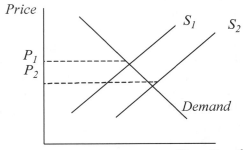

e. Housing prices increased between 1997 and 2006, and then decreased between 2007 and 2009. How might changes in expectations of future price changes affect demand for housing?

Expectations of future increases in prices would cause current demand to increase (from D1 to D2). Expectations of future decreases in prices would cause current demand to decrease (from D2 to D1).

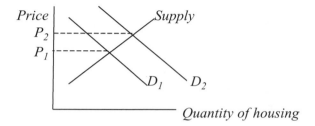

f. Each of the following has been suggested as a potential cause of the increase in housing prices from 1997 to 2006. For each, determine whether this would affect the supply curve or the demand curve for housing, then decide whether it would increase or decrease the appropriate curve.

1) An increase in population.

An increase in population would increase the demand for housing. More people means that more houses will be demanded at any given price. This shifts the demand curve to the right.

2) An increase in building costs.

An increase in building costs would decrease the supply of housing. At any given price of housing, developers would be willing and able to construct fewer houses. This would shift the supply curve for housing to the left.

3) A decrease in interest rates.

A decrease in interest rates would increase the demand for housing. Lower interest rates make having a mortgage more affordable. This would shift the demand for housing to the right.

4) Changes in expectations of prices of housing.

If potential buyers expect prices of housing to increase, demand for houses may increase. This would cause demand to shift to the right. There may by a reduction in supply as some individuals wait to place their houses on the market. Both changes would contribute to rising prices.

The next part of Activity 3 asks students to determine whether the data supports the view that changes in fundamentals such as population or building costs could have been responsible for the rapid increase in housing prices. Display Visual 3b: Potential Causes of Rising Housing Prices and discuss the answers.

g. The graphs in Visual 3b show the relationship between real home prices and other relevant variables from 1950 through 2009.

1) Does the first graph support the view that increases in real home prices from 1997 to 2006 were justified by increases in building costs?

No, the data show that the real cost of building a home doubled between 1950 and the mid-1970s as the building cost index rose from about 50 to 100. Prices then fell slightly until 1990. They have been relatively constant since then. There is no evidence that rising building costs could be responsible for the rapid increase in housing prices.

2) Does the second graph support the view that increases in real home prices were justified by increases in population?

No, population appears to have steadily increased since 1950. There has been no significant change in population trend that could explain the increase in housing prices.

3) Does the third graph support the view that increases in real home prices were justified by changes in long-term interest rates?

This is a little more complicated than the other two cases, but it doesn't appear that changes in long-term interest rates explain the dramatic increase in housing prices. Long-term interest rates peaked in the early 1980s and have trended downward since, although with some volatility. But interest rates fell during a time of constant home prices (1980-1997), rising home prices (1997-2006) and falling home prices (after 2006).

Another complication is that adjustable rate mortgages are more affected by changes in short-run interest rates, and this graph only shows long-run interest rates.

4) Does the fourth graph support the view that increases in real home prices were justified by changes in short-term interest rates?

This is an excellent opportunity for students to integrate specific content knowledge, quantitative skills, and critical thinking skills.

Some people blame the Federal Reserve for the rapid increase in housing prices because of its decision to keep short-term interest rates low. What does this graph tell us? Critics of the Federal Reserve point to the period from 2000 to 2003, when the federal funds rate fell from 6.5 percent to only 1 percent. During this time, housing prices rose significantly. But housing prices actually began their historic rise around 1997. The graph shows that the federal funds rate increased from below 5 percent in 1998 to over 6 percent in 2000.

In addition, the Federal Reserve began increasing rates after 2003. The federal funds rate rose from 1 percent in 2003 to 5.25 percent in 2006, even as housing prices hit their peak. But students should be careful how they interpret this information. While it appears that housing prices increased despite higher short-term interest rates, it is important

to remember that adjustable rate mortgages often had teaser rates that lasted two to five years. This means that it would take some time before existing mortgages would reset and be affected by the higher interest rates.

[It could be that the rise in short-term interest rates contributed to the beginning of the decrease in housing prices. See the discussion in Activity 4 below.]

4. Tell students that the previous activity supports the view that the rise in housing prices represented a bubble. Define a price bubble as a situation in which the increase in price is not justified by any fundamental factor affecting supply or demand and therefore is not sustainable. A price bubble is often caused by contagion, that is, prices increase because people observe them going up and therefore think they will continue to go up. This causes people to purchase houses with the expectation that they will be able to sell them for a higher price in a relatively short time. A bubble is therefore often referred to as a speculative bubble.

5. Hand out Activity 4: The Fall in Housing Prices. Briefly go over the answers.

   a. The run-up in prices led many developers to build houses without specific buyers on the expectation that the housing boom would continue.

   This would increase the supply of housing, which is represented by a rightward shift in the curve. This would lower the equilibrium price of housing or lead to a slowing of the rise in prices.

   b. The Federal Reserve began increasing interest rates in order to stave off inflation. This caused the interest rate charged on many adjustable mortgages to increase, leading to an increase in mortgage defaults and foreclosures.

   This could affect both the demand and supply of housing. Increased interest rates would reduce the demand for housing. This shifts the curve to the left and lowers the price of housing for sale. The increased rates would also increase the supply of housing. As adjustable rates went up, many families found themselves unable to make their monthly mortgage payments. This caused an increase in foreclosures. Banks, attempting to recoup their investment, put more foreclosed houses on the market, thereby increasing the supply of housing. This put additional downward pressure on the price of housing.

In the third quarter of 2009, the Mortgage Bankers Association reported that nearly 5,000,000 homeowners were at least one payment behind on their mortgage. This accounts for almost 10 percent of all mortgages. An additional 4.5 percent of mortgages were in foreclosure.

   c. Expectations of future housing prices change as current prices begin to decrease.

Buyers may consider waiting to buy if they expect lower house prices in the future. Sellers might sell now because they expect prices to fall in the future. Both have the effect of lowering housing prices.

6. Tell students that they are now beginning to understand what lies behind the run-up and subsequent collapse of housing prices. Tell students that there were changes in the mortgage industry, other than those discussed to this point, that are related to what banks do with loans after they made them. Show Visual 4: Changes in Ownership of Mortgages. Tell students that they are going to learn how two additional aspects of mortgages helped spread the housing crisis to financial markets. These two factors are securitization and **leverage**.

7. Securitization. Tell students you are a banker with five home mortgages. You would like to sell those loans to an investor in order to be able to make additional loans. Show students five pieces of

different colored paper. Tell them each piece of paper represents a mortgage. Each student is an investor looking to invest in the home-mortgage market. Each student will be given an amount to invest. Assign five students $100,000 and each of your remaining students $50,000. (You may choose to hand out play money in the above amounts or simply designate the five students that have $100,000 to invest. You should tell the students with $50,000 that they will have to sit on the sidelines for the moment.)

Part I

   a. Tell students you are willing to sell each of the mortgages for $100,000. Ask who is able to purchase a mortgage. Only the five investors with $100,000 have enough money. Everyone else is unable to take part in the investment.

   b. Now tell them that in return for the investment, the investor will receive the mortgage payments from the homeowner. This will include money to pay back the principal ($100,000) and to pay interest on the loan. The investor can expect to receive a total of $120,000 if the homeowner makes all of the mortgage payments, resulting in a $20,000 profit.

There is a possibility that the borrower will be unable to pay the mortgage. Perhaps the owner becomes sick or hurt or loses employment. In the event the homeowner is unable to pay, the investor will have to sell the house. After paying for legal and real estate expenses, in addition to all other costs, the investor will only receive $40,000. In other words, the investor will lose $60,000 on the original investment.

   c. Tell students that there is a 1 out of 6 chance that the owner will default. If they decide to purchase the mortgage, you will roll a die for each mortgage, and, if a 1 comes up, the owner defaults and the investor only receives $40,000. If a 2 through 6 comes up, the owner makes all payments and the investor receives $120,000.

Ask students if they understand how the process will work.

d. Before rolling the die, tell students that you will give each of the potential investors the opportunity to pay $5,000 to know ahead of time whether or not the homeowner is going to default. This means that for $5,000 you will roll the die and see what number turns up. (Tell students this is the equivalent of checking a homeowner's credit, income and employment history. In the real world, it won't eliminate the possibility of a default, but it can significantly lower it.) If the die turns up a 1, the student won't have to purchase the mortgage (and therefore will lose $5,000 rather than $60,000). If a 2 through 6 comes up, the student will earn a profit of $15,000 ($20,000 minus the $5,000 fee).

e. Now go to the students with $100,000 and ask each of them if they would like to pay $5,000 to receive information on whether the borrower will default. If the first student says yes, write $5,000 in the third row for "Cost of checking income and employment" for Investor 1 on Visual 5a: Mortgage Investments. Then roll the die. If a 1 comes up, the homeowner will default. Enter $0 for both the Revenue received and Cost of mortgage for Investor 1, because investors obviously will choose not to purchase a mortgage if they know the borrower will default. This results in a loss of $5,000. If a number other than 1 comes up, put $120,000 in the Revenue received box and $100,000 in the Cost of mortgage box. This results in a profit of $15,000.

If the student decides not to pay the $5,000 for the default information, write $100,000 in the Cost of mortgage box for Investor 1. Next, roll the die. If it is a 1, put $40,000 in Revenue received. If it is a 2 through 6, put $120,000 in that box.

Then calculate the profit or loss for the investor.

Do this for all five investors. Briefly discuss the process with the class. Ask the five investors if they thought they were taking a lot of risk. Were they nervous before the roll of the die? Which method would they prefer? Why?

Part II

Ask students with $50,000 if they would like an opportunity to invest in the housing market. Tell them their only alternative is to earn 2 percent in a bank account.

f. Now tell students that there is a change in the mortgage industry. The previous method of selling mortgages placed a very big risk on investors. In addition, smaller investors were not able to participate. Therefore, the bank has developed an investment vehicle called a **mortgage-backed security**.

g. Take the five colored pieces of paper and put the papers into a pile and tell students that you have "pooled" the five mortgages into one mortgage-backed security.

h. Now take scissors and cut each of the mortgages into 10 pieces and divide them into 10 piles. Each of the piles will have one small square of each of the five different colors. The mortgage-backed security is backed by the five mortgages. (Tell students that in the real world, mortgage-backed securities may include hundreds of houses.) The security was then divided into 10 "shares." Instead of cutting 10 pieces, you might cut one piece out of each one and tell students that it is a sample.

i. Tell students that each share will sell for $50,000. This will result in the same revenue to the bank as before ($50,000 x 10) = ($100,000 x 5) = $500,000. As before, homeowners will pay their monthly mortgages or default. The money collected from the homeowners will be divided into 10 equal amounts, and investors will receive one-tenth of the entire amount for each share they own.

Therefore, if all five homeowners make all of their payments, investors will receive $60,000 per share. ($120,000 x 5 = $600,000, then $600,000 ÷ 10 = $60,000). This would result in a profit of $10,000 per share. ($60,000 revenue minus $50,000 initial investment.)

On the other hand, if one of the homeowners defaults, the total amount collected for the mortgage-backed security equals $520,000 = ($120,000 x 4) + $40,000. Dividing by the 10 shares results in a payment of $52,000 for a profit of $2,000 per share. The process is similar if two or more mortgages default.

j. Now ask one of the investors with $50,000 if he/she would be willing to pay $5,000 in order to know if mortgage 1 (say, blue) will default. The student should say no because it is no longer worth the cost. If one house defaults, the individual will still earn $2,000. Thus the incentive to spend the $5,000 is less (although some may decide it is still worth it). Therefore, there is no longer as strong a financial incentive for an individual investor to worry about whether the homeowner will be able to pay or will default.

k. Now roll the die once for each mortgage. Fill in the appropriate box on Visual 5b: Mortgage-backed Security with either $40,000 or $120,000 depending upon whether the borrower defaulted or not. Sum the revenue received from all five mortgages, enter the total, and divide by 10 to determine how much holders of each share will receive. Next fill out the bottom part of Visual 5b to determine the profit or loss for each share.

l. After completing this exercise, you will want to do two things. First, explain to students that this is an illustration of the securitization of mortgages in which many investors and financial firms were involved. Second, summarize the positives and negatives of securitizing mortgages.

Positives

- Spread risk. Investors didn't have "all their eggs in one basket." A default by a single homeowner would not be as devastating. Many mortgage-backed securities held hundreds of mortgages.

- Took an illiquid asset (mortgage) and converted it into a liquid investment (shares in the mortgage-backed security). Investors could buy and sell the shares just like stocks.

- Allowed smaller investors to take part in investing in the mortgage industry.

- All of these may mean that more money flows into the mortgage market which should lower the cost of mortgages.

Negatives

- Reduced the incentive for investors to be concerned about the creditworthiness of the borrowers.

- Reduced the incentive for banks and mortgage brokers to be concerned with the creditworthiness of the borrowers. The effect of default or foreclosure is borne by someone else.

- Exported the investments and therefore, the risk, around the world. The mortgage-backed securities were purchased by institutional and individual investors around the world. Therefore when home owners began to default on their loans, it wasn't felt only locally, like with most previous real estate busts, but now it had a financial effect around the world.

8. Leverage. A second feature of the mortgage industry that contributed to the financial crisis was the extreme leveraging by banks and investors. Investors leverage an investment by borrowing or using other

investors' money in addition to their own. This activity illustrates the potential increase in profits and the increase in risk.

Hand out Activity 5: Leveraging. Have students read it and fill in the charts. Briefly discuss the answers.

Total money available	Cost per bottle at store	# of bottles bought	Total cost (cost per bottle x # bottles)	Selling price per bottle at game	Total revenue (# bottles x price)	Profit
$10.00	$1.00	10	$10.00	$1.10	$11.00	$1

Total money available	Cost per bottle at store	# of bottles bought	Total cost (cost per bottle x # bottles) + interest of $1	Selling price per bottle at game	Total revenue (# bottles x price)	Profit
$100.00	$1.00	100	$101.00	$1.10	$110.00	$9

Total money available	Cost per bottle at store	# of bottles bought	Total cost (cost per bottle x # bottles) + interest of $1	Selling price per bottle at game	Total revenue (# bottles x price)	Profit
$100.00	$1.00	100	$101.00	$0.80	$80	-$21

Ask students to compare the outcome with and without "leveraging."

In the second scenario above, leveraging allowed the student to make nine times as much profit as when she was only able to use her own funds.

While leveraging magnified the potential profits in the second scenario, it magnified losses in the third scenario. In this case, not only did the student have her entire capital of $10 wiped out, she was no longer able to pay back all of the borrowed funds. Therefore some of the impact of the fall in water prices was exported to the lender of funds. In fact in this case, the lender lost more money ($11) than the student ($10). (If the student had not leveraged, the most the loss would have been is $8 minus $10 or a total of $2.)

Tell students that banks and financial institutions were leveraged up to 30 times their own capital in the mortgage-backed securities market (this would be the equivalent of the student borrowing $300 to buy water). Therefore, when homeowners started to default and the price of housing fell significantly, these firms faced huge losses. In addition, other investors and institutions not directly involved in owning mortgage-backed securities were affected.

CLOSURE

Activity 6: Events Linking Housing Prices to the Financial Crisis includes the five main events linking the housing crisis to the financial crisis (these statements are in bold, capital letters). For each main event there are two contributing factors (in lowercase letters). Either provide each student with a copy of this activity or use one copy in front of the entire class, and discuss the relationships.

An alternative is to cut out each of the boxes before presenting this to the class. Tell students that they are to put the five main pieces in the order in which they occurred and then choose which two contributing factors belong with each main piece.

ASSESSMENT

Multiple-choice questions

1. Which of the following statements concerning home prices, adjusted for inflation, is false?

   a. Housing prices increased every year from 1997 to 2006.

   b. The index of home prices surpassed 200 in 2006.

   *c. In 2008, home prices fell to their lowest level in 30 years.

   d. Home prices remained relatively unchanged between 1960 and 1975.

2. Which of the following is a characteristic of many subprime mortgages?

   a. Borrower has good credit.

   b. Require a 20 percent down payment.

   *c. Borrower more likely to default than on a prime mortgage.

   d. Borrower supplies documentation on income and employment.

3. Mortgage-backed securities

   a. can lower individual investor risk through diversification.

   b. exported the U.S. housing crisis throughout the world.

   c. consist of a large number of individual mortgages.

   *d. all of the above.

   e. none of the above.

Constructed-response question

What are the pros and cons of subprime mortgages? What aspects of investor-owned, as opposed to bank-owned, mortgages contributed to the financial crisis? How?

Subprime loans mean that more people will qualify for loans. It also means that some of those individuals may have problems keeping up with the payments on those loans, particularly if the interest rates significantly increase. The increase in subprime loans prior to and during the financial crisis meant that there were more foreclosures.

If banks continue to own the mortgages they have made, they will be very concerned about the quality of the loans and less likely to make loans that will not succeed. If the mortgages are sold to investors, the issuers may be less concerned with the qualifications of the borrowers. The increase in securitization of loans before the crisis meant that the original issuers of the loans were less concerned with quality. Therefore, when pressure arose, there were more failures than there might otherwise have been.

ACTIVITY 1
HOUSING PRICES

The following graph displays data on an index of real (adjusted for inflation) housing prices in the United States for the years 1950 through 2009.

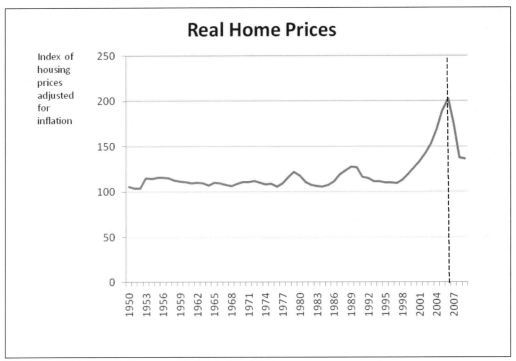

Source: Case-Shiller Home Price Index,
www.irrationalexuberance.com

A. Describe the general trend in real home prices from 1950 through 1997.

B. Describe the general trend in real home prices from 1997 through 2006.

C. Describe the general trend in real home prices from 2006 through 2009.

D. Predict what the value of the real home price index would have been in 2009 if the general trend in prices had continued at the 1950 to 1997 pace.

E. What might be some reasons for the observed trend in real home prices from 1997 through 2006?

F. What might be some reasons for the observed trend in real home prices from 2006 through 2009?

Activity 2
Taking Out a Mortgage

In order to understand the role of housing in the financial crisis of 2007 to 2009, it is important to know how the mortgage market works. A house is the most expensive purchase most people ever make. Very few people can afford to pay the entire price of a house out of their savings. Therefore, almost all homebuyers borrow money by taking out a mortgage from a bank or another financial institution. There are many different types of mortgages, but all function in basically the same way. An individual borrows money and uses this to pay the previous owner of the house. The borrower makes a monthly payment, which can cover part of the principal (the original amount borrowed) and the interest (the payment to compensate the lender for the use of the funds).

In some cases, homeowners are unable to make the mortgage payment. After the borrower has missed a few payments, the loan is referred to as "delinquent." If the borrower stops paying altogether the loan is said to be in "default" and eventually the lending institution will put the house in "foreclosure." At this point, the financial institution takes ownership of the house and will attempt to sell it to another buyer.

The conditions under which mortgages are given have changed significantly over the last few decades. The chart below compares some of the important features of prime and subprime mortgages. Many people still take out prime mortgages, but during the dramatic run up in housing prices from 1997 to 2006, subprime mortgages increased significantly.

	Prime	Subprime
Down payment	People save before purchasing a house and usually pay an amount equal to 20 percent of the purchase price. This means that the typical mortgage equals 80 percent of the purchase price.	People purchase a house with little or no down payment. This means that the mortgage may equal 100 percent of the purchase price.
Interest rate	The interest rate is fixed at the time the mortgage is taken out and remains unchanged throughout the term of the loan (usually 20 to 30 years). This means that homeowners will have the same monthly mortgage payment for the life of the loan.	The interest rate is adjustable. This means that the interest rate on the loan can go up or down depending on economic conditions. Adjustable rate mortgages often come with a "teaser rate," a low introductory rate that "resets" to a higher adjustable rate after two to five years. With adjustable rate mortgages, the monthly mortgage payment will vary and can eventually be significantly higher than when the loan was originally taken out.
Documentation	Individuals who want to borrow money from banks to purchase a house have to show that they are good credit risks. This means showing that they have a steady stream of income and a good record of paying off other debt, such as car loans and credit card bills.	Individuals are able to take out mortgages even if they have credit problems and are unable or unwilling to provide documentation on work history and income levels. Often banks and mortgage brokers accept "self-reported" information on these factors instead of contacting employers and creditors.

ACTIVITY 2, CONTINUED
TAKING OUT A MORTGAGE

The term subprime mortgage has been given to mortgages in which the borrower has some credit problems and does not have adequate funds to make a significant down payment. In addition, these mortgages are often not supported by full documentation on income and employment status.

A. The U.S. government made increased home ownership by lower income individuals a public policy goal. Which type of mortgage, prime or subprime, would be more likely to result in the government's goal? Why?

B. If someone defaults on a mortgage, why is it better for the bank if the borrower had put down a 20 percent down payment as opposed to no down payment?

C. Compare the level of risk to banks and financial institutions between prime or subprime mortgages. Who do you think is more likely to become delinquent on their mortgage payment and face foreclosure, someone with a prime or a subprime mortgage? Why?

D. During the run-up in housing prices, banks and mortgage brokers significantly increased the number of subprime mortgages. Why might banks be willing to take on more risky loans during times of increasing prices? (Hint: What does a bank do if someone defaults on a mortgage?)

ACTIVITY 3
THE RISE IN HOUSING PRICES

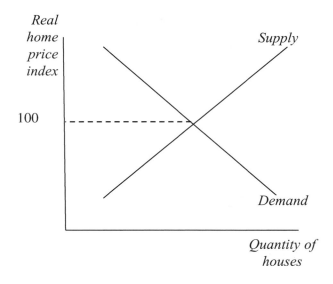

A. Between 1997 and 2006, housing prices increased dramatically. Would an increase or decrease in demand cause this? Is this illustrated by a rightward or leftward shift of the curve?

B. Between 1997 and 2006, housing prices increased dramatically. Would an increase or decrease in supply cause this? Is this illustrated by a rightward or leftward shift of the curve?

C. Between 2007 and 2009, housing prices fell dramatically. Would an increase or decrease in demand cause this? Is this illustrated by a rightward or leftward shift of the curve?

D. Between 2007 and 2009, housing prices fell dramatically. Would an increase or decrease in supply cause this? Is this illustrated by a rightward or leftward shift of the curve?

E. Housing prices increased between 1997 and 2006 and then decreased between 2007 and 2009. How might changes in expectations of future price changes affect demand for housing?

ACTIVITY 3, CONTINUED
THE RISE IN HOUSING PRICES

F. Each of the following has been suggested as a potential cause of the increase in housing prices from 1997 to 2006. For each, determine whether this would affect the supply curve or the demand curve for housing.

1) An increase in population.

2) An increase in building costs.

3) A decrease in interest rates.

4) Changes in expectations of prices of housing.

G. The graphs below show the relationship between real home prices and other relevant data from 1950 through 2009. Answer the question that follows each graph.

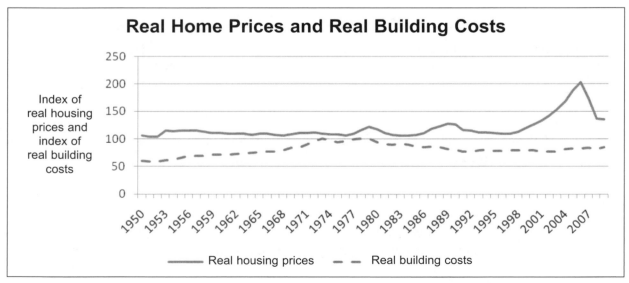

Source: www.irrationalexuberance.com

1) Does the graph support the view that increases in real home prices from 1997 to 2006 were justified by increases in building costs?

TEACHING FINANCIAL CRISES © COUNCIL FOR ECONOMIC EDUCATION, NEW YORK, NY

ACTIVITY 3, CONTINUED
THE RISE IN HOUSING PRICES

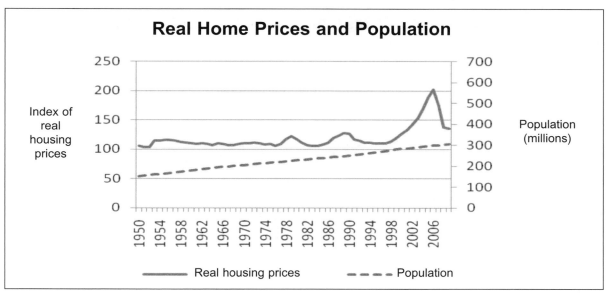

Source: www.irrationalexuberance.com

2) Does the graph support the view that increases in real home prices were justified by increases in population?

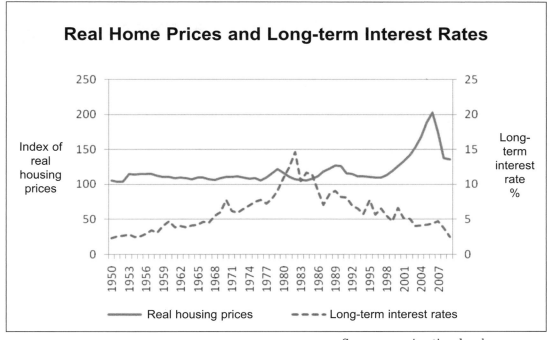

Source: www.irrationalexuberance.com

3) Does the graph support the view that increases in real home prices were justified by changes in long-term interest rates?

ACTIVITY 3, CONTINUED
THE RISE IN HOUSING PRICES

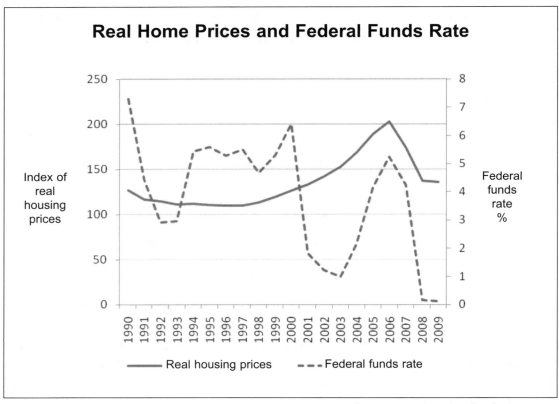

Source: www.irrationalexuberance.com
www.federalreserve.gov

4) Does the graph support the view that increases in real home prices were justified by changes in short-term interest rates?

ACTIVITY 4
THE FALL IN HOUSING PRICES

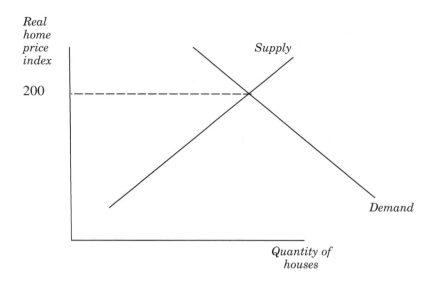

This represents the housing market as it existed in 2006. Following are three explanations for why housing prices fell from their peak. For each of the explanations, explain whether it affects the supply curve or the demand curve and in which direction the curve shifts.

A. The run-up in prices led many developers to build houses without specific buyers on the expectation that the housing boom would continue.

B. The Federal Reserve began increasing interest rates in order to stave off inflation. This caused the interest rate charged on many adjustable mortgages to increase, leading to an increase in mortgage defaults and foreclosures.

C. Expectations of future housing prices change as current prices begin to decrease.

ACTIVITY 5
LEVERAGING

It is 90 degrees and sunny and you are at your brother's Little League game. There are hundreds of people in attendance. After a few innings, the water fountain at the field stops working and people are getting hot and thirsty. You remember that there is a convenience store around the corner where you could buy water for $1 a bottle. After asking around, you figure you could sell water for $1.10 per bottle. You have $10 in your wallet. You figure that you will have time to make only one trip to the store and back.

Fill in the chart below to show the amount of profit or loss you can make by selling bottled water. Assume that you are able to sell all of the bottles you purchase.

Total money available	Cost per bottle at store	# of bottles bought	Total cost (cost per bottle x # bottles)	Selling price per bottle at game	Total revenue (# bottles x price)	Profit

While the situation will make you a small profit, you wish that you had remembered to bring more money to the field. You have $50 in your piggy bank and that would have allowed you to make a much bigger profit. Just then, one of your mother's friends offers to lend you $90 to go to the store and buy water. All you have to do is pay him back $91 before the game ends. Use the chart below to calculate your expected profit or loss if you accept the offer and can sell all of the bottles of water for $1.10 each.

Total money available	Cost per bottle at store	# of bottles bought	Total cost (cost per bottle x # bottles) + interest of $1	Selling price per bottle at game	Total revenue (# bottles x price)	Profit

So you make the deal, run to the convenience store and return with 100 bottles of water. Unfortunately when you return you discover that the water fountains are now working. Because of this, people are only willing to pay you 80 cents for a bottle of water. Use the chart to calculate your expected profit or loss.

Total money available	Cost per bottle at store	# of bottles bought	Total cost (cost per bottle x # bottles) + interest of $1	Selling price per bottle at game	Total revenue (# bottles x price)	Profit

ACTIVITY 6
EVENTS LINKING HOUSING PRICES TO THE FINANCIAL CRISIS

HOUSING PRICES RISE
Interest rates are low.
Standards are lowered to allow more people to qualify for mortgages.
INVESTORS AND FINANCIAL INSTITUTIONS ADOPT FINANCIAL INNOVATIONS
Individual mortgages are pooled and securitized.
Institutions leverage their funds at 30 to 1.
HOUSING PRICES PEAK AND BEGIN TO FALL
Interest rates begin to rise.
Developers build houses speculating that they will be bought.
MORTGAGE DELINQUENCIES AND FORECLOSURES RISE
Adjustable rate mortgages reset to higher rates for millions of homeowners.
Subprime mortgage holders have difficulty making mortgage payments.
INVESTORS AND FINANCIAL INSTITUTIONS SUFFER MAJOR LOSSES
Mortgage-backed securities lose value.
Institutions scramble for funding.

VISUAL 1
HOUSING PRICES

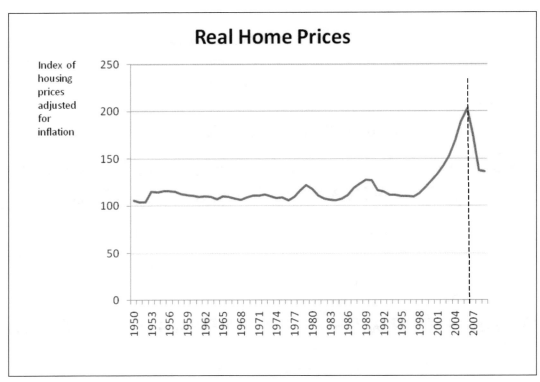

Source: Case-Shiller Home Price Index, www.irrationalexuberance.com

VISUAL 2
TAKING OUT A MORTGAGE

Prime	Subprime
20% down payment	As little as 0% down payment
Fixed interest rate (usually 20 to 30 years)	Adjustable interest rates and low teaser rates
Strict documentation of credit, income, and employment	Little if any documentation needed

A. The U.S. government made increased home ownership by lower income groups a public policy goal. Which type of mortgage, prime or subprime, would be more likely to result in the government's goal? Why?

B. If someone defaults on a mortgage, why is it better for the bank if the borrower had put down a 20 percent down payment as opposed to no down payment?

C. Compare the level of risk to banks and financial institutions between prime and subprime mortgages? Who do you think is more likely to become delinquent on their mortgage payment and face foreclosure, someone with a prime mortgage or a subprime mortgage. Why?

D. During the run-up in housing prices, banks and mortgage brokers significantly increased the number of subprime mortgages. Why might banks be willing to take on more risky loans during times of increasing prices?

VISUAL 3A
THE RISE IN HOUSING PRICES

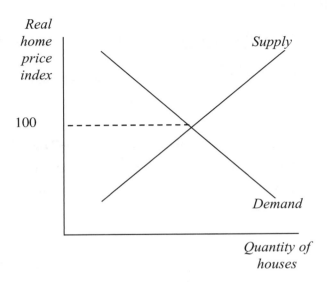

VISUAL 3B
POTENTIAL CAUSES OF RISING HOUSING PRICES

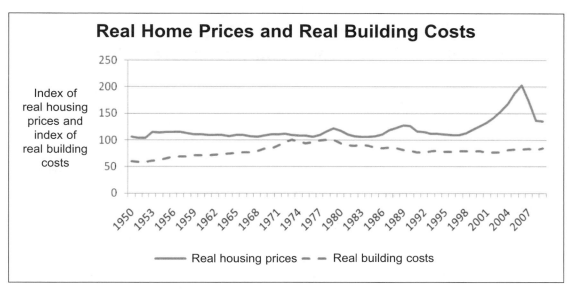

Source: www.irrationalexuberance.com

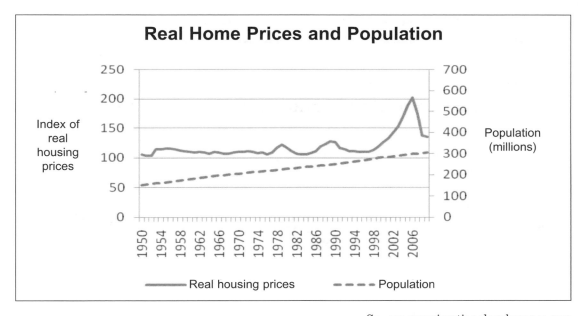

Source: www.irrationalexuberance.com

VISUAL 3B, CONTINUED
POTENTIAL CAUSES OF RISING HOUSING PRICES

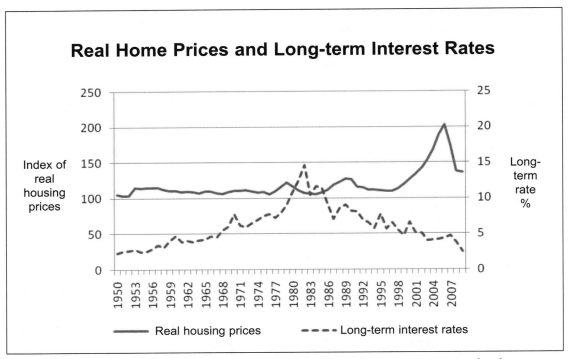

Source: www.irrationalexuberance.com

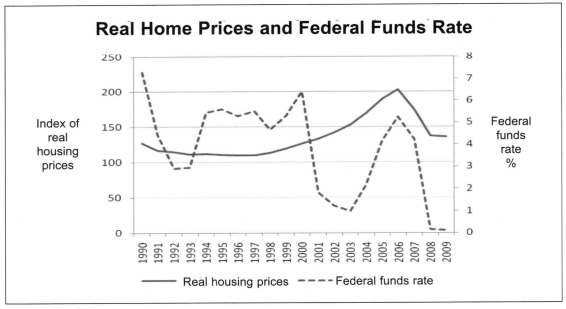

Source: www.irrationalexuberance.com
www.federalreserve.gov

Visual 4
Changes in Ownership of Mortgages

	Bank-owned mortgages		Investor-owned mortgages
Ownership of a loan	After issuing a mortgage, the bank collects monthly payments from the borrower and uses the receipts to make additional loans. A portion of the payments is bank profit.		After issuing a mortgage, banks sell the loans to a larger bank or investment company. Hundreds of mortgages are bundled and the resulting pool of mortgages is divided into "shares." These shares are called mortgage-backed securities. The shares are then sold to investors. Investors expect to earn profits when homeowners pay the principal and interest on their mortgages.

VISUAL 5A
MORTGAGE INVESTMENTS

Investors

	1	2	3	4	5
Revenue received					
Cost of mortgage					
Cost of checking income and employment					
Profit or loss					

VISUAL 5B
MORTGAGE-BACKED SECURITY

	Revenue received
Mortgage 1	
Mortgage 2	
Mortgage 3	
Mortgage 4	
Mortgage 5	
Total	
Per share (total ÷ 10)	

Profit or loss per share

Revenue received	
Cost of investment	$50,000
Profit or loss	

THE INSTRUMENTS AND INSTITUTIONS OF MODERN FINANCIAL MARKETS

LESSON 7
THE INSTRUMENTS AND INSTITUTIONS OF MODERN FINANCIAL MARKETS

LESSON DESCRIPTION

Students work in small groups to make flash cards to display terms commonly used in modern **financial markets**. Each group of students begins by learning one group of terms. The students pass their flash cards from group to group until everyone has had an opportunity to study all of the terms. The students then play an Instruments and Institutions of Modern Financial Markets quiz bowl game. Finally, students proceed to comprehend these terms in the context of mock newspaper articles. Knowing these terms can help students understand reports about modern financial markets as well as news stories explaining the causes of financial crises.

INTRODUCTION

Financial institutions exist to accept savings of individuals and institutions and transfer those resources to other individuals and institutions that may have productive uses for funds. Traditional commercial banks have fulfilled those functions relatively well, but have experienced challenges from time to time. Our automobiles, vacations, housing, and higher education are often funded with someone else's savings. Our apartments and office buildings and factories are paid for by money that has been indirectly borrowed from savers who have placed their savings in a financial institution.

Financial systems have played a significant role in enabling economic growth around the world. The thousands of small information technology and Internet companies would have had a difficult time beginning their entrepreneurial lives without an effective financial system. Companies engaged in international trade can concentrate on producing high quality products and use financial innovations to avoid the potential challenges of changing currency values. Even mutual funds have allowed the average saver to own a diverse set of equity investments that they would be unlikely to match on their own.

As financial institutions and markets have evolved, a need for a significant economic role for government has also become evident. Traditionally, unregulated and uninsured commercial banks have been subject to severe bank runs and costly failures. The costs of those failures are not solely borne by the owners and employees of the troubled institutions. The customers who lose their savings, employees of companies that can no longer borrow and thus must reduce their work forces, and the retirees dependent upon the income from saving all pay part of the cost. That is the justification for an economic role for government. Certainly our financial system is more efficient and safer than it was years ago. But obviously it can still fail at times. The design of regulation that permits innovation and flows of funds to where they are most needed is not easy or obvious. Financial markets can fail. The crisis of 2007-2009 is a financial crisis at its core.

As we learn from the crisis, new and creative regulation and competition will surely emerge and financial markets will likely work well once again. To understand that new markets, new instruments, and new institutions will be created and grow and to grasp the reasons for our current financial crisis and the necessary changes in the economic role of government, a sound basis of understanding of the instruments, the institutions and the characteristics of modern financial markets is necessary.

CONCEPTS
- Economic institutions
- Credit
- Insurance
- Financial markets
- Risk and return
- Moral hazard

OBJECTIVES

Students will:

1. Learn terms commonly used in modern financial markets.

2. Explain the meaning of financial terms as used in news articles about the recent financial crisis.

CONTENT STANDARDS

*   A market exists when buyers and sellers interact. This interaction determines market prices and thereby allocates scarce goods and services.

*   Prices send signals and provide incentives to buyers and sellers. When supply or demand changes, market prices adjust, affecting incentives.

*   Institutions evolve and are created to help individuals and groups accomplish their goals. Banks, labor unions, markets, corporations, legal systems, and not-for-profit organizations are examples of important institutions. A different kind of institution, clearly defined and enforced property rights, is essential to a market economy.

*   There is an economic role for government in a market economy whenever the benefits of a government policy outweigh its costs. Governments often provide for national defense, address environmental concerns, define and protect property rights, and attempt to make markets more competitive. Most government policies also have direct or indirect effects on people's incomes.

*   Federal government budgetary policy and the Federal Reserve System's monetary policy influence the overall levels of employment, output, and prices.

TIME REQUIRED

One or two class periods

MATERIALS

*   Activity 1. Terms of Modern Financial Markets (one copy per student)

*   Activity 2. Financial Crisis News Stories (one copy per student)

*   Visual 1: Terms of Modern Financial Markets (transparency and one copy per student)

*   Visual 2: Instruments and Institutions of Modern Financial Markets Quiz Bowl Game Board (transparency)

*   Visual 3: Instruments and Institutions of Modern Financial Markets Quiz Bowl Game Score Sheet (transparency)

*   Visual 4: Question List for Quiz Bowl Game (reserved for teacher use)

*   Six or seven note cards and one marker for each of the five groups

*   Optional: Small prizes for the Instruments and Institutions of Modern Financial Markets quiz bowl game

PROCEDURE

1. Explain to students that understanding the world of modern **financial markets** requires learning a new language. Participating fully in such markets requires that a person know the appropriate terms.

2. Distribute a copy of Activity 1: Terms of Modern Financial Markets to each student and give the students a few minutes to look over the terms and definitions displayed. Assure the students that they will be able to learn the terms and definitions a few at a time.

3. Display Visual 1: Terms of Modern Financial Markets and distribute a copy of the visual to each student. This visual lists the terms in two columns: Instruments and Institutions in the first column; Technical Terms in the second.

4. Spend a few minutes of direct discussion of the more complicated terms from each category. Terms that are likely to need clarification include: asset-backed securities, credit default swaps, hedge funds, private equity funds and **moral hazard**.

Asset-backed securities are typically made up of a group of small and illiquid assets that are difficult to sell individually. These investments played a role in the 2007-2009 financial crisis as many investment banks were buying the mortgages of American homes and then combining them to create investments that included parts of many mortgages (some very risky and some not).

The selling of credit default swaps in an unregulated market was also a contributor to the 2007-2009 global financial crisis because failing financial institutions were unable to pay investors on their credit default contracts.

Hedge funds are typically marketed to a small number of professional or wealthy investors, which allows the funds to undertake investments that would not be allowed by law for more conventional investments like mutual funds. You may want to say a few words about mutual funds if this is a new term for your class.

Private equity funds can be understood as funds that buy large shares of private companies in order to gain control of them, make changes to them, and sell them at a profit or list them on a stock exchange.

Moral hazard can be described as the increase in **risk** that investors and borrowers might take if they do not bear all of the costs of that risk. For example, investment firms may take more risk in the future, if they know that a government will pay for some of their losses if they occur. Thus government bailouts may make future failures more likely.

5. Randomly divide the class into five groups of equal size. Distribute note cards and markers for making flash cards. Assign each of the five groups a set of six or seven terms from Visual 1.

6. Tell the students to write a term on one side of each flash card and the definition of the term on the other side. When the

groups have prepared their flash cards, ask them to quiz one another within their group to practice learning the terms and definitions.

7. Once you think all of the students have had a chance to learn the terms from their group, ask the students to pass their cards to the next group. Group 1 to Group 2; Group 2 to Group 3; Group 3 to Group 4; Group 4 to Group 5; and Group 5 to Group 1. After a period of time, rotate again and continue this process until all of the students have had an opportunity to learn the terms from the five groups.

8. Now you are ready to conduct the Instruments and Institutions of Modern Financial Markets quiz bowl game.

   Display Visual 2: Instruments and Institutions of Modern Financial Markets Quiz Bowl Game Board.

   Tell the students that, in their groups, they will compete in the quiz bowl game. The answers to the questions or statements on the board will be terms from Visual 1. Allow the groups to keep Visual 1, if you distributed a copy, in front of them; however, the note cards and sheet of definitions from the activity must be put away.

   To get started, call on a student from Group 1 to select a category and point value. Mention that there are two "Daily Doubles" in the game (the groups that choose one of these can "bet" up to as many points as they have at the time; however, not less than the value of the question on the board). Use Visual 4: Question List for Quiz Bowl Game to read the definition associated with the group's choice. Give the group a couple of moments to consult with their partners and answer. (The answers are in parentheses following each question.)

   The teacher announces if the answer is correct or incorrect. If the term is correctly identified, enter the points on the team's score using Visual 3: Instruments and Institutions of Modern Financial Markets Quiz Bowl Game Score Sheet and cross the question box off of Visual 2 so another group may not select it. If the term is not correctly defined, subtract the number of points indicated on Visual 2 and discuss the correct answer.

Call on a student from Group 2 to select a category and point value and proceed in this manner until all of the questions have been asked and discussed (each group will get to try five terms).

Declare the group that earned the most points the winner. Optional: Award prizes (or extra credit) to members of the winning team.

9. Tell the students that they've learned the terms necessary to understand modern financial markets and are now ready to apply this knowledge to a news story.

   Provide each group with a copy of Activity 2: Financial Crisis News Stories. Tell the students that one of the most important reasons to understand the terms they've been studying is to better understand the economic news around them. Mention that these short excerpts from news stories have been adapted from real stories and that they should practice applying what they have learned on them. Have each group work through the activity and determine which missing terms correctly complete the sentences. Once again, all of the answers will come from Visual 1.

   Solutions to Activity 2:

   1) Fannie Mae and Freddie Mac

   2) Nationalized

   3) Debt

   4) Foreclosure

   5) Mortgage

   6) Subprime mortgages

   7) Investment bank

   8) Mortgage-backed securities

   9) Bonds

   10) Mortgages

   11) Commercial bank

   12) Bank run

   13) Liquidity, or liquidity risk

   14) Federal Deposit Insurance Corporation (FDIC)

CLOSURE

Review the key terms in the lesson. In particular, focus on the terms that the teams missed in the quiz bowl game.

Bring to class several actual news articles that use one or more of the terms featured in the lesson. Read excerpts from the news articles out loud and ask students to explain them in their own words using the definitions they have just learned. Show students that after having taken part in this lesson they are in a much better position to understand economic and financial events. They've just taken the steps necessary to learn a new language—that of modern financial markets.

ASSESSMENT

Multiple-choice questions

1. Which of the following would be considered the most liquid asset?

   a. a house

   *b. a checking account

   c. a share of common stock

   d. a government bond

2. Which of following is a type of insurance investors can purchase to protect themselves against an investment failure?

   a. mortgage-backed security

   b. asset-backed security

   c. hedge fund

   *d. credit default swap

3. Which investment vehicle is typically concerned with buying private companies so that they may be restructured?

a. hedge fund

b. common stock

*c. private equity fund

d. investment bank

Constructed-response questions

1. Explain how the bailouts of large financial firms conducted by the U.S. government might represent a moral hazard.

A moral hazard exists if one investor makes a decision about how much risk to take while some other person or institution bears the cost if the investment fails or performs less well than expected. As a result, the investor may take more risk. The investor knows that he or she will receive higher returns if the investment works; riskier investments normally pay higher rates of return. The investor also knows that he or she will not pay all of the costs if the investment fails. Thus, large financial firms will be likely to take higher risk investments and earn higher returns when they know that a government will step in to provide a bailout if the investments fail.

2. Explain why some consumers may choose to take out a subprime mortgage rather than a conventional loan.

Consumers who choose alternative mortgages generally have an issue in their financial situation that forces them to take these loans with a higher interest rate rather than a conventional mortgage. Lenders see these customers as riskier because of their low credit scores, lack of employment documentation, lack of savings, or high debt load, among other reasons. The consumer may not have a better choice and the only way that a house can be purchased is through a subprime loan.

A second reason is that if the borrower expects housing prices to continue to rise, the borrower may be able to refinance when interest rates rise following an initial low interest rate. A third reason may be that the borrower expects to move before or about the same time interest rates would

reset and thus is not concerned with the higher cost. A fourth reason might be that the consumer has decided to purchase a house that is more expensive or larger than he or she can truly afford. They are pushing their own limits in hopes that the house will increase in value or that their own financial circumstances will change.

ACTIVITY 1
TERMS OF MODERN FINANCIAL MARKETS

Asset-backed security: A security whose value and income payments are derived from and backed by a specified pool of underlying assets. Pooling the assets into financial instruments allows shares to be sold to general investors and may be intended to reduce risk. The pools of underlying assets can include common payments from credit cards, auto loans, and mortgage loans.

Bank run (bank panic): A series of unexpected cash withdrawals caused by a sudden decline in confidence or fear that the bank will fail, that is, many depositors withdraw cash almost simultaneously. Because the cash reserve a bank keeps on hand is only a small fraction of its deposits, a large number of withdrawals in a short period of time can deplete available cash and force the bank to close and possibly go out of business.

Bond: A loan to a government or corporation in return for a promised repayment at a specified interest rate.

Capital: The wealth—cash or other financial assets—used to establish or maintain a business. Within companies, it is often characterized as working capital or fixed capital.

Central bank: The principal monetary authority of a nation, which performs several key functions, including issuing currency and influencing the supply of credit in the economy. The Federal Reserve is the central bank of the United States.

Commercial bank: A bank that offers a broad range of deposit accounts, including checking and savings deposits, and extends loans to individuals and businesses.

Common stock: An ownership share of a corporation. A common stock offers no guarantee that it will hold its value or pay dividends.

Credit: What individuals and institutions borrow. When you borrow money, you promise to pay in the future. A "line of credit" is permission from a bank to borrow money up to an established limit.

Credit crunch: A situation created when banks and other lenders suddenly and significantly reduce their lending to each other, to individuals, and to businesses, because they are uncertain about how much money they will have to lend and whether the borrowers will be able to pay loans back.

Credit default swap: A type of insurance against a security falling in value. For example, an owner of a mortgage-backed security pays a fee to an institution or investor in return for the promise of much larger payment if the mortgage-backed security falls in value. The risk of default has been "swapped" to the seller of the credit default swap in return for fees.

Debt: Money owed; also known as liability.

Default: Failure to meet the terms of a credit or loan agreement.

Equity: Ownership interest in an asset after liabilities are deducted. For example, the value of your house after deducting the total amount of your mortgage.

Fannie Mae and Freddie Mac: Government-created financial institutions that buy mortgages from banks and then sell those mortgages as investment products. They were created to help make more money available for banks to make more home loans. Because of the housing crisis, both independent companies were on the verge of collapse and were taken over by the federal government in September 2008. Fannie Mae was created in 1938 and Freddie Mac in 1970.

ACTIVITY 1, CONTINUED
TERMS OF MODERN FINANCIAL MARKETS

Federal Deposit Insurance Corporation (FDIC): An independent deposit insurance agency created by Congress in 1933 to maintain stability and public confidence in the nation's banking system. The FDIC protects bank accounts up to $250,000 for each individual depositor (the amount was $100,000 before October 2008).

Federal Reserve System: The central bank of the United States, created by Congress and made up of a seven-member Board of Governors in Washington, D.C., 12 regional Federal Reserve Banks, and their 25 branches.

Foreclosure: The legal process used to force the payment of debt secured by collateral (such as a house) whereby the property is sold to satisfy the debt. Usually this means a family needs to leave their house because they cannot pay their mortgage.

Futures contract: A legally binding agreement to buy or sell a commodity or security at a future date at a price that is fixed at the time of the agreement.

Hedge fund: An investment fund normally with a limited number of investors focusing on a specific type of investment strategy. Hedge funds tend to be subject to less regulation and fewer restrictions than many other investments, such as mutual funds.

Investment bank: A bank that offers financial services such as trading securities, raising capital, and managing corporate mergers and acquisitions. Examples include Goldman Sachs and the former Bear Stearns.

Leverage: Borrowing by an individual or institution to expand the size of an investment. In so doing, the potential return from the investment may increase as well as the risk of the investment.

Liquidity: The degree of difficulty in converting an asset into money.

Liquidity risk: The risk that a bank will not have sufficient cash or liquid assets to meet borrower and depositor demand.

Moral hazard: The phenomenon whereby an investor may take more risk if the investor does not have to bear all of the costs of that risk.

Mortgage: An agreement to pay interest and eventually to pay back a loan made on a house.

Mortgage-backed securities: Investment firms bought many mortgages on homes and put them together in a pool. The firms sold parts of the pool of mortgages to other investors. Those parts (securities) could then be bought and sold in financial markets.

Mutual fund: A group of financial investments often of a specific kind or category, managed by professionals, with many individual or institutional investors.

Nationalization: Government, normally a national government, taking ownership and/or control of a business.

Options: The right, but not the obligation, to buy or sell a specific amount of a given stock or groups of stocks, commodities, currencies, or debt, at a specified price during a specified period of time.

Private equity funds: An investment fund that purchases the majority or all of a company often with a goal of making significant changes in the company's management or operations. It is described as a private equity fund because the fund may purchase shares of stock that are currently traded on a public stock exchange and take those shares off the public market.

ACTIVITY 1, CONTINUED
TERMS OF MODERN FINANCIAL MARKETS

Regulation: A principle, rule or law designed to control or govern how a market, such as the financial system works.

Return (rate of return): Money earned from an investment. The money could be profits, interest, appreciation, or a combination of dividends and appreciation. The rate of return is the ratio of money earned to the amount invested.

Risk: The degree of uncertainty associated with the return on an asset or the value of an asset.

Securitization: The process of taking an illiquid asset, or group of assets, and transforming them into an investment to be sold or traded.

Subprime mortgages: Mortgages that are made to individuals with low incomes, few assets, and perhaps weak credit history. The risk of default on subprime loans is greater than prime loans made to individuals with higher incomes, greater assets, and better credit histories. Some subprime loans were made with very low introductory interest rates with an expectation that the interest rates would increase.

ACTIVITY 2
FINANCIAL CRISIS NEWS STORIES

News Story #1—*Small Street Journal*

(1)_____ are two of the largest financial institutions in the country. They are almost exclusively focused on buying, selling, and guaranteeing single family residential mortgages. These organizations were originally U.S. government agencies, but became public companies in the 1970s. In 2008, the U.S. government (2) _____ these institutions. Dr. John C. Economist called this action "one of the most sweeping government interventions into a private financial market in decades." The overwhelming size and importance to the U.S. housing market of these institutions has resulted in what amounts to an implicit U.S. government guarantee that they will never default on their (3)_____.   When the housing boom began to cool in 2006 and 2007 these institutions began to experience serious financial problems. An increasing number of home owners had fallen into (4) _____; that is, had lost ownership of their homes or been threatened with it because of a failure to keep up with their (5) _____ payments. The wave of problems has also battered cities where (6) _____ riskier loans made at higher interest rates to individuals with poor credit or other problems had been prevalent.

News Story #2—*Widget City Times*

This past weekend the (7) _____ Bear Stearns, which had specialized in trading securities and helping companies with mergers and acquisitions, went bankrupt. Bear Stearns, which was founded in 1923 and had survived the Great Depression, was destroyed by a type of investment that many Wall Street firms had been buying for years. These investments, created by bundling many home mortgages into one pool, were known as (8) _____. These investments resemble (9) _____, instruments issued by governments and corporations that promise to pay a fixed amount of interest for a defined period of time. However, these securities are created when a company such as Bear Stearns buys a bunch of (10) _____ from a lender— that is, from the bank or company that helped a person buy a home—and then uses the buyer's monthly payments, and those of thousands of others, as the revenue stream to pay investors who have bought pieces of this pool.

News Story #3—*The Young Economist*

A rash of customers withdrawing their funds from a (11) _____, commonly called a (12) _____, occurred over the weekend. In the wake of recent news about bank financial problems, customers were worried about the (13) _____, or the ability of these banks to have enough cash on hand to meet their deposit requests. The (14) _____ quickly issued the following statement, "We stand ready to maintain public confidence in the banking system and will insure customers' deposits up to $250,000."

VISUAL 1
TERMS OF MODERN FINANCIAL MARKETS

Instruments	**Technical terms**
Asset-backed security	Bank run
Credit default swap	Capital
Bond	Credit
Common stock	Credit crunch
Mortgage-backed security	Debt
Mutual fund	Default
Option	Equity
Futures contract	Foreclosure
Subprime mortgage	Leverage
	Liquidity
Institutions	Liquidity risk
Central bank	Moral hazard
Commercial bank	Mortgage
Hedge fund	Nationalization
Investment bank	Regulation
Fannie Mae/Freddie Mac	Return
Federal Deposit Insurance	Risk
Corporation (FDIC)	Securitization
Federal Reserve System	
Private equity fund	

VISUAL 2
INSTRUMENTS AND INSTITUTIONS OF MODERN FINANCIAL MARKETS QUIZ BOWL GAME BOARD

Houston, We've Got A Problem	Institutionalize This	Bank On It	Not Your Grandma's Finance	Financial Potpourri
10	10	10	10	10
20	20	20	20	20
30	30	30	30	30
40	40	40	40	40
50	50	50	50	50

VISUAL 3
INSTRUMENTS AND INSTITUTIONS OF MODERN FINANCIAL MARKETS QUIZ BOWL GAME SCORE SHEET

Group	Score
1	
2	
3	
4	
5	

VISUAL 4
QUESTION LIST FOR QUIZ BOWL GAME (Reserved for Teacher Use)

Houston, We've Got a Problem

10—A bank will use this legal process to force payment on your house (or take ownership of it) if you stop paying your mortgage. (Foreclosure)

20—This occurs when banks reduce their lending to other banks and customers because they are worried about being re-paid. (Credit crunch)

30—If a person or company fails to meet the terms of their loan agreement they are said to be in _____. (Default)

40—Not the board game; rather, the uncertainty of the return on an asset. (Risk)

50—A government take-over of a business. Hint: Fannie Mae and Freddie Mac. (Nationalization)

Institutionalize This

10—Federal-government-created, now Federal-government-owned, institutions that buy mortgages from banks. (Fannie Mae and Freddie Mac)

20—The central bank of the United States. It's responsible for setting the nation's monetary policy. (Federal Reserve System)

30—It protects your bank deposit up to $250,000 at each bank. (FDIC)

40—A group of risky investments typically purchased by wealthy investors or institutions. (Hedge fund)

50—Investments in private companies by groups with plans to take over ownership. (Private equity fund)

Bank On It

10—The type of institution that offers services such as checking accounts, savings accounts, and loans to individuals and businesses. (Commercial bank)

20— A loan that banks make to individuals buying a home. (Mortgage)

30—This occurs when many depositors in a bank lose confidence and try to withdraw their money all at once. Hint: This happened in the movie "It's A Wonderful Life." (Bank run)

40—The institution in a nation that performs functions like issuing currency and influencing the supply of credit in the economy. (Central bank)

50—DAILY DOUBLE: A bank that offers financial services such as trading securities, raising capital, and managing corporate mergers and acquisitions. (Investment bank)

VISUAL 4, CONTINUED
QUESTION LIST FOR QUIZ BOWL GAME (Reserved for Teacher Use)

Not Your Grandma's Finance

    10—An agreement to buy or sell a commodity or security later at a price determined today. (Futures contract)

    20—The rights to buy or sell an investment during a specific period of time. (Options)

    30—Similar to home or car insurance but for your investments. (Credit default swap)

    40—DAILY DOUBLE: Wall Street firms bought lots of these from 2001 to 2006. They are created by bundling home loans and repackaging them as this investment. (Mortgage-backed securities)

    50—Home loans offered to people with credit problems, often with higher interest rates than typical home loans. (Subprime mortgages)

Financial Potpourri

    10—A loan to a corporation or government in return for repayment with interest. (Bond)

    20—A share of ownership in a corporation. (Common stock)

    30—How easily something can be turned into money. (Liquidity)

    40—Rules or laws designed to control or govern the financial system. (Regulation)

    50—The process of converting an illiquid asset (or group of illiquid assets) into an investment that can be sold or traded. (Securitization)

UNDERSTANDING FINANCIAL MARKETS, 2007-2009

LESSON 8
UNDERSTANDING FINANCIAL MARKETS, 2007-2009

LESSON DESCRIPTION

This lesson pulls together the events in financial markets from 2007 to 2009 by examining the persons and financial institutions that played key roles in the crisis, including why it occurred, who was affected, and the aftermath. How better to understand the complexities than for students to ask questions of certain people or entities concerning their complicity involving the crises? Students will do so in a mock trial, where witnesses such as Mr. Wally Banker and Mr. Mainy Street will be called to testify in *The People v. Ulysses S. Economy*. Because the people have been harmed, they have filed suit against the economy, personified by Ulysses S. Economy, who feels that he is the victim, not the instigator. The defendant is accused on four counts: the deterioration of consumer confidence, the failure to create jobs, the weakening of GDP growth, and the worsening turmoil in the global economy.

Students with computer access can link to several sites that highlight the market turmoil. These supplemental sites, along with the trial transcript, will be used to complete an exercise that requires them to place 20 decisions and events that are associated with the 2007-2009 financial crisis in correct sequence, beginning with the changes in banking regulations and ending with questions and concerns beyond 2009. The goal is for students to be able to understand, describe, and demonstrate knowledge of this crisis.

INTRODUCTION

In January 2007, the annual unemployment rate was 4.6 percent; the U.S. economy was at full employment. By December 2009, the annual unemployment rate for the nation was 10.0 percent with 17 states experiencing double-digit unemployment. The two states with the highest recorded rates Michigan, at 14.5 percent, and Nevada at 13.0 percent. Real GDP grew at annual rates of 2.3 percent and 2.9 percent in the third and fourth quarters of 2007 and then

began to decrease. The annual rate of change in real GDP was -4.0 percent, -6.8 perent, and -4.9 percent, respectively, in the third and fourth quarters of 2008 and the first quarter of 2009. It fell slightly in the second quarter of 2009 and then began to increase. The Dow Jones celebrated a high of 14,198 on October 11, 2007, only to lose over 50 percent of its value when it reached 6,469 on March 6, 2009. Inflation rates as measured by the CPI, were 4.1 percent, zero, and 2.8 percent during 2007, 2008, and 2009. Main Street, Wall Street, and the U.S. government demand to know how this happened and what can be done about it.

CONCEPTS

- Redlining
- Subprime mortgages
- New financial instruments
- Collateralized debt obligations
- Mortgage-backed securities
- Credit default swaps
- Deregulation
- Fiscal policy stimulus package
- Monetary policy stimulus tools

OBJECTIVES

Students will:

1. Identify the persons, groups, and financial institutions that made decisions that contributed to the financial crisis.

2. Explain how these persons, groups, and financial institutions were affected by the crisis.

3. Sequence the events that comprised the financial crisis of 2007-2009.

CONTENT STANDARDS

- A market exists when buyers and sellers interact. This interaction determines market prices and thereby allocates scarce goods and services.

- Prices send signals and provide incentives to buyers and sellers. When supply or demand changes, market prices adjust, affecting incentives.

- Institutions evolve and are created to help individuals and groups accomplish their goals. Banks, labor unions, markets, corporations, legal systems, and not-for-profit organizations are examples of important institutions. A different kind of institution, clearly defined and enforced property rights, is essential to a market economy.

- Fluctuations in a nation's overall levels of income, employment, and prices are determined by the interaction of spending and production decisions made by all households, firms, government agencies, and others in the economy. Recessions occur when overall levels of income and employment decline.

- Unemployment imposes costs on individuals and the overall economy. Inflation, both expected and unexpected, also imposes costs on individuals and the overall economy. Unemployment increases during recessions and decreases during recoveries.

- Federal government budgetary policy and the Federal Reserve System's monetary policy influence the overall levels of employment, output, and prices.

TIME REQUIRED

Three class periods

MATERIALS

- Activity 1: Witness Brief Cards (cut to distribute to each of nine witnesses)

- Activity 2: Trial Transcript: *The People v. Ulysses S. Economy* (one copy per student)

- Activity 3: "Brief" Notes on Witnesses for the Prosecution and the Defense (one set per student)

- Activity 4a: Financial Crisis Event Cards (one copy per student)

- Activity 4b: Financial Crisis Event Chart (one copy per student)

- Visual 1: What You Will Learn, How You Will Learn, and the Lesson Goal (transparency)

- Visual 2: Key Financial Terms (transparency)

- Visual 3: The Trial of *The People v. Ulysses S. Economy* (transparency)

- Visual 4: Evidence—Exhibit #1: Ratio of U.S. Household Debt to GDP

- Visual 5: Evidence—Exhibit #2: Dow Jones Industrial Average Historical Chart

- Visual 6: Evidence—Exhibit #3: Mortgage Delinquencies and Foreclosures

- Visual 7: Evidence—Exhibit #4: Global Comparison of Output, Prices, and Jobs

- Visual 8: Evidence—Exhibit #5: Monetary Policy Conducted by the Federal Reserve Rescue Efforts

- Visual 9: Evidence—Exhibit #6: Fiscal Policy (Congress and the President) Rescue Efforts

- Visual 10: Evidence—Exhibit #7: Consumer Price Index (Measures Inflation)

- Visual 11: Answer Key to the Financial Crisis Event Chart

- Pair of scissors

PROCEDURE

1. Prepare the classroom by arranging the desks as a courtroom would be situated including desks for a jury, witness stand, judge's bench, prosecution side and defense side with a desk for the defendant. The judge could wear a robe and have a gavel.

2. Display Visual 1: What You Will Learn, How You Will Learn, and the Lesson Goal. Discuss this with the class and make sure

everyone understands the objectives of the lesson.

3. Display Visual 2: Key Financial Terms. Introduce the key vocabulary that students will be introduced to during this lesson.

4. Display Visual 3: The Trial of *The People v. Ulysses S. Economy* and review the characters. Appoint or ask for volunteers to play the roles of judge, bailiff, prosecuting attorney, defense attorney and spokesperson for the jury.

5. Explain to students they will focus on the witness testimony first in preparation for the trial. Distribute Activity 1: Witness Brief Cards, cut into nine sections. (There are nine witnesses in the upcoming trial.) Divide the rest of the class into nine equal-sized teams. Each student on the team will receive an identical Witness Card. Students should read the facts concerning their witness to get a detailed view of the involvement of their witness in the financial crisis. Allow students to discuss their witnesses' testimony. Tell the students that their witness will be asked to testify in the upcoming trial. Although these cards contain a lot of facts about how that group of persons was involved with the crisis, the trial is an edited presentation of the events. Ask for one volunteer in the team to serve as the witness during the trial.

6. Distribute one copy of Activity 2: Trial Transcript: *The People v. Ulysses S. Economy* to each student. During the trial, the attorneys will ask the judge to admit exhibits into evidence. On cue, the teacher will display Visuals 4-10. Students should pay particular attention to the evidence exhibits provided during the testimony.

7. Distribute one copy of Activity 3: "Brief" Notes on Witnesses for the Prosecution and the Defense to each student. Page 1 of the brief is the testimony by witnesses for the prosecution and Page 2 is the testimony by witnesses for the defense. Ask students to write down the key components of the testimony given by each witness as they watch and participate in the trial.

Begin the trial. Students will use their notes as they participate in a discussion of the testimony led by the teacher. The teacher should ask the students what role the witnesses played in the crisis and how they were affected. Count on the teams to help provide the details about their witness.

Ask students whether they agree with the verdict or not. A worthwhile debate could be structured around the issues of what institutions could have done or whether they could have done more.

8. Distribute one copy of both Activity 4a: Financial Crisis Event Cards and Activity 4b: Financial Crisis Event Chart to each student.

9. For Activity 4a, explain to students that the events are in random order and their task is to put them in the order closest to what actually occurred.

This project is effectively done in pairs. It may be of some help to point out that some of the events may have been happening simultaneously or close to it. Exact ordering may not make much difference in those cases. Others clearly happened at different times.

The exact ordering is less important than an overall idea of what happened. The first three boxes lead up to the housing boom. Then interest rates began to rise (along with a number of other events) and the bubble broke. Three events follow in an approximate order and then the recession begins. Part of that recession is a decline in real GDP. Monetary policy is expanded to create new facilities, then TARP, then even more stimulative monetary policy. The beginning of the recession is officially determined and announced. The fiscal stimulus, known as ARRA, begins. The rest follows in order, with the process ending with a full-fledged recovery finally beginning at sometime in the future.

Once they are finished, ask the first pair to present the first five events, ask a second group to present the next five, and so on. Teachers should review the students' work and display Visual 11: Answer Key to the Financial Crisis Event Chart, which shows the correct sequencing.

10. Once you have finished, go around the room having students announce the sequencing beginning with Step 1 and continuing through Step 20, saying, "which led to..." between steps.

CLOSURE

Review the main points of the lesson by again displaying Visual 1: What You Will Learn, How You Will Learn, and the Lesson Goal. Ask students to identify the persons, groups, and financial institutions that made decisions that contributed to the financial crisis.

Persons on Main Street, Wall Street, homeowners, subprime borrowers, bankers, lenders, global economies, policymakers at the Fed, Congress, and the White House.

Ask students to explain how these persons, groups, and financial institutions were affected by the crisis.

Students should cite the evidence exhibits provided during the trial that show increased unemployment, decreased real GDP growth, increased household debt, declining Dow Jones and worldwide declines in real GDP growth, with China and India as the exceptions. Students will also note that an increase in prices was not a concern in 2009. Students should review their trial notes after which they should relay that the depths of the recession affected the economy so dramatically that fiscal and monetary policies were implemented to the tune of trillions of dollars.

ASSESSMENT
Multiple-choice questions

1. In the sequence of events that marked the financial crisis all of the following events preceded the decline of household wealth except:

    a. Deregulation of the financial industry

    b. Increase of the debt load held by households

    c. Bundling of mortgages in the form of mortgage-backed securities

    *d. A fiscal-policy stimulus package that included bailouts of the car industry

2. Identify the economic component that was the most stable during the 2007-2009 crisis.

    *a. CPI

    b. Real GDP

    c. Unemployment

    d. Dow Jones Index

3. What characteristic best describes the subprime market for mortgages?

    *a. These mortgages are provided to persons who have a less-than-stellar credit history.

    b. These mortgages offer holders of the loan an interest rate below the prime rate.

    c. Subprime mortgages are less likely to lead to foreclosures.

    d. Subprime mortgages earn banks less interest.

Constructed-response questions

1. One of the witnesses for the defense in the mock trial suggested the financial institutions were like teenagers without a curfew. How appropriate do you think this analogy is regarding the 2007-2009 crisis?

    Answers will vary but students should site the testimony provided by President Fizzcal Policy regarding deregulation.

2. Although the financial crisis of 2007-2009 has a beginning date, there remains an uncertain future for the U.S. economy into 2010 and beyond. What concerns will likely be on the forefront for policymakers?

    Students should speculate that economic indicators such as high unemployment, slow growth in real GDP, weakening global economies, and a fluctuating stock market are problematic. So too, the currently quiet CPI may be short-lived, given the magni-

tude of both the fiscal and monetary stimulus packages. Although this lesson does not address the budget deficit, students should be mindful that spending on the stimulus packages and bailouts increased the federal deficit, and consequences necessarily result from these actions.

3. Ask students what changes they would make in their own financial fitness to prepare for the future.

    Students may want to consider whether they should be more mindful of their debt load.

EXTENSION

At schools that provide computer access during class, the teacher can instruct students to link to the following sites. Teachers can elect to assign these sites as extension activities, for extra credit, or to enhance discussion.

a. Direct students to access an interactive publication released by the San Francisco Federal Reserve Bank at http://frbsf.org/econanswers/portal.htm. Ask students to review each of the presentations including Financial Crisis, Fed's Response, and Road Ahead. Ask students to review the interactive charts entitled Vicious Cycle and Virtuous Cycle.

b. Direct student to access the following interactive site which presents 10 weeks of financial turmoil: http://www.nytimes.com/interactive/ 2008/09/27/business/economy/20080927_W EEKS_TIMELINE.html. Students should pay particular attention to the seven-minute speech delivered by Treasury Secretary Hank Paulson on September 19, 2008.

c. Direct students to view a 10-minute presentation called *The Crisis of Credit Visualized* that focuses on the decisions made by the financial institutions on Wall Street and by homeowners on Main Street. www.crisisofcredit.com.

d. Direct students to access http://www.nytimes.com/interactive/

2008/10/01/business/20081002-crisis-graphic.html, which describes the important events leading up to the credit crisis of September 17-18, 2008.

ACTIVITY 1
WITNESS BRIEF CARDS

Witness Brief Card #1

You are a **Witness for the Prosecution: Mr. Mainy Street**. You represent the average American.

ECONOMIC FACTS: You are struggling. Unemployment rate has risen from 4.6 percent in January 2007 to 10 percent at the end of 2009. By December 2009, 17 states had double-digit unemployment.

FACTS ON THE CREDIT CRUNCH: Many businesses on Main Street cannot get loans. This credit crunch is killing businesses and hurting families. Two reasons for this are tighter regulations on banks after the crisis and banks fearful of making loans when it is not clear that businesses and individuals will be able to repay.

FACTS ON BAILOUT MONEY: Taxpayers provide money in two ways: through direct bailout payments to automobile companies and financial firms and through fiscal policy designed to stimulate spending in the economy. Congress and the president did not increase taxes, but borrowed the money.

The Federal Reserve Board conducts monetary policy and in doing so has significantly increased the money supply. This injection of new money is intended to provide the liquidity needed for banks and financial firms to survive and to make short- and long-term loans with a goal of helping the economy recover.

FACTS ON AUTO COMPANY BAILOUT: Through congressional legislation, taxpayers funded a more than $80 billion loan package to GMAC, Chrysler, and GM. Part of the money has been paid back to the government.

FACTS ON HOUSEHOLD DEBT: Nationwide, U.S. household debt as a percentage of GDP reached 100 percent in 2009. It had been 50 percent in the mid-1980s. The last time U.S. household debt was this high was in 1929.

Take a look at Exhibit 1, if you don't believe me. A Columbia University professor said, "The problem is not the banks, greedy though they may be, overpaid though they may be. The problem is us.... We've been living very high on the hog. Our living standard has been rising dramatically in the last 25 years. And we have been borrowing much of the money to make that prosperity happen."

ACTIVITY 1, CONTINUED
WITNESS BRIEF CARDS

WITNESS BRIEF CARD #2

You are a **Witness for the Prosecution: Mr. Falling Down Jones.** You represent a key index of stock ownership held by investors.

FACTS ON THE STOCK MARKET: The Dow Jones Industrial Average peaked on October 11, 2007, at 14,198. Less than a year later, the Dow dropped 778 points in one day of trading to close at 10,365. It reached a decade low of 6,469 in March 2009.

FACTS ON THE DOW'S DIVE AND THE LOSS OF WEALTH: Between the middle of 2007 and the end of 2008, Americans lost an estimated average of more than a quarter of their collective net worth. By early November 2008, a broad U.S. stock index, the Standard & Poor's 500 (S&P 500), was down 45 percent from its 2007 high. Total retirement assets, Americans' second-largest household asset, dropped by 22 percent, from $10.3 trillion in 2006 to $8 trillion in mid-2008. During the same period, savings and investment assets (apart from retirement savings) lost $1.2 trillion and pension assets lost $1.3 trillion.

Witness Brief Card #3

You are a **Witness for the Prosecution: Mrs. Risky Subprime.** You represent everyone who got a loan even though they had poor credit history.

FACTS ON THE FORECLOSURES: Foreclosures increased 79 percent from 2006 to 2007 and an additional 81 percent from 2007 to 2008. According to the International Monetary Fund (IMF), by April 2009 loss of wealth from mortgage defaults was $1.4 trillion, compared to $240 billion in October 2007. By the fall of 2009, more than 14 percent of all mortgages were delinquent or in foreclosure.

ACTIVITY 1, CONTINUED
WITNESS BRIEF CARDS

WITNESS BRIEF CARD #4

You are a **Witness for the Prosecution: Mr. Wally Banker.** You represent all of the big brokerage firms on Wall Street as well as the government-subsidized mortgage giants Fannie Mae and Freddie Mac and insurance giant American Insurance Group (AIG).

FACTS ON THE CONNECTION BETWEEN MRS. RISKY SUBPRIME AND MR. WALLY BANKER: Bankers, mortgage brokers, and investors lent money to Mrs. Risky Subprime because a new set of buyers was needed and all the prime buyers were already homeowners. By 2003, traditional lending standards had been exhausted and innovative financial transactions were created in order to earn profits.

ECONOMIC SITUATION POST 9/11: Interest rates were low during the 2001 recession and after September 11, 2001, under the monetary policy conducted by Fed chair Alan Greenspan. From 2000-2003 the federal funds rate dropped from 6.5 percent to 1.0 percent. Investors leveraged their money with loans and mortgages on houses to earn profits.

FACTS ON THE STRATEGY: Financial institutions began selling mortgages in packages to investors. A shadow banking system of sorts was created. Mortgages, some safe, and some risky, were bundled together and sold as mortgage-backed securities (MBS). They derived their value from mortgage payments and housing prices.

Once the foreclosures began, there was a domino effect. Investors disappeared from the MBS markets. These financial instruments were ostensibly insured by AIG by the sale of what were described as credit default swaps (CDS). AIG became vulnerable when so many of the bundled packages failed, which is why the government bailed out the insurance company giant. The goal was not to save AIG for its own sake, but to prevent the failure of many other financial institutions, banks, and businesses.

FACTS ON THE HEALTH OF THE "WALLY BANKERS:" One could argue that September 7, 2008, when Fannie Mae and Freddie Mac were placed into conservatorship (under the control of the federal government), was the beginning of the real credit crisis. The following week brought the collapse of Lehman brothers, the bailout of AIG and the almost total freezing up of credit markets. Lehman Brothers filed for bankruptcy. Goldman Sachs and Morgan Stanley became bank holding companies. Merrill Lynch and Wachovia became part of Bank of America and Wells Fargo, respectively, both with financing from the government. The Fed provided financing for JPMorgan Chase to purchase Bear Sterns. AIG remains intact, thanks to a bailout package from Congress and the Fed. In September, Washington Mutual became the largest savings and loan to fail in U.S. history.

ACTIVITY 1, CONTINUED
WITNESS BRIEF CARDS

WITNESS BRIEF CARD #5

You are a **Witness for the Prosecution: Mrs. Glowbell Economies.** You represent all of the economies around the world.

FACTS ON THE GLOBAL ECONOMY IN TROUBLE: Banks around the world joined the bandwagon that the Wall Street companies were riding. MBS and credit default swaps were enticing investment opportunities for investors everywhere, in spite of the risk. When these instruments began to lose value, buyers were not available. Access to credit was limited and, with the demise of Lehman Brothers, short-term credit was close to nonexistent. International financial activities came to a halt and a global panic began.

FACTS ON OTHER NATIONS: Japan's 2009 real GDP was -5.3 percent and the Euro area was -3.9 percent. Former Soviet countries such as Latvia, Estonia, Lithuania, and the Ukraine were suffering double-digit declines in GDP. Among the few countries that experienced real GDP growth were China at 8.2 percent and India at 5.5 percent.

The Royal Bank of Scotland began to fail. The British government had to pump in over $30 billion to nationalize the bank and protect the U.K. from economic disaster.

WITNESS BRIEF CARD #6

You are a **Witness for the Defense: Mr. Benny Fromthefed.** You represent the U.S. Federal Reserve System.

WHAT DOES THE FED DO? The Federal Reserve System conducts monetary policy and can expand or contract the money supply by using tools that also affect interest rates.

FACTS ON THE FED'S ACTION: Among the many dramatic changes that occurred during this crisis, the Fed lowered the target federal funds rate from 5.25 percent in September 2007, to a range of 0–0.25 percent in December 2008. Through congressional legislation the Fed began paying banks interest on both required and excess reserves. The Fed also created a number of new monetary tools. The evidence file shows the programs the Fed created to add liquidity into the market and to rid the financial institutions of illiquid toxic assets both at home and abroad.

ACTIVITY 1, CONTINUED
WITNESS BRIEF CARDS

WITNESS BRIEF CARD #7

You are a **Witness for the Defense: President Fizzcal Policy.** You represent those responsible for fiscal policy—the president of the United States and Congress.

The president of the United States and the Congress make fiscal policy. This crisis required fiscal policies designed to expand the economy.

FACTS ON RECOVERY PLANS: In October 2008, the legislation called TARP (Troubled Asset Relief Program) provided up to $700 billion to purchase financial assets that would permit banks and other financial institutions to continue to function in a productive manner in a very uncertain financial market. In 2009, a second stimulus package, the American Recovery and Reinforcement Act (ARRA), appropriated an additional amount up to $787 billion. ARRA allowed tax cuts and spending increases amounting to 2 percent of GDP in 2009 and 2.5 percent of GDP in 2010. Fannie Mae and Freddie Mac were given assistance and AIG received an additional commitment. The Federal Deposit Insurance Corporation (FDIC) was offered help in financing the insurance payouts of banks that had closed.

ADDITIONAL FACTS ON THE FDIC: The FDIC is a part of the federal government and serves as the insurance company and auditor of most banks in the U.S. Banks pay a fee to FDIC to insure deposits. The FDIC played a significant role in this crisis by closing and merging failed banks and insuring the depositors.

FACTS ON DEREGULATION: President Jimmy Carter supported eliminating the "redlining" practice that banks used to exclude minorities from qualifying for loans. President Ronald Reagan deregulated banks. President Bill Clinton allowed commercial banks to get into investment banking, and actively encouraged Fannie Mae and Freddie Mac to give minorities and low income groups access to home ownership even if that meant subprime loans. President George W. Bush continued programs to expand home ownership.

FACTS ON TWO OTHER REGULATORY AGENCIES: The Securities and Exchange Commission (SEC) and the Fed. The SEC changed some key banking regulations that allowed for the creation of more subprime mortgages. The Fed, under Alan Greenspan, chose not to regulate the shadow banking system that created MBS and credit default swaps.

ACTIVITY 1, CONTINUED
WITNESS BRIEF CARDS

WITNESS BRIEF CARD #8

You are a **Witness for the Defense: Mr. Ian Flated Prices**. You represent inflation.

Inflation is defined as a period of a general rise in prices caused by either too much money chasing too few goods or costs of inputs rising.

FACTS CONCERNING IMPENDING INFLATION: Prices increased in 2007 and 2008 and then fell slightly in 2009. However, the expansionary fiscal and monetary policy conducted by the government cause a watch-and-worry mentality. Bank reserves have increased dramatically and could lead to an even greater expansion of the money supply.

WITNESS BRIEF CARD #9

You are a **Witness for the Defense: Ulysses S. Economy**. You represent the economy.

FACTS ABOUT THE ECONOMY: People have been experiencing an economy from 2007-2009 that has not lived up to expectations. According to the Bureau of Labor Statistics, unemployment has been dangerously high, with some groups hit harder than others. Among African Americans, the unemployment rate for 2009 was 16.2 percent compared to 9 percent for whites. For Hispanics, the unemployment rate was 12.9 percent. For teenagers, the unemployment rate was a staggering 48.2 percent in 2009.

And then there is the GDP. Spending by businesses and new personal housing construction fell more than 50 percent in the first quarter of 2009. By the third quarter of the same year, investment had grown by 5 percent.

Consumer spending was also down in the third quarter of 2008, with a 3.5 percent decline followed by another decline of 3.1 percent in the next quarter. Household wealth is down almost $16 trillion since it peaked in 2007. Between housing-based losses and the stock market crash, 25 percent of personal net worth was wiped out.

Ulysses S. Economy will testify that he was the victim, not the instigator of the crisis. He claims he was the one who has suffered and wants to return to the days when real GDP was growing at a comfortable rate of 3-3.5 percent.

"I want to get back to the days of full employment. The last time I was close was in April 2008 when unemployment was at 5 percent. I appeal to the jury for a not-guilty verdict."

ACTIVITY 2
TRIAL TRANSCRIPT: *THE PEOPLE V. ULYSSES S. ECONOMY*

Bailiff: All rise. The Honorable Judge Adam Smith presiding.

Judge Adam Smith: *(Dressed in a robe and carrying a gavel. He enters the courtroom and taps the gavel. The judge's name is chosen in recognition of the father of economics, Adam Smith)* You may be seated. Today this court will hear the case of The People v. Ulysses S. Economy. The defendant is accused on four counts:

Count 1 of the indictment is that Ulysses S. Economy has deteriorated consumer confidence.

Count 2 of the indictment is that Ulysses S. Economy has failed to create jobs.

Count 3 of the indictment is that Ulysses S. Economy has weakened real GDP growth.

Count 4 of the indictment is that Ulysses S. Economy has created turmoil in the global economy.

Mr. (Ms.) Prosecuting Attorney, you may now call your first witness.

Mr. (Ms.) Prosecuting Attorney: The prosecution calls its first witness, Mr. Mainy Street.

Baliff: Raise your invisible hand. I mean your right hand. Sorry your honor. Place your left hand on *The Wealth of Nations* and answer the following question: Do you swear to tell the truth, the whole truth, and nothing but the truth?

Mr. Mainy Street: I do.

Baliff: You may be seated.

Mr. (Ms.) Prosecuting Attorney: Who are you?

Mr. Mainy Street: I am your elderly neighbor, your local entrepreneur, your daughter's high school economics teacher, your son's little league baseball coach, a deployed soldier, and a union autoworker. I am all that America stands for: hard-working, giving, and right now, scared about the future of our nation.

Mr. (Ms.) Prosecuting Attorney: Do you feel that Ulysses S. Economy has let you down?

Mr. Mainy Street: Yes, I do. Factories are closing and the economy has stopped flowing. The city and state governments have to eliminate services because without these jobs, folks are not paying taxes. When businesses do try to get loans, banks are tightening the credit options. This credit crunch is killing businesses and hurting families.

Mr. (Ms.) Prosecuting Attorney: What is causing the credit crunch?

Mr. Mainy Street: A couple of things, I think. First, the bailout money banks received from Congress and the president had new restrictions on lending. Second, banks are simply afraid to make loans because they do not know how secure many small and large businesses really are.

Activity 2, Continued
Trial Transcript: *The People v. Ulysses S. Economy*

Mr. (Ms.) Prosecuting Attorney: You mentioned bailout money. Who provides the bailout money and who decides how much money is given and where the money goes?

Mr. Mainy Street: Taxpayers provide the money through fiscal policy. The money is either raised through taxes or by borrowing. In this case, the federal government borrowed the funds. Congress and the president have decided how much and where it goes. Separately, the Federal Reserve conducts monetary policy and has been attempting to increase the money supply to encourage banks to make loans so that businesses might grow.

Mr. (Ms.) Prosecuting Attorney: Do you think that the federal government should have "bailed out" the car companies in Detroit?

Mr. Mainy Street: I know that the automakers are not just in one city. The reach of Detroit extends to every state in so many ways, from auto parts to local dealerships.

Mr. (Ms.) Prosecuting Attorney: Mr. Mainy Street, do you share some responsibility for this situation?

Mr. Mainy Street: Yes, I do. My friends and I have been on a buying spree. Just look at household debt, if you don't believe me.

Mr. (Ms.) Prosecuting Attorney: Your honor, I would like to have entered Exhibit #1 into evidence. *(Teacher displays Visual 4)*

Judge: Are there any objections?

Mr. (Mrs.) District Attorney: No, your honor.

Judge Adam Smith: So ordered.

Mr. (Ms.) Prosecuting Attorney: *(Shaking his hand at the witness)* Mr. Mainy Street, some have said that the problem is not the banks, greedy and overpaid though they may be. The problem is us... We've been living very high on the hog. Our living standard has risen dramatically in the last 25 years. And we borrowed much of the money to make that prosperity happen. What do you have to say for yourself?

Mr. Mainy Street: I am embarrassed, humiliated, and sorry, but then again, I am not on trial here, right?

Mr. (Ms.) Prosecuting Attorney: There are no further questions, your honor.

Judge Adam Smith: You may call your next witness.

Mr. (Ms.) Prosecuting Attorney: The prosecution calls its next witness, Mr. Falling Down Jones.

Baliff: Raise your right hand and place your left on *The Wealth of Nations.* Do you swear to tell the truth, the whole truth, and nothing but the truth?

Mr. Falling Down Jones: I do, but please bear in mind that I don't have all the answers.

ACTIVITY 2, CONTINUED
TRIAL TRANSCRIPT: *THE PEOPLE V. ULYSSES S. ECONOMY*

Baliff: *(Under his breath)* That's bull.

Judge Adam Smith: Baliff, did you say something?

Baliff: No, your honor. Sorry.

Judge Adam Smith: You may be seated Mr. Falling Down Jones.

Mr. (Ms.) Prosecuting Attorney: Who are you and what do you represent?

Mr. Falling Down Jones: I represent 30 stocks that make up the Dow Jones Industrial Average. I am a key index of stocks owned by investors.

Mr. (Ms.) Prosecuting Attorney: How have you been affected by Ulysses S. Economy?

Mr. Falling Down Jones: I was making a pretty amazing run for awhile. I peaked in 2007 then fell dramatically.

Mr. (Ms.) Prosecuting Attorney: Your honor I would like to enter as evidence Exhibit #2. *(Teacher displays Visual 5)*

Judge: Are there any objections?

Mr. (Mrs.) Defense Attorney: No, your honor.

Judge: So ordered.

Mr. (Ms.) Prosecuting Attorney: Do you share some responsibility for this situation?

Mr. Falling Down Jones: Yes, I do. Many investors were too bullish on the market, buying stocks with high P/E ratios (that is, the price of a stock divided by the earnings per share). That means that the price of the stock did not necessarily represent the true value of the company. A lot of folks lost a lot of wealth that they had built up for their children's education and their own retirement.

Mr. (Ms.) Prosecuting Attorney: How much wealth was lost?

Mr. Falling Down Jones: Between June 2007 and December 2008, Americans lost more than a quarter of their collective net worth. Savings and investment assets (apart from retirement savings) fell by $1.2 trillion and pension assets shrank by $1.3 trillion.

Mr. (Ms.) Prosecuting Attorney: So Ulysses S. Economy has let you down?

Mr. (Mrs.) Defense Attorney: Objection your honor. Leading the witness.

Judge Adam Smith: Objection overruled. Proceed.

Mr. Falling Down Jones: Yes Ulysses S. Economy has let me down, but I am trying hard to make a comeback. Since December 2009, I have been consistently over 10,000 points. Most days.

Mr. (Ms.) Prosecuting Attorney: There are no further questions your honor.

ACTIVITY 2, CONTINUED
TRIAL TRANSCRIPT: *THE PEOPLE V. ULYSSES S. ECONOMY*

Judge Adam Smith: You may now call your next witness.

Mr. (Ms.) Prosecuting Attorney: The prosecution calls its next witness, Mrs. Risky Subprime.

Baliff: Raise your right hand and place your left on *The Wealth of Nations.* Do you swear to tell the truth, the whole truth, and nothing but the truth?

Mrs. Risky Subprime: I do, trust me.

Baliff: You may be seated.

Mr. (Ms.) Prosecuting Attorney: There are many people who feel that you are to blame for starting this crisis. You made some bad choices about buying a new house and now you want to blame Ulysses S. Economy for losing your house?

Mr. (Mrs.) Defense Attorney: Objection your honor. Is the prosecuting attorney asking a question or giving us an opinion?

Judge: Objection sustained.

Mr. (Ms.) Prosecuting Attorney: Mrs. Subprime, are you aware that there are many who blame you as the single reason causing Ulysses S. Economy to fall precipitously?

Mrs. Risky Subprime: I am aware of that, yes.

Mr. (Ms.) Prosecuting Attorney: Were you aware that the mortgage papers you signed obligated you to make your payments on time and in full?

Mrs. Risky Subprime: Yes, but you don't understand.

Mr. (Ms.) Prosecuting Attorney: What is it that I don't understand, Mrs. Risky Subprime?

Mrs. Risky Subprime: *(Seeming weepy)* One minute I am renting a nice house that I can afford and the next minute I learn that there are some too-good-to-be-true loans available to folks like me who live from paycheck to paycheck. They promised that housing prices would continue to rise and I would have no problem refinancing. I had no money to pay down on the loan, but the banker said I could buy the house without paying any money upfront. Sound borrowers are called prime borrowers but I am less than prime. They call me subprime. Imagine how that makes me feel.

Judge Adam Smith: Mrs. Risky Subprime, do I need to call a recess?

Mrs. Risky Subprime: No honor, I can finish my testimony.

Judge Adam Smith: Very well. Proceed.

Mrs. Risky Subprime: So sure, I signed the papers because I trusted the loan officer who shook my hand and said, "Congratulations, you have just bought a house." I paid a good many months but then my mortgage

ACTIVITY 2, CONTINUED
TRIAL TRANSCRIPT: *THE PEOPLE V. ULYSSES S. ECONOMY*

adjusted from an initial low payment to a much higher payment. I got behind and I didn't have the income to pay my bills and my mortgage. Walking away from my obligation wasn't right but because I didn't have a down payment to lose, it was easier than I thought it would be, plus I had no choice. The bank was foreclosing on my loan. In 2010, more than 10 percent of all mortgages are delinquent and 4.5 percent are in foreclosure.

Mr. (Ms.) Prosecuting Attorney: Your honor, allow me to enter into evidence displays of the foreclosure rates. *(Teacher displays Visual 6)*

Judge Adam Smith: So ordered.

Mr. (Ms.) Prosecuting Attorney: Why did the bank lend you money?

Mrs. Risky Subprime: I really don't know, but I wish they hadn't. You will have to ask Mr. Wally Banker about why he lent me money. Overall, Ulysses S. Economy let me down, but I know that I let Ulysses S. Economy down, too.

Mr. (Ms.) Prosecuting Attorney: There are no further questions your honor.

Judge Adam Smith: Mr. (Ms.) Prosecuting Attorney, you may call your next witness.

Mr. (Ms.) Prosecuting Attorney: The prosecution calls Mr. Wally Banker.

Baliff: Raise your right hand and place

your left on *The Wealth of Nations*. Do you swear to tell the truth, the whole truth, and nothing but the truth?

Mr. Wally Banker: I do, you can bank on it.

Baliff: You may be seated.

Mr. (Ms.) Prosecuting Attorney: Where do you work?

Mr. Wally Banker: Wall Street.

Mr. (Ms.) Prosecuting Attorney: Who do you represent?

Mr. Wally Banker: I am Goldman Sachs, Lehman Brothers, Bear Sterns, JP Morgan Chase, and other big banking powerhouses. I am also mortgage giant Fannie Mae and Freddie Mac and insurance giant AIG.

Mr. (Ms.) Prosecuting Attorney: Why did bankers and mortgage brokers and investors lend money to Mrs. Risky Subprime?

Mr. Wally Banker: The quick answer is that we needed buyers and all the good prime buyers were already homeowners. By 2003, traditional lending standards had been exhausted. We needed innovative financial transactions in order to make a profit.

Mr. (Ms.) Prosecuting Attorney: Why did you need buyers? What do houses bought on Main Street have to do with Wall Street?

Mr. Wally Banker: We took advantage of borrowing low-interest-rate

ACTIVITY 2, CONTINUED
TRIAL TRANSCRIPT: *THE PEOPLE V. ULYSSES S. ECONOMY*

money and turned it into a lot more money.

Mr. (Ms.) Prosecuting Attorney: Go on.

Mr. Wally Banker: Investors wanted a part of this action so lenders began selling mortgages in packages to investors. We created a shadow banking system of sorts. We took these mortgages, some safe, some not so safe, and some downright risky, and bundled them together. These repackaged mortgages were sold and resold again and again all with the idea that they were insured from loss. These bundles derived their value from mortgage payments and housing prices. But when subprime borrowers failed to make their payments, foreclosures began and the bundles became unwanted, illiquid, and toxic.

Mr. (Ms.) Prosecuting Attorney: What would have happened with just one foreclosure?

Mr. Wally Banker: One would not have been bad. The bank would have taken ownership of the house and put it up for sale. The problem is that with so many foreclosures, more houses were put up for sale and exceeded the number of houses people wanted to buy. Even folks who could afford their houses walked away from their obligation because their house was suddenly worth less.

Mr. (Ms.) Prosecuting Attorney: How significant are the foreclosures?

Mr. Wally Banker: As Mrs. Subprime testified earlier, foreclosures hit home. By the end of 2009, more than 14 percent of all mortgages were either delinquent or in foreclosure.

Mr. (Ms.) Prosecuting Attorney: How did billionaire Warren Buffet characterize the insurance on these mortgage bundles provided though credit default swaps in a letter to his shareholders in 2002?

Mr. Wally Banker: He called them "financial weapons of mass destruction."

Mr. (Ms.) Prosecuting Attorney: Just a few more questions. You mentioned earlier in your testimony the companies you represented. What has happened to those companies?

Mr. Wally Banker: Lehman Brothers filed for Chapter 11 bankruptcy, Goldman Sachs and Morgan Stanley became bank holding companies. Merrill Lynch and Wachovia no longer exist independently after they were purchased by Bank of America and Wells Fargo, respectively. The Fed provided financing for JPMorgan Chase to purchase Bear Stearns. AIG remains intact thanks to a multi-billion dollar bailout from Congress and the Fed, as do Fannie Mae and Freddie Mac thanks to an up to $200 billion bailout from Congress.

Mr. (Ms.) Prosecuting Attorney: That is a lot of money for some very big companies that made risky financial transactions. Why should taxpayers bail you big guys out?

ACTIVITY 2, CONTINUED
TRIAL TRANSCRIPT: *THE PEOPLE V. ULYSSES S. ECONOMY*

Mr. Wally Banker: Tough question but easy answer: These companies were too big to fail. The domino effect would have led to a totally failed economy, a depression. Wall Street and Main Street are not on parallel paths to a healthy economy; they intersect.

Mr. (Ms.) Prosecuting Attorney: Mass destruction indeed. No further questions.

Judge Adam Smith: You may call your next witness.

Mr. (Ms.) Prosecuting Attorney: The prosecution calls its next witness, Mrs. Glowbell Economies.

Baliff: Raise your right hand and place your left on *The Wealth of Nations.* Do you swear to tell the truth, the whole truth, and nothing but the truth?

Mrs. Glowbell Economies: I do.

Mr. (Ms.) Prosecuting Attorney: Where do you live Mrs. Glowbell Economies?

Mrs. Glowbell Economies: Everywhere beyond the United States. You can find me in Europe, China, India, everywhere.

Mr. (Ms.) Prosecuting Attorney: Where does the problem begin?

Mrs. Glowbell Economies: Banks worldwide jumped on the bandwagon that the Wall Street companies were riding. Just like Mr. Wally Banker testified, those new subprime mortgage packages were enticing investment opportunities for investors everywhere, in spite of the risk. When some of the mortgages inside these instruments failed, buyers were not available. Banks became nervous. Access to credit was limited and with the demise of Lehman Brothers, short-term credit was close to nonexistent. International trade came to a halt and a global panic began.

Mr. (Ms.) Prosecuting Attorney: Have other countries been affected?

Mrs. Glowbell Economies: Yes. If I may, I would like to direct your attention to data provided by *The Economist* magazine.

Mr. (Ms.) Prosecuting Attorney: Your honor, allow me to enter this chart into evidence as Exhibit #4. *(Teacher displays Visual 7)*

Judge Adam Smith: Are there any objections?

Mr. (Mrs.) Defense Attorney: Yes, your honor, I do not see what the GDP of other nations in the world has to do with my client.

Judge Adam Smith: If you do not understand the connection, I suggest you return to your high school economics class. The chart is admitted into evidence but your objection is noted. Proceed.

Mr. (Ms.) Prosecuting Attorney: What countries have been hurting the most?

ACTIVITY 2, CONTINUED
TRIAL TRANSCRIPT: *THE PEOPLE V. ULYSSES S. ECONOMY*

Mrs. Glowbell Economies: As you can see, Japan and the Euro area were hit hard. The former Soviet countries such as Latvia, Estonia, Lithuania, and the Ukraine suffered double-digit declines in real GDP. Among the few countries that experienced real GDP growth were China at 8.2 percent and India at 5.5 percent.

Mr. (Ms.) Prosecuting Attorney: Your honor, the prosecution rests.

Judge Adam Smith: Mr. (Mrs.) Defense Attorney, you may call your first witness.

Mr. (Mrs.) Defense Attorney: Thank you, your honor. I would like to call Mr. Benny Fromthefed.

Baliff: Raise your right hand and place your left on *The Wealth of Nations*. Do you swear to tell the truth, the whole truth, and nothing but the truth?

Mr. Benny Fromthefed: You bet I do.

Mr. (Mrs.) Defense Attorney: What is your relationship with the defendant?

Mr. Benny Fromthefed: I spend the better part of my day trying to get Ulysses S. Economy back on track by using the tools I have available to me at the Fed as well as creating a number of new ones, all with the goal of injecting liquidity into the market.

Mr. (Mrs.) Defense Attorney: Your honor, I would like to enter the follow-ing chart into evidence as Exhibit #5. *(Teacher displays Visual 8)*

Judge: Are there any objections?

Mr. (Ms.) Prosecuting Attorney: Yes, your honor. These numbers are likely to predudice the jury. I cannot possibly see how they will convict the defendant when they realize how much money was needed to prevent an economic crisis.

Judge Adam Smith: Your objection is noted but the evidence is admitted. Proceed.

Mr. (Mrs.) Defense Attorney: *(Looking at the visual)* You have obviously made an exceptional effort to avoid a collapse of the defendant. For those persons in the jury who cannot see, please tell us the total amount of money that has been committed by the Fed and how much money has been spent.

Mr. Benny Fromthefed: At the peak, the largest programs supplied $1.5 trillion of funds. In addition, I supplied $120 billion to specific institutions. The Fed's assets have increased from about $900 billion to almost $2.5 trillion. That is significant evidence that I have been trying to save the financial system and stimulate the economy.

Mr. (Mrs.) Defense Attorney: Thank you for that information. You obviously felt that there was a great need. When did you first notice that Ulysses S. Economy was heading into trouble?

ACTIVITY 2, CONTINUED
TRIAL TRANSCRIPT: *THE PEOPLE V. ULYSSES S. ECONOMY*

Mr. Benny Fromthefed: In August 2007 but especially in September 2008.

Mr. (Mrs.) Defense Attorney: Some have suggested that the government has provided too much of a safety net for risky decisions others make, the too-big-too-fail financial institutions in particular. Merrill Lynch, Lehman Brothers, Bear Stearns, Goldman Sachs, Morgan Stanley, Fannie Mae and Freddie Mac held the American people hostage by holding $9 trillion in debt. They ran amok because there was no government regulation of the shadow banking system they had created. What do you say to that?

Mr. Benny Fromthefed: Yes, the government is the parent and these companies are teenagers.

Mr. (Mrs.) Defense Attorney: Please explain.

Mr. Benny Fromthefed: The government failed to give these teenagers a curfew and then, when they went astray, the government bailed them out. The safety net expected to be provided by the "parents" was so comfortable that the teens were not afraid to take thrill-seeking risks. Decisions are easy to make if there are no consequences to bear.

Mr. (Mrs.) Defense Attorney: Do you think that the defendant will one day soon pay his debt to society by creating jobs, sustaining growth, fostering international trade, and restoring consumer confidence?

Mr. Benny Fromthefed: I do. I see green shoots of a healthy, back-on-track economy. If anyone can make it right, it is Ulysses S. Economy.

Mr. (Mrs.) Defense Attorney: I have no other questions for this witness. I would now like to call the President of the United States, Fizzcal Policy.

Baliff: Raise your right hand and place your left on *The Wealth of Nations.* Do you swear to tell the truth, the whole truth, and nothing but the truth?

President Fizzcal Policy: Absolutely.

Mr. (Mrs.) Defense Attorney: Mr. President, what is your relationship with the defendant?

President Fizzcal Policy: I work alongside Congress to create taxing and spending policies to get the defendant back on track.

Mr. (Mrs.) Defense Attorney: Your honor, I would like to enter into evidence data from the Congressional Budget Office that shows the policies and the money the witness is referring to. This will be Exhibit #6. *(Teacher displays Visual 9)*

(The attorney views the table and looks embarrassed.) Your honor, I apologize. There appears to be typographical errors on the exhibit in the final column. Surely those numbers are not hundreds of billions.

ACTIVITY 2, CONTINUED
TRIAL TRANSCRIPT: *THE PEOPLE V. ULYSSES S. ECONOMY*

President Fizzcal Policy: *(Interrupting)* Actually, those numbers are correct. This is a big package because this is a big problem.

Mr. (Mrs.) Defense Attorney: The initial efforts (the TARP) did not spend all that it could. Were you covering up?

President Fizzcal Policy: No, not at all. It is correct. Some of the institutions have repaid the money that was provided. I expect that the final amount of spending will be about $110 billion. Most of the institutions have recovered.

Mr. (Mrs.) Defense Attorney: Sounds like there are multiple layers of what the term "bailing out" means, yes?

President Fizzcal Policy: I'm afraid so.

Mr. (Mrs.) Defense Attorney: What do you say to the criticism that your policies continue to provide too much of a safety net for financial institutions, given that they allow them to make risky decisions with the government on standby with bailout money?

President Fizzcal Policy: I think that has some merit. We need to continue looking at that issue.

Mr. (Mrs.) Defense Attorney: What do you say to the criticism that over the past several years both the Office of the President and Congress have been too willing to deregulate banks and other financial institutions?

President Fizzcal Policy: I think that has some merit, too. No one wants government control over business practices until problems arise. When that happens, everyone begins to point fingers. Congress writes the legislation and, perhaps with the guidance of the president, new laws are made.

Mr.(Mrs.) Defense Attorney: When did the deregulation of financial institutions begin?

President Fizzcal Policy: You could begin as far back as President Jimmy Carter, who supported eliminating the "redlining" practice banks used to exclude minorities from qualifying for loans. You could look at President Ronald Reagan, who deregulated banks so new business investment would emerge. You could look at President Bill Clinton, who allowed commercial banks to get into investment banking. Clinton actively encouraged Fannie Mae and Freddie Mac to give minorities and low-income groups access to home ownership, even if that meant subprime loans. And President George W. Bush continued efforts to increase the number of citizens owning their own homes.

Mr. (Mrs.) Defense Attorney: You're naming both Republican and Democratic presidents, yes?

President Fizzcal Policy: That is correct, not to mention the 435 members of the House of Representatives and 100 members of the Senate representing both political parties.

ACTIVITY 2, CONTINUED
TRIAL TRANSCRIPT: *THE PEOPLE V. ULYSSES S. ECONOMY*

Mr. (Mrs.) Defense Attorney: Are those the only policymakers who made decisions affecting the defendant?

President Fizzcal Policy: No. You could leave the White House and Congress and head over to two agencies in the bureaucracy: the SEC and the Fed. The SEC changed some key banking regulations that allowed for more subprime mortgages. The Fed, under Alan Greenspan, chose not to regulate the shadow banking system that fostered the creation of bundled mortgage packages that became toxic upon high foreclosure rates.

Mr. (Mrs.) Defense Attorney: Do you think that the defendant will one day soon make wise decisions that will lead to more jobs and economic growth here and abroad?

President Fizzcal Policy: I do. I instituted another stimulus in 2009. Look again at Exhibit 6. The total amount of spending will be almost $800 billion when it is finished. As of early 2010 about one-half has been spent—about a third on individual tax reductions and about a third on state and federal spending. The rest is in direct aid to individuals in need and tax cuts for businesses.

Mr. (Mrs.) Defense Attorney: How confident are you that your policies will help the defendant?

President Fizzcal Policy: Very confident, but Ulysses S. Economy can play tricks on policymakers.

Mr. (Mrs.) Defense Attorney: Do you think that the American people will ever be able to forgive the defendant?

President Fizzcal Policy: I do believe that one day soon consumer confidence will return. The index measuring consumer confidence as published by the Conference Board showed consumer confidence is rising. That's a start.

Mr. (Mrs.) Defense Attorney: Your honor, I now call the next witness to the stand, Mr. Ian Flated Prices.

Baliff: Raise your right hand and place your left on *The Wealth of Nations*. Do you swear to tell the truth, the whole truth, and nothing but the truth?

Mr. Ian Flated Prices: I do.

Mr. (Mrs.) Defense Attorney: You seem a little more quiet than usual, not your usual hyper self. What is your involvement with the defendant?

Mr. Ian Flated Prices: You are right. I have been quiet since November 2008, despite flaring up in late 2007 and throughout 2008. Of course, most economists want me settled down in a 1–2% range.

Mr. (Mrs.) Defense Attorney: Your honor I would like to enter this Consumer Price Index data into evidence. (*Teacher displays Visual 9*)

Judge: So ordered.

Mr. (Mrs.) Defense Attorney: So Mr. Ian Flated Prices, you are supportive of the defendant?

ACTIVITY 2, CONTINUED
TRIAL TRANSCRIPT: *THE PEOPLE V. ULYSSES S. ECONOMY*

Mr. Ian Flated Prices: Yes, I am.

Mr. (Mrs.) Defense Attorney: Are you concerned at all about your presence in the defendant's life given the enormous amounts of stimulus money injected into the defendant from Congress and the president, and the amazingly large amounts of bank reserves created by the Fed?

Mr. Ian Flated Prices: I'll admit that my presence can be destructive because I make currency worth less. I can make a strong dollar weak. On the positive side, if the dollar weakens, the trade deficit shrinks as U.S. exports become more affordable for foreign buyers. I cannot guarantee you that I will leave the defendant alone, but I know there are a lot of policymakers watching me closely, especially at the Fed.

Mr. (Mrs.) Defense Attorney: Your honor, I have no more questions for this witness. I call the defendant to the stand, Mr. Ulysses S. Economy.

Judge: Mr. Economy, you do realize that you can exercise your Fifth Amendment right not to testify against yourself?

Mr. Ulysses S. Economy: I understand my rights, your honor, but I want to testify in this very important trial.

Judge: Very well. Proceed.

Baliff: Raise your right hand and place your left on *The Wealth of Nations*. Do you swear to tell the truth, the whole truth, and nothing but the truth?

Mr. Ulysses S. Economy: I will tell you the truth but I will do so slowly. The Business Cycle Dating Committee of the National Bureau of Economic Research announced that I have been in a recession since December 2007.

Mr. (Mrs.) Defense Attorney: You have been accused of some serious offenses. People have been enduring an economy from 2007 to 2009 that has not lived up to expectations.

Mr. Ulysses S. Economy: *(Interrupting the attorney and putting his hands up in the air in resignation)* Believe me, I know. Spending by business and new personal housing construction fell more than 50 percent in the first quarter of 2009.

Mr. (Mrs.) Defense Attorney: What component of GDP is growing?

Mr. Ulysses S. Economy: Government spending.

Mr. (Mrs.) Defense Attorney: And how do you expect foreign buyers to buy our exports? As Mrs. Glowbell Economies testified, the GDPs of other nations have experienced extraordinary declines. Between housing and the stock market crash, 25 percent of personal net worth was wiped out. What do you have to say for yourself?

Mr. Ulysses S. Economy: *(Looking at the jury.)* I know that you are disappointed in me but I am the victim here.

ACTIVITY 2, CONTINUED
TRIAL TRANSCRIPT: *THE PEOPLE V. ULYSSES S. ECONOMY*

I shouldn't be accused of committing the offenses; I am the one who has suffered. If you must find me guilty, please choose to rehabilitate me instead of just letting me stagnate. Provide me with sound monetary and fiscal policy tools. Tighten regulations on financial institutions but not at the expense of reducing loans for both businesses and consumers. Give businesses a reason to open up factories instead of burdening them with new costs. If you let me remain free to expand, I promise to get back on track.

Mr. (Mrs.) Defense Attorney: Your honor, the defense rests.

Judge: *(Instructions to the jury)* You have heard the evidence in the case of *The People v. Ulysses S. Economy*. On Count one of the indictment that Ulysses S. Economy has deteriorated consumer confidence, how do you find?

Spokesperson for the Jury: Guilty.

Judge: On Count two of the indictment, that Ulysses S. Economy has failed to create jobs, how do you find?

Spokesperson for the Jury: Guilty.

Judge: On Count three of the indictment, that Ulysses S. Economy has weakened GDP growth, how do you find?

Spokesperson for the Jury: Guilty.

Judge: On Count four of the indictment, that Ulysses S. Economy has worsened turmoil in the global economy, how do you find?

Spokesperson for the Jury: Guilty.

Judge: *(Looking at Ulysses S. Economy)* You have been found guilty on all counts of the indictment. Many want to lock you up and throw away the key. After all, you have destroyed the income and wealth of millions of people around the world.

I have determined your sentence. *(Pause)* I will free you and let you expand, grow again, and restore yourself as the leading economic power in the world. However, I am also likely to establish some new laws and regulations to guide you and to help prevent a recurrence of the experience we have all just gone through.

It is not just a coincidence that Adam Smith's *The Wealth of Nations* was published the same year that Thomas Jefferson authored the *Declaration of Independence*. Just remember all that you are and all that you can become is because of the American people. We are adjourned. *(Strike gavel)*

ACTIVITY 3
"BRIEF" NOTES ON WITNESSES FOR THE PROSECUTION

 **Mr. Mainy Street**

 **Mrs. Risky Subprime**

 **Mr. Wally Banker**

 **Mr. Falling Down Jones**

 **Mrs. Glowbell Economies**

ACTIVITY 3, CONTINUED
"BRIEF" NOTES ON WITNESSES FOR THE DEFENSE

 **Mr. Benny Fromthefed**

 **President Fizzcal Policy**

 **Mr. Ian Flated Prices**

 **Mr. Ulysses S. Economy**

ACTIVITY 4A
FINANCIAL CRISIS EVENT CARDS

Easy credit and low interest rates	ARRA	Real GDP booms. Employment races ahead. The recovery is fully under way.	Interest rates begin to rise	Housing bubble breaks
Foreclosures increase at a record rate	Recession begins	Unemployment rate reaches 10.1%	Housing boom begins	Fed begins special monetary facilities
TARP	Real GDP decreases	Fed lowers federal funds rate to between zero and 0.25%	Deregulation	Recession is formally declared
Stock market low - Dow stops at 6,750	Real GDP begins to expand	Fed begins to lower target federal funds rate	Stock market peak - The Dow hits a market high of almost 15,000	Securitization expands

Activity 4b
Financial Crisis Event Chart

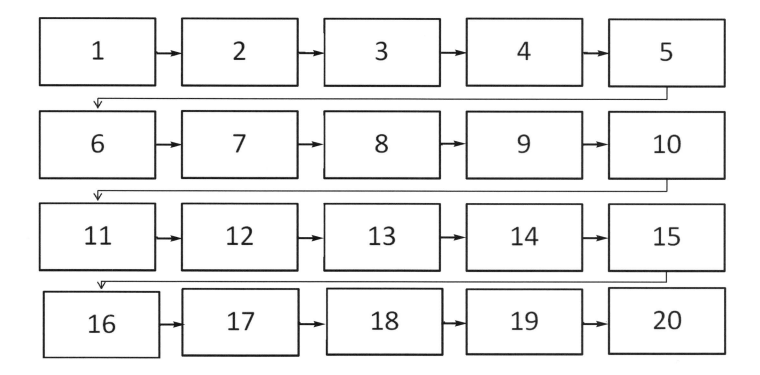

VISUAL 1
WHAT YOU WILL LEARN, HOW YOU WILL LEARN, AND THE LESSON GOAL

WHAT YOU WILL LEARN

You will be able to identify the persons, groups, and financial institutions that played a role in decisions that contributed to the financial crisis.

You will be able to explain how these persons, groups, and financial institutions were affected by the crisis.

You will be able to sequence the events that comprised the financial crisis of 2007-2009.

HOW YOU WILL LEARN

You will participate in a mock trial where witnesses such as Mr. Wally Banker and Mr. Mainy Street will be called to testify in the case of *The People v. Ulysses S. Economy.* The defendant is accused on four counts including the deterioration of consumer confidence, the failure to create jobs, the weakening of real GDP growth, and the worsening of turmoil in the global economy.

You will correctly order 20 events that occurred during 2007-2009 in correct sequence beginning with the changes in banking regulations and ending with questions and concerns beyond 2009.

THE LESSON GOAL

You will be able to understand, describe, and demonstrate knowledge of this most recent crisis.

VISUAL 2
KEY FINANCIAL TERMS

Credit default swap: A type of insurance against a security falling in value. For example, an owner of a mortgage-backed security pays a fee to an institution or investor in return for the promise of much larger payment if the mortgage-backed security defaults. The risk of default has been "swapped" to the seller of the credit default swap in return for fees.

Mortgage-backed securities: Investment firms bought many mortgages on homes and put them together in a pool. The firms sold parts of the pool of mortgages to other investors. Those parts (securities) could then be bought and sold in financial markets.

Toxic assets: An informal term describing financial assets that have an unknown value. For example, if some or many of the mortgages included in a mortgage-backed security are in foreclosure, the value of that security may be very difficult to determine. It might be described as toxic, that is, no one wants to buy or own it because no one is sure of its value.

Redlining: A practice that some mortgage companies and banks engaged in that made persons who lived in certain geographic areas less likely to qualify for loans. These areas were often largely minority areas. Mortgage companies defended the practice by saying that these mortgages were more likely to become delinquent and subject to foreclosure. The practice has been severely limited by recent laws.

VISUAL 2, CONTINUED
KEY FINANCIAL TERMS

Subprime mortgages: Mortgages that are made to individuals with low incomes, few assets, and perhaps weak credit history. The risk of default on subprime loans is greater than prime loans made to individuals with higher incomes, greater assets, and better credit histories. Some subprime loans were made with very low introductory interest rates with an expectation that the interest rates would increase.

Shadow banking system: Financial institutions, including investment banks, private equity funds, and hedge funds, that accept investments, make loans and create and sell new securities. This process of acting as an intermediary between those who wish to save and those who wish to borrow is outside the traditional banking system and subject to much less regulation.

Deregulation: Acts that eliminated many of the congressional mandates, rules and regulations under which the financial industry operated, giving the financial industry much more flexibility.

VISUAL 3
THE TRIAL OF *THE PEOPLE V. ULYSSES S. ECONOMY*

CHARACTERS IN THE COURTROOM

Judge Adam Smith
Bailiff and Jury

Prosecuting Attorney
Defense Attorney

Witnesses for the Prosecution

Mr. Mainy Street
Mrs. Risky Subprime
Mr. Wally Banker

Mr. Falling Down Jones
Mrs. Glowbell Economies

Witnesses for the Defense

Mr. Benny Fromthefed
President Fizzcal Policy

Mr. Ian Flated Prices
Ulysses S. Economy

VISUAL 4
EVIDENCE—EXHIBIT #1: RATIO OF U.S. HOUSEHOLD DEBT TO GDP

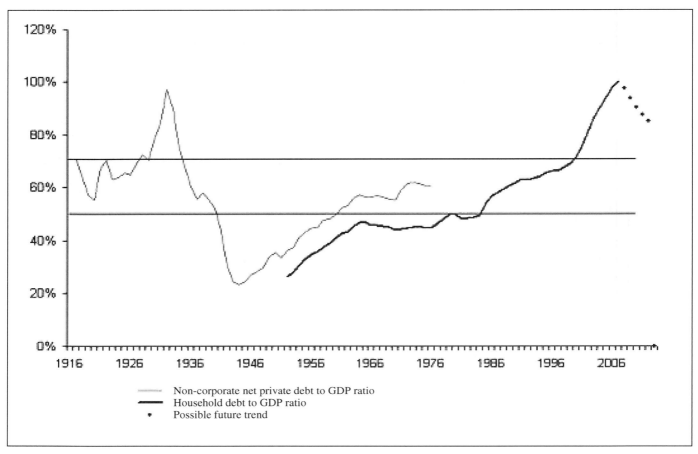

Non-corporate net private debt to GDP ratio
Household debt to GDP ratio
• Possible future trend

Source: Credit Suisse, February 26, 2009

VISUAL 5
EVIDENCE—EXHIBIT #2: DOW JONES INDUSTRIAL AVERAGE HISTORICAL CHART

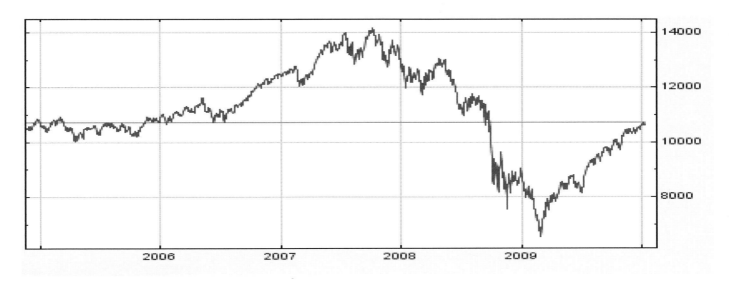

Source: http://www.advfn.com/p.php?pid=qkchart&symbol=DOW1%AINDU

VISUAL 6
EVIDENCE—EXHIBIT #3: MORTGAGE DELINQUENCIES AND FORECLOSURES

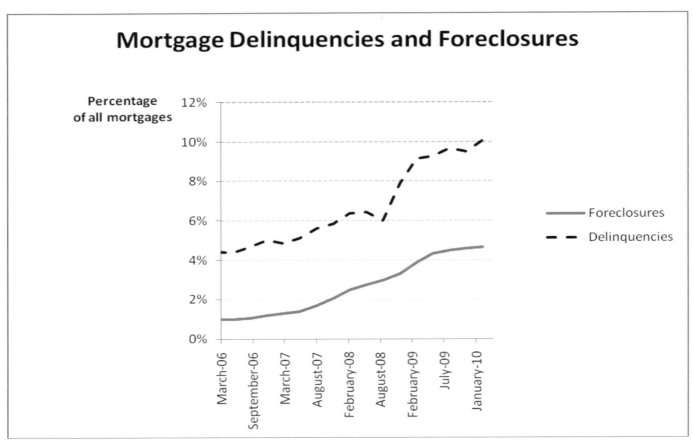

Source: Historical National Delinquency Survey Data, Mortgage Bankers Association, 2010

VISUAL 7
EVIDENCE—EXHIBIT #4: GLOBAL COMPARISON OF OUTPUT, PRICES, AND JOBS

Percentage change over previous year for first three columns

Country	GDP 4th Quarter 2009	Industrial Production	CPI	Unemployment rate (%)
United States	-2.5	-5.1	-0.3	10.0
China	+8.2	+19.2	-0.8	9.2
Euro area	-3.9	-11.1	-0.3	10.0
Estonia	-13.0	-13.7	-0.4	15.2
India	+5.5	+11.7	+9.8	9.1
Iceland	-6.3	+10.1	+12.0	8.0
Japan	-5.3	-3.9	-1.3	5.2
Latvia	-16.9	+2.4	+3.3	20.9
Lithuania	-15.0	+8.3	+4.7	11.7
Ukraine	-17.0	+8.6	+16.5	8.8

Source: *The Economist*, online edition, June 24, 2010, and World Bank, Countries Data Research, www.worldbank.org

VISUAL 8
EVIDENCE—EXHIBIT #5: MONETARY POLICY CONDUCTED BY THE FEDERAL RESERVE RESCUE EFFORTS

Program	Amount at maximum
Central Bank Liquidity Swaps	$582 billion
Term Auction Facility	$493 billion
Commercial Paper Funding Facility	$349 billion
Term Securities Lending Facility	$45 billion
Total	$1,500 billion
Total Aid to Specific Institutions	$120 billion
Total Assets of Federal Reserve increased from $900 billion in the fall of 2008 to almost $2,500 billion in 2010.	

Source: Federal Reserve System

VISUAL 9
EVIDENCE—EXHIBIT #6: FISCAL POLICY (CONGRESS AND THE PRESIDENT) RESCUE EFFORTS

Program		Authorized	Net spent to date
Troubled Asset Relief Program, 2008	Total	$700 billion	$344 billion
Purchase of Preferred Shares of More Than 700 Financial Companies		$205 billion	$75 billion
Additional Assistance to Citigroup and Bank of America		$45 billion	$0 billion
AIG (American Insurance Group)		$70 billion	$70 billion
Automotive Company Assistance		$85 billion	$82 billion
Other		$294 billion	$118 billion
American Recovery and Reinvestment Act, 2009	Total	$787 billion	$373 billion
Individual Tax Reductions			$127 billion
State Fiscal Relief			$76 billion
Direct Aid to Individuals			$75 billion
Government Spending			$55 billion
Business Tax Reductions			$41 billion

Source: Federal Reserve. Treasury, FDIC, CBO, White House
Note: Figures as of March 2010

VISUAL 10
EVIDENCE—EXHIBIT #7: CONSUMER PRICE INDEX (MEASURES INFLATION)

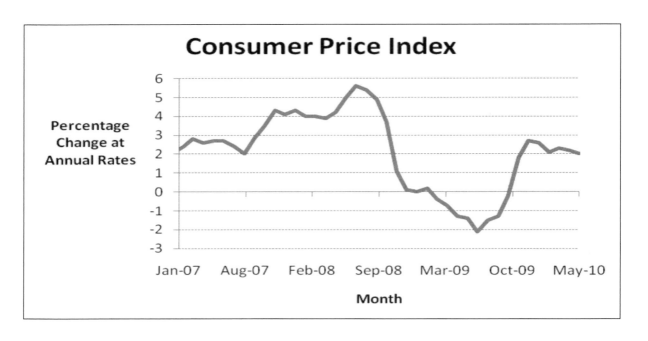

Year	Jan	Feb	Mar	Apr	May	Jun	Jul	Aug	Sep	Oct	Nov	Dec	Annual
2007	2.1	2.4	2.8	2.6	2.7	2.7	2.4	2.0	2.8	3.5	4.3	4.1	2.8
2008	4.3	4.0	4.0	3.9	4.2	5.0	5.6	5.4	4.9	3.7	1.1	0.1	3.8
2009	0.0	0.2	-0.4	-0.7	-1.3	-1.4	-2.1	-1.5	-1.3	-0.2	1.8	2.7	-0.4
2010	2.6	2.1	2.3	2.2	2.0								

Source: U.S. Bureau of Labor Statistics, June, 2010

VISUAL 11
ANSWER KEY TO FINANCIAL CRISIS EVENT CHART

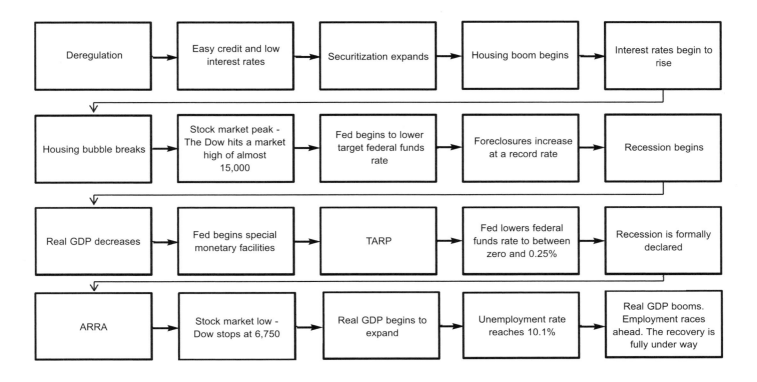